Crossing Borders

Florida A&M University, Tallahassee

Florida Atlantic University, Boca Raton

Florida Gulf Coast University, Ft. Myers

Florida International University, Miami

Florida State University, Tallahassee

University of Central Florida, Orlando

University of Florida, Gainesville

University of North Florida, Jacksonville

University of South Florida, Tampa

University of West Florida, Pensacola

Crossing Borders

A Memoir

Kate Ferguson Ellis

University Press of Florida

Gainesville/Tallahassee/Tampa/Boca Raton

Pensacola/Orlando/Miami/Jacksonville/Ft. Myers

Copyright 2001 by Kate Ferguson Ellis
Printed in the United States of America on acid-free paper
All rights reserved
All photographs courtesy of the author

06 05 04 03 02 01 6 5 4 3 2 1

Library of Congress Cataloging-in-Publication Data
Ellis, Kate Ferguson, 1938–
Crossing borders : a memoir / Kate Ferguson Ellis.
p. cm.
ISBN 0–8130–2284–3 (cloth: alk. paper)
1. Ellis, Kate Ferguson, 1938– 2. Victims of crimes—United
States—Biography. 3. Anorexia—Patients—United States—
Biography. 4. Women college teachers—United States—
Biography. I. Title.
HV6250.4.W65 E4   2001
362.88'0929–dc21
[B] 2001041577

The University Press of Florida is the scholarly publishing
agency for the State University System of Florida, comprising
Florida A&M University, Florida Atlantic University, Florida
Gulf Coast University, Florida International University, Florida
State University, University of Central Florida, University of
Florida, University of North Florida, University of South
Florida, and University of West Florida.

University Press of Florida
15 Northwest 15th Street
Gainesville, FL 32611–2079
http://www.upf.com

Cover photo by Joseph Tabacca

Here at this deep unconscious level lies
the drive to remain incarnate for purposes
unknown to the conscious mind.

Rachel Naomi Remen, M.D.

I am who I am because of who you are.

African proverb

Contents

Acknowledgments

I am grateful for the support of the following people:

Christina, Sara, Susan, Keith, and Kathleen, for sticking with me till it happened

Robert, Jackson, and my classmates in the New School graduate writing program for more of the same

Rachel and Jackie, for careful readings that made a real difference

Peter, for his generosity with his laser printer

Members of the Black Atlantic seminar at Rutgers University, for giving me a place in which to work out "my own private Black Atlantic"

And finally, my creative writing students at Rutgers over the years, for making demands that let me teach myself to write.

Not Even on My Map

1

"Oh, good. You're awake now."

My head felt heavy, but my eyes took in a white ceiling streaked green with water and mold. Where was I? Not in New York, where my bedroom's white walls were covered with bookshelves and photographs of my son as a baby, a student at Stanford, a smiling bridegroom. Loud voices speaking Yoruba leapt toward me from the darkness outside, pulling me across the Atlantic to the house of my friend Nike in Nigeria. But my room there was yellow. Its window looked out onto a tiled back porch with baskets of yams and mottled oranges by the kitchen door. Was someone calling for help? Giving birth to a baby?

As she walked toward my bed, I recognized Seyi, Nike's daughter—the yellows and blues of her head tie in a free fall, down to the hem of her batik wrapper. A few feet away, her two friends remained seated on another bed, its thin mattress covered with striped ticking. How long had they been there?

"Yeah, I'm awake," I said to her. My torso felt sweaty under the stiff sheet, and my fingers found strips of gauze and adhesive tape at my chin and again at the edge of my hairline. My other arm was pinned to the bed by a cast that ran all the way from my knuckles to my armpit. I knew to wiggle my toes to make sure my spine was still intact. "But what's all this?"

"You got some stitches," Seyi said. "And I guess you broke your arm. You don't remember any of it?"

"Any of what? How did I get here?" Her two friends walked toward us as if they wanted to hear the answer too.

"Folusho put you over his shoulder and carried you. The other car hit your side, not his."

I hadn't seen another car. Maybe I'd closed my eyes as we were heading home along the hilly, potholed road to Nike's house after a four-hour ceremony on the edge of town. I remember walking back to the car, a blanket wrapped around my shoulders, the chilly air still clinging to the red-brown earth. A rooster was summoning the day, but the few vehicles that swooped noisily toward us still had their headlights on. The front seat is the place of honor in Nigeria, so as the guest I got in next to Folusho. Seyi and her older brother sat in the back, eyes closed, heads tilted toward the window behind them. I must have put my hand on the dashboard as the other car—or truck, or whatever it was—came toward us.

I tried to picture chubby Folusho, his gold-rimmed glasses glinting in the middle of his round face, checking my limp body for signs of life, then pulling me carefully out of the wrecked car. When I'd climbed in beside him, I was a bit anxious, though not about his driving skills. I was worried that we would run out of fuel. Fuel is Nigeria's primary resource, but it is kept so scarce that no one ever seems able to buy a full tank, and pushing a car, as we did both coming and going, is almost the normal way to start it.

"Does your mom know there's been . . . an accident?" I asked Seyi. My voice sounded reassuringly familiar.

"No," she said, a look of wariness flitting across her smooth, dark face, a version of her mother's wide-cheeked beauty. "We wanted—I mean, Folusho wants to find out what's happening with the car before we tell her anything."

Nike was away in Nairobi attending an exhibition of her artwork. Her six-foot batik squares, dyed indigo and filled with the sprawling shapes of kings, drummers, and pounders of yams, command the prices that denote a world-class artist. Would she be angry, as her children seemed to assume? My father hadn't blamed me when I sent our Pontiac skidding into a lamppost one snowy night in Toronto right after getting my license. But then Daddy always said he hated cars that displayed your wealth—a prejudice that Nike, who'd grown up with no shoes in a tiny village, clearly did not share. Besides the Peugeot we had apparently wrecked, she owned two Mercedes and two bright-yellow vans with the logo of her art school, the Nike Centre for Art and Culture, emblazoned in red and blue on the sides.

"How bad is the damage?" I asked hesitantly.

"Smash-o," said Seyi, hitting a fist against her palm. "Do you want to call my mom when you get back home?"

"No," I reassured her. "But she'll know soon enough that something happened." We all looked at my enormous cast.

"I know. It's just that Folusho feels so bad. I wish Olabayo had driven, but you know he likes to tell his brother what to do. Folusho is . . . uh . . . not so good behind the wheel." You could have warned me, I thought, but there was no use mentioning it now. Seniority in a family is all-important in Nigeria, and rebellion by the children at the bottom is unheard of. Olabayo, the "been-to" oldest brother, was just back from four years of college in the States.

We four had set out around midnight. After parking beside the main road, edged in silent, two-story houses, we continued on foot toward the one still-lit structure. The minister and his small flock had claimed the roofless space within an unfinished house. Inside its cinder-block walls, we were separated from the night sky only by sheets of corrugated tin, supported by poles driven into the bare ground. Loops of electrical wiring carried a current to a long neon tube above the altar and to a naked bulb over our heads. The wooden benches were narrow and without backs. Having left our shoes outside by the door, we wrapped blankets over our clothes and stretched out to wait among the other bodies, apparently sleeping, on the benches' hard surfaces.

I knew that the service itself would not start for at least an hour, and I've learned since then that on any night of the week it is possible to find a small, charismatic Christian church determined to outshout its rivals through a sputtering PA system. I was apprehensive when I heard that the service might last till dawn, but not wanting to decline the offer of my hosts to show me a part of their complicated culture that most visitors don't see, I readied myself by dousing my body with mosquito repellent.

I had almost fallen asleep despite the unsteadiness of my bench on the uneven ground, when a minister in a yellow robe roused us with a "Praise the Lord! Alleluia!" through a microphone held too close to his mouth. Like figures at the last judgment, the sleepers around me jumped up and shouted back, most of them women in long white robes and ballooning hats made from the same fabric. They began with singing, but soon they threw themselves into frenetic dancing and fast clapping, shouting, shaking, and running around the benches or writhing on the packed dirt floor.

The level of sound rose slowly, and I tried for a while to clap and dance too. The punctuating cries of "*oruko Jesu*" told me that the God being called upon was the one I had known as I was growing up and with whom I was again on speaking terms. An Anglican childhood makes it hard to dance and praise the Lord at the same time, but I felt too self-conscious to be the only person sitting down, so I swayed a bit and moved my arms and feet, hoping that my past would not be too visible.

After a while I decided that no one was watching me, so it was safe to take a break. Coming from New York City, where the bravura of performers beating sticks on plastic tubs competes with the rumble of subways, I would have been happy simply to listen to the powerful drumming. But just as I was getting comfortable, I felt the indignant stare of a woman who in Nigeria would be called old, though she was probably close to my own age.

When she first approached me, I scrambled to my feet as if caught in a posture of disrespect. She nodded, and the minister's voice drew her back into a burst of responsive shouting. I tried for a while to surrender to the apparently boundless energy around me, then danced over to the edge of the makeshift structure and sat down again. Twice more we repeated this speechless call and response, the demand from her fierce black eyes leaping out and then receding into the hollows of a bony, depleted body, wrapped from armpit to knee in a white cloth.

An hour before the final "alleluia," my mosquito repellent was no longer working, and I was ready to go home. Light was beginning to gather at the horizon beyond our little structure. Why was my sense of "enough" so different from anyone else's? Yet I couldn't help wondering if that woman was sending me a message, a warning of disaster that I might avert by dancing, full-out. Or perhaps she had detected my deepest fear about this place I so wanted to love—that it could kill me and was summoning a spirit to avert its realization. I never saw her again, but whenever I saw danger averted during the rest of my stay in her country, I thought of her and wondered who was at work.

The next morning, Nike's children and their friends in even greater numbers—including Folusho with his worries about what his mother would say—were back at the hospital. I still don't know who was at fault, but the image of this round-faced African carrying me, on foot along the side of the road by the dawn's early light, cast him as my rescuer rather than someone who might have killed me. No one was willing to stop and help him, he said, because people who try to help can find themselves accused or blamed in the legal melee that usually follows such sudden disasters.

My erstwhile family brought me things that hospitals supply in the States: a towel and a facecloth from Nike's linen closet, large and thick the way her Western visitors like them, and several covered, plastic containers filled with rice and beans, chicken, fried plantains, and of course tea bags since they knew I had the strange habit of drinking hot tea every few hours. This required a boiling ring plugged into the outlet behind my bed, but the taste of the final product, sweetened with lumps of sugar and whitened with powdered whole milk from a tin, revived me more than any other form of attention I got over the next two days.

Leading the entourage of visitors was Olabayo, the head of the household in his mother's absence. In this capacity he'd promised to serve as my guide to his country, at least until his friend Funsho (to whom he assumed I was engaged) could take over. Funsho—or Foley, as most people called him—was at that moment still living in my apartment in New York, completing an unexpected commission for some traditional carving and then planning to come home to Nigeria when it was finished.

It had been my idea to leave New York ahead of him. I'd decided to spend the whole of my sabbatical in his country and to find out, on my own, whether I could really be part of such a radically different culture. When I told my friends about the man I'd met in Africa the previous summer, they advised caution. A younger man was cool—but exactly how much younger? They don't have birth certificates in rural Nigeria, but weren't there other ways I could find this out? And what about past entanglements? Foley's father had had numerous children by eight wives.

"What do people do who have no family to bring them food?" I asked Olabayo when he arrived with my evening meal.

"People like that," he said, "probably don't even get to a hospital."

I think it was the third day when I asked a nurse who was mopping my floor if anyone had said anything about my going home. By then, I was sleeping as much out of boredom as out of tiredness, and though someone from Nike's school sat on the other bed most of the time, we had little to say to each other beyond rough translations of the greetings Nigerians value so highly. I was eager to get back to my room at Nike's house, where I could be alone.

"I think you can go whenever you want," the nurse said without looking up. "I'll ask the head nurse when I finish this."

I didn't hear from her again, so I asked Olabayo when he showed up that afternoon. "They'll be perfectly happy to keep you here," he said. "We pay by the day, you know."

"So d'you think I can leave now?"

"We need to ask someone, but if you feel up to it—"

"Let's pack up and go, then."

When we walked into the crowded waiting room, the eyes of everyone were on me. Most of the faces belonged to mothers wearing bright prints and head ties like Seyi's—-almost every mother had a baby tied to her back, another on the way, and a third child running around or being sharply told in Yoruba to sit still. The two men who were there had the lined faces and missing teeth that signify old age. They sat rigid, hands spread on their knees, their heads lowered, their breathing uneven. As a white person, I was a curiosity, a reaction I was trying to get used to—and figure out. The boy sitting next to his mother did not shout, "*Oyibo! Oyibo!*" the way children usually do when they see me, but that was the feeling in the room.

"Don't you take her away!" came from the head nurse seated behind a desk in the corner. "She wants to stay with us now, hmm?" She laughed and the other nurses joined in.

I looked at Olabayo and then smiled at her. "What can I do? We have to do what the men say, don't we?"

"Well, you have to come back and see us soon," said another nurse whose voice reminded me of Jamaica. "And don't forget to bring us something."

"What sort of something?" I asked, wondering if this was an expected part of a hospital visit.

"Whatever you like," they answered coyly.

"What sort of thing?" I asked Olabayo as we drove away.

"People here always like money. Especially if they know you're from America," he said, a smile opening below the three tribal marks that crossed each cheek, a sign of his seniority. "Or if they know you've been there, like me."

"Well, I have to make what I've got last for six months." I'd known when I left the States this time that the money I'd brought would be all I would have: a thousand dollars for rent for Nike and fifteen hundred for everything else. It had been strapped to my waist as I walked through customs, and most of it was now safely stowed, I hoped, in the suitcase under my bed. You can't use a credit card in Nigeria, and sending cash is too risky. The banks are unreliable and give a hopelessly low rate of exchange.

"Before we go back to the house," Olabayo said, changing the subject, "I want to take you to the chief of police. You can see the Peugeot too. We may not be able to repair it."

"It's that bad, huh?"

"God was with you," said Olabayo. "Believe me."

I'm not sure why the chief of police had to be seen. He looked about my father's age and was balding under his military hat. His air of pride in his double chin and large stomach—both indicators of prosperity in his country—were features my exercise-conscious father would never have endorsed. Standing in front of his gray cement, two-story office building in the busiest section of Osogbo, surrounded by the limbs and entrails of wrecked cars including our Peugeot—its front gouged and twisted on the passenger side—the chief echoed Olabayo's comment about forces beyond our control.

"I see wrecks every day," he said. "And really, if you were not standing here next to me, I would not believe that the person in the passenger seat of that vehicle could still be alive. Someone must be looking after you, my dear."

"That scares me," I said to Olabayo on the way home.

"You mean, what the chief of police said? How come?"

"This is not my first close call."

"What do you mean?"

"Something like this happened a long time ago. It's just really weird, that's all."

"Lots of weird things happen here," he said, and I could tell he was dropping into a memory of his own. Perhaps someone he knew had not been as lucky as I was. Or perhaps Olabayo himself had been even luckier. Nevertheless, I was glad that he did not press for details. I'm not even sure how much I had told Foley about what had happened to me in the lobby of my building in New York. I've always felt awkward and in-authentic bringing it up, as if I were asking for attention and pity like the panhandlers on the subway who tell you they have AIDS or that they were veterans of the Vietnam war.

But as I sat for the rest of the day on the porch that faced Nike's court-yard—a protected enclave of swept cement and sprawling bougainvil-lea, its high wall edged in fins of broken glass—or when I lay down for a nap in my yellow room off the kitchen, I wondered if Olabayo and the chief of police could be right. Were there lessons I had not learned from my first close call and could not learn anywhere but here, in the country of the man I might marry? That question took me back twelve years to the most frightening time in my life.

I was on the uptown train, coming home from a Christmas party in Greenwich Village. It was a week after John Lennon had been killed thirty blocks from where I lived, so perhaps he was on my mind. As the train pulled into my stop at 103rd Street, I noticed a pair of teenage boys who then got off with me. Neither one looked more than fourteen. The taller boy wore a black leather jacket with multiple zippers. His hair was cut flat across the top and sharply angled, a style newly popular with black teenagers. The other one I don't remember, except that he was shorter and wore Army fatigues.

As powdery snow swirled around my feet, I could hear thuds of boots that I knew were theirs. Except for a Korean grocery half a block behind me, the stores on Broadway were all closed, safely hidden behind their solid metal grates. Could it have been my beautiful shearling coat that set me apart as a "have," a person with the resources to stay warm in any weather? My bare hand shook as I pulled my keys out of my pocketbook. Cutting between parked cars, I wanted only to get behind my front door as fast as I could, to put distance between myself and their approaching feet.

When I reached the entrance to my building, I could see inside the lighted lobby, but it was empty. Our doorman had been fired by the building's new owners, who wanted to scare tenants out of the rent-controlled apartments where they'd lived since the forties and fifties. A rent strike that I'd helped to organize was still going on. Just as I was putting my key into the inside door, on the other side of which lay safety, I heard the outer door slam shut behind me. There was no lock on it. The landlord had broken that too.

"Don't scream, lady." The tall one knocked me against the wall while his less imposing friend put a gun to the side of my head. This could have been my last moment alive. And yet the gun looked like a toy, not real at all.

"Don't kill me," I whispered. "Please don't kill me."

Waiting for the sound of the trigger being pulled, I withdrew from my body, felt its temperature falling, one last moment of life followed by another. "I got a gun between my legs," the tall one breathed into my neck, his hands tugging on his zipper. "An' I'm gonna use it." It sounded like a line he'd heard in a movie, one he'd been waiting for a moment like this to use. I stood frozen against the barrel of the real gun, cold against my hairline. The sound of the opening zipper grated against my eardrums like a fingernail being drawn down a blackboard.

Then a hand pushed down on the top of my head and a thick, sour-tasting penis was jammed into my mouth, the gun still against my hairline. The muscles in my legs and back hurt so much I could hardly register what happened next, or how long I held that painful position, half kneeling, half squatting. When the semen spurted into my mouth, I felt the floor disappear under me like a sudden drop in a broken elevator. Then I was on my hands and knees, gagging and spitting onto the filthy tile floor. At the sound of the zipper's closing I looked up at its groaning owner. The tiny microphones of his Walkman were still in his ears.

"C'mon man, let's chill!" The one with the gun grabbed my pocketbook. The two of them made a lurch for the door, and my fingers locked around the handle of my bag. No! No! They weren't going to get that too. Not after what they had done. My life was in that pocketbook and I wanted it—not just my wallet but a book and a beautiful necklace from the friends I had just visited. My fingers gave way, then the rest of me, and my shoulders rolled out over the floor.

As the boy with the gun turned back and fired, the scream I heard seemed to come from far away. I pulled myself up to a sitting position on the marble step in front of the door. The pain was on the right side, not the left. "It's okay," I remember thinking, blood trickling down under my sweater onto my skirt. "It's not my heart." Gravity lifted, letting me fly up for a moment to look from a great height at the black and white pattern of the tiled lobby floor.

Then gravity returned as I tried to stand up, my fingers still gripping my key. Once on the other side of the door, I inched over to the wall and leaned against it, holding my skirt and gagging. For a moment the tiles rocked in front of me as blood ran through my fingers, but I knew that if I didn't look down, I could walk to the stairwell. Putting my full weight onto the wooden banister, I made my way down the flight of stairs to the super's door and pressed with all my strength against his doorbell. When Eugenio's face appeared I said, "Ring 911. I've been shot. Please hurry."

In the months, and then the years, that have followed that night, I sometimes asked myself the question Ralph Ellison's narrator asks in *Invisible Man:* "What did I do to get so black and blue?" It's true that I'd let the Civil Rights movement pass me by, but for years I'd been a supporter of the Black Panthers, and if those feelings had faded, they had not disappeared. Perhaps it was pay-back time for the way I'd acted toward my mother, courting danger to show her I didn't need the safety of a taxi or a man's protecting arm. But my wish to break rules whenever I see them is a habit I can't break, or don't want to. In any case, it has taken me to Nigeria, where I've learned some things that I wish my mother could have understood.

2

The shooting happened in 1980, my first year as a tenured professor at Rutgers after a seven-year struggle to achieve that enviable status. Home from the hospital, I spent the next month listening to requiems: Mozart, Brahms, Verdi, Fauré, Berlioz—I could sing along with all of them. As an usher in the late 1950s I'd heard them performed at Carnegie Hall, and gradually I'd replaced my old LPs with CDs. It was as if I'd been preparing for my recovery from that horrible night in my lobby ever since leaving Toronto and coming to my adopted city at age eighteen. My first serious purchase back then had been a stereo set— the tuner, turntable, and speakers I'd set up in the one-room Village walk-up that was my first, and perhaps my favorite, home from my time as an usher till my marriage in 1965.

The loneliness of those weeks of recuperation made me glad that, in my ignorance, I had not asked for a medical leave. I went back to teaching sooner than I should have, determined to reconnect to my old routine, as I'd always done whenever I hit bottom. Once when I had given the students a writing assignment to do in class, I put my head down on the desk. My next conscious moment was of being woken up by the woman who taught the next class. I looked up and saw unfamiliar faces where I had last seen my own students. I always fell asleep as soon as I got settled on the homeward-bound train, and once someone quietly removed all the bills from my unguarded wallet, leaving—thank goodness—a token for the subway home. Luckily, New York's Penn Station was the final stop.

Three years later a young woman who had come to New York to study acting was stabbed to death on her roof, not far from mine. I got the news on a Friday and spent the weekend crying off and on, remembering my own dancer self in the Village of the fifties and sixties. A candlelight vigil, held on a bleak winter Saturday afternoon, drew a crowd of my neighbors to the sidewalk in front of her building. The indistinct face of her assailant, the super's son, looked out contemptuously under the headlines of the *News* and the *Post*. Wax from my candle dripped onto my glove, and when I came home, I put on the Brahms Requiem and opened the window so that its ethereal notes could reach her across the intervening space. That Sunday I went to my neighborhood Episcopal church, a nineteenth-century building with beautiful Tiffany windows, and prayed for her. It was my first visit to a church since my wedding.

Sometimes during those first years after the attack I'd ask myself why I, and not so many others, had been saved. For what? You might say I was depressed, that my world and my sense of safety in it had been shattered, but it hadn't. When I looked for anger at "those guys," there was only a numbness that felt familiar, and I wondered why. I'd cry when I saw a headline of a young boy killed on the streets, usually an honor student, the apple of his mother's eye. Violent death and the nearness of it were what they, and now I, knew. But I could not cry for myself.

What does come back are the faces and words of the people who helped me through it, starting with Eugenio, who let me in when I rang his bell. The building management hired a new super shortly after the shooting, so I can't even ask Eugenio's wife, Maria, if the blood that drained out of me ruined their mattress—or tell her I'd planned to buy them a new one. I remember the relief of sinking down, enveloped by the deep rose walls of their bedroom, and Maria putting a blanket over me because I said I was cold. I remember that their children were up and running around. I remember keeping my eyes open because that slowed the descent.

"Okay. *Rapidamente, por favor,*" came Eugenio's voice from the other side of the beaded curtain. "They say they're coming now. You kids, you go back to bed."

Oh, good. I closed my eyes just for a minute, but immediately I began to sink again. So I focused on the crucifix hanging between the door and a dresser with a tilted mirror and began to do shallow breathing, holding my ribs still, the way I'd learned to do in my Lamaze classes years ago—as if filling my body with air, a little at a time, would keep me afloat. Drawing in too much at once would widen the hole through which everything was escaping. It would have been easy to keep my eyes closed and let myself fall. I had no idea how far from the bottom I was.

"Do you want us to call your son?" Maria was asking me from the foot of the bed.

"No, don't, it's awfully late. I'm okay." It's hard to believe I said that, but I distinctly remember doing so.

A sharp ring of the doorbell sent a bustle to the door as the children ran down the hall. Then a man and a woman in uniforms pushed their way through the curtain, the man carrying a stretcher, the woman a stethoscope. The woman spoke in a take-charge voice. "How you doing, girl?"

"Fine." I could close my eyes, now that they were there. Eugenio talked to the two of them in Spanish, and then the man said, "Okay, honey, we're going to get you to the hospital as quick as we can. But right now we gotta stop the bleeding." They pulled my coat away from me and wrapped something around my chest, a cross between a zippered life jacket and the inflatable strip of fabric that tightens around your arm when a nurse takes your blood pressure. I felt lighter—able to float—as it pressed against me where it hurt.

"Let's go, let's go." The man's voice came from a place far ahead of me. "Looks like a close one. Do we have a time when she got here?"

"They'll have it on the 911 call," his partner said. "Don't move now. We're going to lift you up."

When we reached the lobby, there was my fifteen-year-old son in his winter coat, his shoelaces still untied. "I'm going to be fine, sweetheart," I said, as he took my very cold hand, and I know I believed it. If I had died on the operating table, I would not have seen it coming. Kevin climbed into the back of the ambulance, keeping hold of my hand as we sped up Amsterdam Avenue. (Three years later, when asked to write about a memorable experience for his application to various colleges, he wrote a one-page essay describing the worst night of his life.) Even now, the possibility of him growing up without a mother is a thought to which neither of us is able to give voice.

At the door of the emergency room at St. Luke's, the driver ordered a knot of waiting people to stand back. Cold air slapped my face as I was lifted into the whirling red light and wheeled under the neon glare of the emergency room. Out of the corner of my eye, I could see resigned bodies slumped in plastic chairs, dug in for a long night. Then I was flying, feet first, past snatches of conversation I couldn't quite make out. Lights on the ceiling flew backwards the way the sand pulls away under your feet when you're watching a wave slip back into the ocean.

Our destination was a room with pale green walls and four or five pairs of hands that immediately began undressing me. A woman, completely covered and masked in green, moved toward me with a pair of scissors. "What are those for?"

"We're going to cut off your sweater—"

"No! Please! I knitted it myself. Pull it over my head."

"If you insist." A needle jabbed my back and then someone lifted my hips and removed my skirt and pantyhose. "We'll deal with this," said the woman in green, holding up my semen-stained skirt, "once we've taken care of the lung." She made it sound like it wouldn't take too long. "Maybe you'll be able to send the guy who did this to jail."

"Just lie still now," came a male voice, "'cause we're about to do something that's going to hurt. You've got a lot of fluid in your lung and we need to drain it. If we get it out, that'll be it. If not, we're going to send you up to the operating room." It sounded matter-of-fact till they started cutting. Then the pain took over. I don't remember it ending, or how long I screamed—"Give me something! Please! Please, something!" The nurse with the scissors held my hand, guiding me through the wall of fire. "Steady now," her soothing voice intoned. "Just a little longer." Then there was a mask over my face, ether.

"Please hurry!" was the last thing I remember saying. "I have to get home before my son wakes up."

"I can't believe it," came the voice of Lourdes, my neighbor, the first words I heard when I woke up in the ICU. "This isn't Kate."

I tried to ask her what made me unrecognizable, but I couldn't open my eyes. A while later—a few hours or perhaps a few days—I heard the name of a friend from San Francisco, then someone from London. How quickly the news must have traveled. I pictured a map like the ones in airline offices, a dot of red light going on as each person found out, a web of lights and lines clustering and growing denser—and thought to myself, I can relax now; that web of light will hold me up.

The first face that came and went belonged to Rick, who looked quite round-shouldered gliding past my bed. Only Kevin could have summoned his dad from Boston, but why would he do that? Rick and I had not spoken in the eight years since our custody fight over our child, and in the ghostly space now surrounding the two of us, he did not break this silence.

"Is my son here?" were the first words I actually spoke.

"I haven't seen him today," said a sweet Irish nurse who was setting up a jug of water and a plastic-wrapped glass on my bedside table. "I saw him talking to your mother and father out in the waiting room, but that was a couple of days ago. He's a fine-looking lad, isn't he? Nice and tall, like his grandfather." *Mum and Dad, here?* For the first time I felt fearful. Was I going to die?

"His father is tall too," I said. "Are my parents still here, do you know?"

"I didn't see them today," said the nurse, "but I can't really say for sure."

"How long have I been here?"

"Three days, I think. We moved you out of intensive care this morning. Now you can see all your visitors. Only the family is allowed into intensive care."

"Do I have visitors?"

"Oh, yes, people have been here practically round the clock. They're pulling for you. It makes a difference, I say."

My body felt remote, the way it did once in Muir Woods when an acid trip let me slide up and down the evolutionary scale several times in a few hours, as I became a fern, a redwood, a human being learning to walk. Now I was tightly wrapped in tape from waist to armpit and being rolled over and jabbed with long needles every few hours. Someone tied a sanitary pad between my legs but I kept bleeding onto the rubber sheet—the last period I would ever have. On the floor was a lung machine, its tubes inserted into my chest through my back. It almost seemed alive as it bubbled and sloshed, comforting me the way the sound of a mother's blood must reassure an unborn child.

Kevin tried to sound cheerful, but he looked exhausted when I saw him for the first time since I'd slipped out of the framework of hours and days and holidays. "Dad and I spent Christmas together," he said, pulling up a chair.

"Did you find your present from me?"

"Sure. Thanks, Mom." It was something with a Polo logo hovering somewhere. Kevin, in the ninth grade, was already a preppie, reproducing in every detail the looks and gestures of the boys who hadn't signed my program cards at holiday dances. "There's some stuff waiting for you under the tree."

"What did your dad give you?"

"A book he designed for Little, Brown on the Civil War." Rick was a good father, just as I thought he would be when we first met. "He had to go back to work on Tuesday, though." Kevin had spent Christmas worrying, he told me later, about who would pay the rent and the bills "if the worst happened."

"Where are Granny and Granddaddy?"

"They left," he said. "I think they were only here overnight. Granddad said something about coming back down when you get out of the hospital."

"You mean they went back to Toronto? Are you serious?"

"You know them—" said Kevin, with the nonchalance he has always managed to muster about my parents.

"But a person isn't out of danger as long as they're in intensive care. The doctors told me you could catch pneumonia and—"

"Don't yell at me, Mom. *I* was here."

"I'm sorry, sweetie. I didn't mean to blow up at you."

"I know," he said with a kind of parental patience. "But there's nothing you can do about Granny and Granddaddy. It looked to me like Granny was a bit unsteady on her feet. You know how she . . .uh . . . gets."

My parents didn't abandon me entirely, of course. They came back to New York on a chilly Friday afternoon three weeks later. Daddy picked me up from the hospital and took me in a taxi to the St. Moritz for the weekend. They had booked a room with windows facing Central Park, with an adjoining one for me. Mummy was "resting."

Sitting up in bed in her navy blue dressing gown with white piping, a cigarette in her hand, pillows behind her—a Piranesi print of Roman ruins, framed in gold, hanging above the mahogany headboard—my mother looked a lot more drawn than Daddy, as if she had taken on the aging process for both of them. Every few years she went to Creed's and bought herself another dressing gown exactly like the one she had on. It was one of the items my father liked her to wear. Penny loafers were another. Nothing frilly.

"What took you so long, you two?" she asked us in the same shaky voice in which she would tell me, late at night on my infrequent visits home, how like two teenage lovebirds she and Daddy still were. "I was about to call the police."

"Your mother's a big worrier, you know," my father said cheerfully after kissing her on the forehead. We hung up our coats and I hugged my mother's angular body. From twenty stories up I could see the tops of the trees in the Park. Sitting down on the other bed, I caught sight of my face in the ornate mirror over the dresser. When I leaned back, my mother came into the frame. Her hair, once the shade of auburn I've created for years with Clairol, was now thinning along with the rest of her. We had never looked more alike.

"We stopped at my apartment so I could get some stuff," I said. "I needed to get my old down coat, since the one I was wearing has a couple of holes in it." The realization that my coat was ruined beyond repair was the moment when "permanent damage" became real for me. The coat was a dark brown shearling from Scotland, the most luxurious one I'd ever owned. I'd bought it in a store not far from the hotel. Perhaps my parents would take me there and buy me a new one.

From the way she had reacted to our taking an extra half hour to get to the St. Moritz, I could tell that my mother had found her way to a bottle of something. My father had probably forgotten to put the key to the refrigerator-bar in his pocket. "I thought we'd have lunch here in our room," she said to our joint reflection. "I'm not feeling all that well and you probably want to take a nap too."

"I am tired," I said, "and I'm hungry too." I ordered sandwiches for all of us and then checked out the room next door that was to be mine for three days. With its framed botanical prints and flattering lights around the bathroom mirror, it inserted itself gently between me and the past three weeks. For the next twenty-four hours, I slept on and off, leaving my heavy curtains open. Twice during the night I pushed aside the thin nylon billowing gently in front of the air conditioner and peered down into the ordered affluence of Central Park South.

Around eleven the next morning, my mother knocked on the door between our rooms and woke me up. "I'm going shopping," she said. "Is there anything you want?"

"Actually there is," I said, pushing back the blanket and slowly moving my body toward the door. "My pocketbook was stolen, you know. If you could get me a replacement that would be great."

"All right. Any particular style?"

"Well, yes." My mother had a flat calf bag with a pale leather lining. It looked a bit like a briefcase, but an elegant one. "I'd like one sort of like yours."

"This one? I'm afraid it's a little out of your price range." *My price range?* Was she talking to a daughter whose funeral she had barely escaped, or what? When I joined the women's movement in the late sixties, I tried to figure out the source of my mother's belief that her children were among the hordes lying in wait to devour everything that was hers if she let them. I decided that it was because she had never earned money herself; it appeared magically and so it could disappear the same way.

"Well, you could get a cheaper version of the same thing. Is Daddy going with you?" Over the years Daddy had sometimes splurged on me: a down payment on a car after I'd totaled my VW bug, for instance—a gesture that gave me a warm feeling I knew Mummy would not share.

"No, he has something to do downtown. I won't be gone long. I'm sure I can find you something nice."

I opened up the armoire concealing the TV and watched a nature program followed by a Julia Child rerun on public television—a crown roast encircled with potatoes. Now *there* was a woman whose husband let her do what she wanted. I was just sliding back into sleep when I heard my mother's key in her door. "I found a terrific dress at Bonwit's," she announced through the open door between our rooms, "and a lovely purse for you too."

I looked warily at the two lilac-sprigged shopping bags at the foot of her bed. "But first I need something to pick me up. Do you want anything?"

"I'm fine for now, thanks." While my mother disappeared into the bathroom I peered into the shopping bags and pulled out a light brown leather purse with a shoulder strap. It was shaped like a feed bag and was probably popular in places where people had horses.

"How do you like it?"

"It's not," I said slowly, "quite what I asked for."

"Well, it was the closest they had," she said. "I didn't think you wanted a color, and in leather, I thought this was the nicest one they had. The stores are getting ready for spring, you know, even though it's the middle of winter. I'm just going to have one drink," she added, as if suddenly aware she was not alone. "You can tell your father that one was all I had."

"I will if he asks," I said, still working on my disappointment about the bag. She slipped into her new dress and I zipped it up the back. It was navy, with bugle beading around the neckline and down the front. "That *is* a nice dress," I managed to say.

"I thought so, too. I can sometimes wear a four, but I'm long-waisted, so I'm hard to fit unless it's a really good dress. But I can wear this year-round, really. It was on sale too."

When my father came back, his rough cheeks cold and a bit mottled from his walk up Fifth Avenue, he gave us each a hug before hanging up his snow-dampened coat and black Persian lamb hat. "Wait till you see my new dress," my mother told him triumphantly. "And the nice new purse I got for your daughter."

By this time I had no interest in feigned enthusiasm for Daddy's benefit. I was already trying to figure out how I could find the sales slip so I could return the bag. It would not be the first time I had gotten rid of my mother's presents, and I know she knew it. Most of the others I'd simply given away: red satin palazzo pants, a black quilted satchel with a gold chain for a handle, several pieces of pearl jewelry. But I'd never find a taker for this one.

I picked up the sprigged shopping bags as if to put them out of the way. Nothing there. "Now dear, don't you go trying to figure out the price of my dress. I'm not going to tell you."

"Mabel, you didn't do anything foolish, did you?"

"No, darling," she said with an alcoholic drawl. "I haven't done anything foolish in years."

"Not since the day you married me, right?" Daddy leaned over and squeezed her arthritic, manicured hand.

"Oh, I've done some foolish things now and then," she added, as I assessed the likelihood that the sales slip was still in my mother's purse. "Your mother and father like to be silly sometimes. Right, dear?"

"The best decision I ever made was marrying your mother. That's what I always say. And just look what it produced." My father's willingness to generate cheerfulness under any and all circumstances made it difficult to know what his real feelings were, or if he would even acknowledge such a category. "If you girls like," he went on, "we could go to a show tonight. You think you're up to it?"

"I guess. We'll be sitting down, after all." Daddy called the front desk and soon had four tickets for *A Chorus Line*. Kevin had plans with his friends during the day, but we'd all have dinner together and then head for Broadway—just the kind of evening Mum and Dad always had in New York.

In the afternoon Daddy and I went for a short walk in Central Park. Several times, I was on the verge of asking him why he and Mummy had retreated to Toronto so abruptly, but he did most of the talking, as he tended to do. He admired the ducks in the lake and greeted locally grown children who wore matching coats, leggings, and velvet hats like the ones my sisters and I once wore, while their Caribbean nannies and I exchanged bored or embarrassed glances. "I just love little kids," he kept saying to us, his audience, as if trying to assure us all that he was still alive.

"I know how you love living in New York," was his usual opening, followed by his own memories of the city in the thirties, when the Cotton Club was *the* place to be for a bachelor who wanted to have fun, and when you could walk in Central Park at any hour. He always told me how happy he was that I was doing so well, adding that it was important to love your work and how much fun teaching must be. I could count on one hand the number of times we had gone beyond this script, when I'd found a way to break through his litany of observations with a thought of my own. But this was not one of those times.

When we got back to the hotel, my mother was sitting on the bed, fully dressed except for her shoes, and reading the latest *House and Garden*, her old favorite, which she must have bought in the lobby.

"Hi, dear," Daddy said, looking enormously pleased. "Your daughter and I have been having a good chat." It would have been callous, surely, to have derailed that by insisting on an answer to the question that kept pushing other thoughts out of my mind: Why had they left the hospital so quickly?

After ordering tea from room service, we all took naps, so I had to suspend my search for the hidden sales slip. I was also beginning to realize that being out of the hospital was very different from being in it. A friend who'd grown up in a rough Brooklyn neighborhood told me, a few years later, that recovery time from the kind of surgery I'd had could be calculated as a month for every hour on the operating table. I'd been there eight hours—and it's with gratitude and admiration that I still think of the people who scrubbed up and put on face masks and willingly spent that much time on their feet, who gave me their whole attention and refused to give up.

"It was touch-and-go there a few times," one of the doctors said to me later. "But you made it." Not *we did it* but *you made it*. And right then I decided that something would come of this incredible joint effort, some new possibility that would not have come to me had this encounter not taken place.

I was woken up by Kevin knocking on the door, there to present me with the black dress, panty hose, and pumps I'd asked him to bring. Once dressed, I focused once again on my mission of finding the sales slip. I managed to pop into my parents' bathroom on the pretext of borrowing a little of Mummy's eye shadow, and looked in the wastepaper basket. No luck there. Then as Daddy poured Scotches for them (part of Mummy's "ration") and sodas for Kevin and me, I scoped out the Piranesi-embellished wastebasket between their wide, double beds. Not there either.

There was only one other possibility. It had to be in her own pocketbook, the model for the one I wanted. I saw her take it and her drink into the bathroom and close the door. She suspects me, I thought. She's going to flush it down the toilet.

"I'm ready for dinner now," she said coming out, the sound of swirling water behind her. "I hope everyone else is." As we walked to the elevator, I noticed that she was carrying a small needlepoint evening bag. "You go ahead," I said to the two of them. "I forgot something." I let myself back into my room just as the maid was coming in to straighten up things for the night. One minute more and she might have closed the door between the two rooms, locking the key on the other side.

"It's all right," I said to her. "I'm getting something for my mother." I swooped into the next room, grabbed the coveted bag, and there was my prize. I had to stand in front of the mirror for a few minutes, taking deep breaths to calm myself before I could go back down to the bustling red, gold, and marble lobby. The cost of the bag was $141 and change. So that was *my price range.* Nothing I couldn't have managed on my hard-won tenured professor's salary.

We had decided on an early dinner at Tavern on the Green, the restaurant tucked into Central Park, before we headed down to the theater district. "We'd like to order our drinks right away," my mother said immediately to the hostess, who disappeared to get our waiter. After a few minutes, Mum announced loudly, "This is an awfully slow restaurant. I've never heard of a place that didn't serve their drink orders quickly. After all, it's the way they make their money."

"Mabel, the waiter is coming as fast as he can."

"I don't see anyone," she said, and signaled to the hostess. "We would like to order something to drink if you would be so kind as to send us our waiter."

"He'll be with you right away." The woman's oval face was expressionless behind her smooth foundation and heavy mascara. She was probably used to vocal, demanding diners.

My mother was allowed one drink before dinner and another one with dinner. When she had gone through these two and barely touched her entrée, she began signaling passing waiters for a third. A waiter finally came over and she tried to hand him her empty glass. "Mabel, that's it." my father said. "The waiter isn't going to get you anything more unless I say so. Now just eat your dinner." The waiter backed away, smiling, and my mother started looking for another ally.

How could I not have noticed before that my obsession with being thin had been handed down to me? Five years before, my parents had marked their fortieth anniversary by having their photograph taken, alone and with all of us, in the clothes in which they were married. They never ate any dessert except fresh fruit and rationed out bread as if we were living under the Siege of Leningrad. Maybe that was why Mummy drank so much. Eating was vulgar but drinking was not. And it kept you from getting hungry.

"Does she eat any better at home?" I asked my father.

"Not really," he said with the puzzled look that I would see more and more often as his "little Mabel," who'd been so bright in college, lost her ability to register what others were saying. He called it Alzheimer's, whose origins are mysterious, rather than using the more obvious A-word. "And her doctors don't seem to be much of a help either."

"Do you not like your lobster, Granny?" Kevin asked.

"No," my mother said, slowly. "The only thing I enjoy is this—" she held out her empty glass.

I touched my own bony hip as I watched her moving her food around on her plate and shifting her attention between the gliding waiters inside and the miniature Christmas lights that covered the trees outside the restaurant like a second, crystalline bark, visible to diners through floor-to-ceiling glass. "What a lot of work it must be keeping all those little bulbs lit," she said. "I wonder how they do it."

"This was a wonderful place to come to," my father said to me as our plates were cleared away. "We'll just have some coffee now, Mabel, and have a lovely time with our daughter and grandson."

My mother glared at him. "I *am* having a lovely time." She reached across the tablecloth and squeezed my hand. Then she put down her empty glass and reached for a cigarette. We were sitting, as always when we ate as a family, in the smoking section.

I was so hungry that I almost forgot about my pocketbook. Of course I'd had to take it with me and act as though I was planning to have a lifelong relationship with it. But when I got up from the table, I saw that an unruly sprig of watercress, coated with oil and vinegar, had landed on its lip. I surreptitiously rubbed the spot with a corner of my flowered napkin—dipped in my water glass—but too late. Defeat stared up at me from the mouthlike opening of this now even more hated purse.

Even before we got out of the cab at the theater I realized that the play had been a mistake. I needed to lie down, and soon. What had made me think that, once released from the hospital, I would be fully recovered? I was still stitched and bandaged, and the skin that would soon be a scar was tightening around me so much that I felt I was being sliced in two. "I need to go home," I told everyone at the end of the first act. "I wish I could stay, but I can't."

"I'll go with you," my mother piped up. "I think the play is rather boring anyway."

The next morning my mother noticed the spot. "Don't worry," she said. "A good leather cleaner will take it right out. Which reminds me, we were slow this year in getting our Christmas checks to you kids." She handed me an envelope, which I tucked into the purse's wide, equine mouth. Our checks were usually generous, written by Daddy in multiples of a hundred. But this one, I noticed in the cab going up Central Park West, was written by Mummy for $358.40, an amount that struck me as odd till I realized she'd subtracted the cost of the bag from the sum she must have given to Ellen and Janet.

3

With Foley still in New York and Olabayo presiding over his mother's house in her absence, it was Michael, one of Nike's art students, who took care of me after the car crash. While I was in the Okin hospital, he had promised to do for me all the things I would not be able to do for myself till my cast came off: cook my meals, make my bed, wash my hair, even cut my fingernails and toenails. His job, for which he got free room and board at Nike's, included cooking and sweeping the floors each morning with a traditional broom made of palm leaves. Why Nigerians prefer these brooms, which require bending close to the ground, to a "real" broom with a long handle, is one of that country's many mysteries.

And yet, despite Michael's excellent care and my periodic forays into town or into the countryside with Seyi, Folusho, and Olabayo, I soon began to feel imprisoned in Nike's elegant house. With the use of only one arm, I was as helpless, if not as drained of energy, as I had been after my surgery in New York. As I waited for my tea one morning on the porch—the promise of a scorching day already hanging on the red bougainvillea that breathed in the shadow of the wall around the house—a thought came to me that reminded me of that earlier, unhappy time: this must be what it's like to be old.

Michael looked as frail as I felt in his worn jeans and batik T-shirt, one of the items Nike's students learned to make to sell to Westerners.

"Let me know if you need anything," he would offer hesitantly whenever he brought my tea.

"Some digestive biscuits maybe?" Digestive biscuits were part of my Anglophile childhood, and Nigerian markets are suffused with the lingering aura of empire ebodied in the toffee, English lavender, shortbread, and Pears soap that insistently pulled me back to my post-war Toronto childhood.

"I'll see if we still have any. You know, the fuel is very hard to get now, so we can't drive into town whenever we want something." *Fuel* in his mouth had two syllables.

"Is it worse than usual?"

He had never seen lines as bad as these. "We have to go in the evening and sleep overnight in the vehicle."

As a long-time New Yorker living one block from the world's largest subway system and surrounded by all-night Korean markets, I had never really faced the possibility of not being able to buy food whenever I wanted it. In this place, not only was I dependent on others to do this for me, but it was also a serious question whether they could.

"I'll be taking care of you," Michael would assure me as he did his best to keep my hunger at bay, "only till Foley comes."

The grin on his face was a reminder that everyone in this tightly knit community associated with Nike assumed I had decided to become "one of us" fairly soon through marriage. "*Katie, Katie, iyawo Foley,*" they would chant whenever two or three were gathered together, and their language was only the outer layer of what I did not know about Nigeria. There are no Yoruba words to mark the various degrees of commitment between men and women that are so important in my country. *Iyawo* covers them all—lets people know whose woman you are, be you a date or a wife of forty years. Perhaps Foley had told them to call me that. It was certainly fine with me, but what expectations did it entail?

I was two months into the six-month stay for which I had applied for a semester's leave from my department at Rutgers. Professors, especially ones with tenure, are expected to spend all their spare time doing writing and research. On the application for this leave, I'd described the book I wanted to work on, never mentioning where I planned to do it.

But I had my laptop, which meant that with a sufficient quantity of reading material I could work anywhere—or so I thought when I'd filled two cardboard boxes with books and xeroxed articles (which Foley put in the back of a cab for me) and headed for the airport. Seventeen hours later I was greeted by Nike's driver at the famously dangerous Lagos airport, having paid a hefty sum in bribes and excess baggage to get all of my things through customs, including my laptop, a boom box tape player, and lots of Bach, Vivaldi, Aretha Franklin, Bob Marley, and Ladysmith Black Mambazo.

Theoretically, I was in an ideal situation to get work done: no telephone, TV, movies, or visitors to distract me. But, in fact, I had no sense that I was doing anything. Perhaps it was the uncertainty of what there would be in the kitchen when I got hungry. Perhaps it was my cast and the infantile level of competence into which it threw me. Or the mosquitoes, which attacked more vehemently once I started working my way through a case of Night Train, a sweet red wine I found in Nike's pantry that helped me to sleep at night. *This is a test,* I told myself. The powers above want to know if I really want to marry a man who will tie me to *this place.*

"How did you two meet?" people ask. That's another story.

My first trip to Nigeria took place two months after my son's June wedding in 1993. The wedding gave me something to do at the beginning of my summer holiday from teaching, but beyond that, I had no plans. I'd been trying to write something about being shot, but it wasn't coming easily, and I dreaded the prospect of spending a summer alone with it. I was used to pressure and deadlines—but now with tenure, I didn't really have any. Then I heard that my friends Felicia and her husband, Max, were taking a group to Nigeria.

I was eating lunch that day in late April with Felicia and her secretary, Marguerite, in a coffee shop with leatherette booths near Felicia's midtown office. Felicia heads up an organization that works with inner-city youth, and I was one of her volunteers. She and I had known each other for almost ten years, though I didn't really think of us as close friends. Felicia was too wary of white people for that.

The two of them had finished eating by the time I joined them and were looking at a mimeographed brochure that invited its readers to Nigeria. "Come and go," it said, "where peaceful and refreshing waters flow." It went on like this:

Osun in Western terms is a patron saint. In Yoruba tradition Osun is the *orisa* of harmony and love, the ancestral principle of fertility, incarnated as the river Osun. People come to her to renew their spirits and rejuvenate their bodies by walking in her sacred groves and washing in her abundant waters.

A week later, I read these words to Janet, my sister who worked at the World Bank, and she warned me to stay away from abundant waters in the tropics. "There's a parasite that lives there called bilharzia," she said, "that can attach itself to your body and kill you." I was sorry to hear that. Bathing in rejuvenating waters appealed to me strongly.

Up till then, I'd never thought of Africa as a place where I would enjoy myself. My idea of traveling involved cities with long, interesting histories: London or San Francisco, places where academics can find others like themselves, expatriate hangouts like Paris and San Miguel de Allende. I've rented a home base in all of those places and used it, not as a point of departure for further travels, but as the nucleus for a kind of community that eludes me in New York. I don't visit. I burrow in. Africa wasn't even on my map.

"How much are you charging?" I asked Felicia.

"Eighteen hundred," she said, "if you get your check in by the first of June."

"And that includes everything?"

"Pretty much. Max will get everyone a visa, and we'll stay with our friend Nike, which brings the cost down considerably. We want to take some of our teenagers if we can raise enough money. You want to contribute? Marguerite is fund-raising for Warren."

"Sure," I said, though I wasn't completely happy about being asked. I was not the only white person who volunteered for Felicia, but fund-raising was the area to which I seemed most naturally suited. It was also the one place where telling my story was okay. I could tell potential donors about what had happened in my lobby, and how, thorough this organization, I had now mentored many kids the age of my assailants. It made me a valuable resource, an exceptional white person, perhaps even an exemplary one.

"Are you going too?" I asked Marguerite.

"Nah, I got too many debts. But you could go. You got a passport, right?"

"Sure. Canadian."

"Well, of course, Canadian," said Marguerite, with whom I exchanged St. Patrick's Day cards and drank Irish breakfast tea in honor of the few drops of Irish blood that linger—she insists—in her gene pool from "way back when." Canadians, I liked to say, are even whiter than American white people. The only person whiter than me was the Queen of England.

"You'd like Nigeria," Felicia said, picking up her check. "It used to be run by the Brits also."

"How often have you been there?"

"This'll be my third trip," she said. "The first time was in the seventies. Max and I went back last year and stayed with Nike. She runs an art school there. A great woman. And she'll feed us stuff we can eat too. The food there is unbelievably hot. The first time we almost starved to death 'cause we just couldn't handle all the pepper." She blew air out through her mouth and waved her hand in front of it.

"How long is the flight?"

"About fourteen hours. Usually there's one stop somewhere, so it adds up to about twenty hours altogether." For $1,800, this *was* a good buy.

"And it really would be okay with you all if I went?"

"Why d'you think not, Kate? White people have gone to Africa before."

"Well, sure. I was just, you know, checking."

By the time I fell asleep that night I knew I would go. I was past having any more children, but perhaps a goddess of fertility connected with a river would bring something—or someone—new into my life. I'd spent too many summers waking up in the heat of New York with nothing to do that involved anyone but myself. My mother spent her summers arranging flowers from the flower beds around our summer home, making sure the lawn was mowed and sprinkled, that vegetables from the garden were brought in baskets to the back door, and that the swimming pool was kept clean.

Instead of a husband, a house in the country, and a life like my mother's, I had my work, or so I liked to think. Writing makes solitude a necessity rather than a burden, a pleasure even, as you imagine people reading the words you have just put down and delighting in your choices. When I felt discouraged I would call up these imaginary readers who would tell me how my words had illuminated some problem they had hitherto been unable to see clearly. The book I'd written to get tenure at Rutgers, *The Contested Castle*, was finally out, but so far my efforts to define what the shooting had meant to me had led to nothing but miscarriages, the very condition the goddess Osun was suppose to be capable of remedying.

I got my check to Felicia by the first of June.

Felicia and Max and the nine other Americans on the trip were not the only ones with me on the road or during my sojourn in Nigeria that pointed me to an African marriage. There was Nike, as I later learned, pulling some strings. But first of all there was Ifayemi who wrote the letter of invitation that we needed to present to the military officers who screen arriving visitors at the Lagos airport. Ifayemi was a Yoruba high priest who told the authorities that he would teach us about his deities. I still believe that he was responsible for setting in motion the sequence of events that brought Foley and me together. Of course I had to be there to let him do this, and for that I have Felicia and Max to thank.

To meet Ifayemi, we had to drive to the far edge of Osogbo, which we did two days after our arrival at Nike's house. This meant piling into her two yellow vans and joining a traffic jam that inched across intersections presided over by military men in small kiosks. It meant breathing in miles of exhaust fumes as we passed the sprawling outdoor markets and ramshackle shops that sold bolts of patterned cloth, pots and pans, jewelry, hair for weaving, soap powder, and plastic sandals, while cars honked and people hawked fried items from glass-sided containers they balanced on their heads. The sight of children carrying huge loads on their heads astounded me: pails of water, sacks of rice, and branches for firewood balanced on a twisted circle of cloth. Women did this also, men rarely.

On our first night at Nike's house, I'd found a book on Yoruba art that listed four virtues central to the Yoruba way of life. Patience is one, along with caution, composure, and respect. Nothing revealed more clearly the difference between the culture I'd brought with me and the one I was taking in through the windows of the van than our silent driver, Matthew. We call patience a virtue, but we don't have much patience with it, in practice. If you're willing to endure dizzying levels of carbon monoxide and steeply angled roads that get washed away regularly, those conditions will persist. And then, whose fault will that be?

The unpaved roads on the outskirts of the town were deeply gullied and terraced from the rains that pummeled the land and everything on it for a few hours every day during the rainy season. I could not imagine anyone taking a car willingly along these roads, but Matthew got our group to Ifayemi's house at the end of a hilly dirt road with no sense that he had done anything that looked heroic to at least one of his passengers. As we climbed out, a cluster of children gathered a few feet away to stare at us.

Ifayemi's home was much humbler than Nike's elegant compound, which was visible from the road over a wall edged in broken bottles that glittered menacingly under the fierce equatorial sun. No wall surrounded Ifayemi's home, only a cement porch that ran the length of the house, its carved wooden pillars supporting the corrugated tin roof that extended over it. I could see signs of cooking behind the house as children ran up to us and then dashed back, laughing, to the safety of a mother's bare legs. It was five o'clock and getting cool, though not yet dark in the sudden way that happens in Nigeria at the same time every night. Our dinner would be waiting for us when we got home.

We filed into a long anteroom with dingy green walls. Ifayemi got up to greet us from a carved wooden chair that looked like a throne. He may have had electricity, but no lights were on. As we settled onto two rattan couches and the floor in front of them, I was aware of Max wanting all of us to be impressed with Ifayemi, whose profuse black beard spread out above a T-shirt that covered his Buddha-like belly. Ifayemi must have sensed Max's wish, but he didn't seem to care. He was not what I would call warm.

"As Max has probably told you," he began, "our deities are very different from yours. They are not faultless, like yours. They simply have powers that we humans do not possess, because they, like our ancestors, are no longer mortal. They see more than we can see, and they will guide us if we ask them in the right way." That meant offering a sacrifice of certain animals and a specific sum of money. If we wanted a reading—an *ebo*, as it's called—we should let him know and he would tell us how much it would cost.

None of this bothered me. I'm not an animal rights activist, and Christianity makes use of the idea of sacrifice too. What put me off was Ifayemi's parting comment. "You have to be willing to take it all seriously," he said as we pulled ourselves to our feet. "You can't just come like a tourist." Well, that counted me out. How could I come as anything else?

Dinner was waiting for us when we got home, and so were Nike and her students, eager to hear how our visit had gone. I decided to say nothing unless I was asked, but I knew that sooner or later someone would ask. The three teenagers (to whose plane fare I had contributed) were using words like "gross"—drawing the vowel out to its maximum length—but nevertheless they were curious, especially about the slaughter of animals. I saw that if I did not sign up for a reading, I might be the only one.

After dinner I went out to the back porch and found Max talking to Yetunde, one of Nike's students who had prepared our meal. She was cutting up some entrails, which I hoped were not for a future dinner. The back porch is where a lot of food gets prepared, even in a wealthy African home. Nike's kitchen is big enough for only a small gas stove, a sink, and some cabinets for dishes. A fridge and a freezer throb noisily in a room next to it. I stood in the doorway and took in the pile of hairy yams clustered by the back door. A basket held pineapples and greenish oranges ready to be sliced or turned into juice.

"Oh, good," Max said, "you're someone I want to talk to." My instinct, when someone says those words to me, is to assume I've been caught doing something wrong. Max must have seen a worried look in my face because he quickly added, "I need to schedule appointments for readings, and I'm realizing you haven't told me what you thought."

"Well, I thought what Ifayemi said was interesting, but I just don't know if it's appropriate for a person like me." I didn't say "a white person" but he knew what I meant.

"Why not? The way I see it, everyone who decided to come is meant to be here. And that means doing everything."

"But how can I not be a tourist, especially if I already have a religion?"

"Most people here have taken on religions that came from the outside," he said. "But they practice this one too. Don't ask me how that works, but it does. Really. So let me ask you something. You're about my age, aren't you?"

"Yeah."

"So now you've pretty much figured out how to get what you can in your life using whatever you know." I nodded. "So you have your son, a nice job, a great apartment, lots of stuff. But I bet there are things you want that you haven't been able to get using what you know, right?"

"Sure," I said, hoping he wouldn't ask me what they were.

"Well, I've consulted the *orisas* whenever I've had a major decision to make. Like having Marie," he said, referring to his eight-year-old daughter, who was with us on the trip. "You know I have two grown kids from my first marriage. Believe me, the *orisas* have always led me in the right direction."

"That's terrific," was all I could think of to say. The headlights from a car driving into the courtyard shone on us for a moment and then switched off. Max was offering me a gift, and here I was acting like an animal who's grown up in a dark place and now can't see in the light. Why not do something different for a change? Maybe something new would unfold.

"Okay," I said into the silence. "I wanted to go with you all, but I guess I needed a push."

"Good for you, girl. I guarantee you won't regret it."

"Did you ever do a reading, Yetunde?" I asked, wondering if she might be a potential friend. Her English was good and she seemed to enjoy being asked questions.

"More than once," she said. "Max is right. You will not regret it." She held up a handful of the squiggly white entrails, and I quickly turned away.

Max smiled at me. "Not your idea of a good meal, huh? Mine neither, I have to admit."

We were both tourists, then, he and I. Food came from the supermarket, not from the stomach of an animal. As the three of us stood up to go inside, a small gold crucifix around Yetunde's neck caught the light from the kitchen window. Perhaps she could explain to me what it meant to do an *ebo* while wearing it. Perhaps the God I had been rediscovering, since my visit to my neighborhood Episcopal church to pray for the girl who'd been stabbed, was not as narrow-minded as he has been made out to be. Perhaps it would be fine with him if I found out what he had been doing in Africa before Christianity came along.

For our readings, two days later, I bought my first African outfit, a *boubou*, or caftan made from a traditional Nigerian cloth called *adire*. The process of making its indigo dye and creating its intricate designs was one of the crafts that Nike taught at her school, and she complimented me profusely on my "new look," undoubtedly hoping I would buy more.

The preliminary reading was brief and efficient. What was blocking my path would be removed if I sacrificed two pigeons, a chicken, and a goat. The ritual would last maybe an hour and the cost, which included these animals, would be roughly thirty-five dollars: less than half the cost of one of my weekly therapy sessions back home!

For the *ebo* itself, Matthew drove us across town, two at a time. After supper the night before, following a trip to a cocoa processing plant with Max and the rest of the group, I had read more in Nike's art book about the practice of divination, known as *Ifa*, which is central to Yoruba religion. Nike herself didn't enjoy reading, she told me, since she'd stopped attending school in the sixth grade. But she had many Western visitors as paying guests, people she'd met on her travels to Europe and the States, and her comfortable mattresses and long dining room table gave us a sense of really being in Africa without having to encounter the more difficult features of life there.

There was one supreme creator, the book explained, who had brought all the other deities into being to help him. Their role was to guide us human beings toward happiness. The theology had some similarities to Christianity, but especially to the version of it that I'd learned about in a conversation with Felicia right after I'd met her. She had been talking about how hard it had been for her when, at the age of eleven, her mother died. "But even then I knew," she said with a smile that radiated certainty, "God didn't want me to be that miserable."

"You grew up with a God who wanted you to be happy? The one I grew up with wanted us to be good. I mean, he'd forgive you your trespasses and all that, but it always seemed a lot easier to disappoint him than to please him."

"Of course he wanted us to be happy," she said. "You think we was put on those slave ships to punish us for something we did wrong?"

My partner for the trip that day was Jean, a professor of performance art from the University of Michigan who had joined us with her nine-year-old daughter and was doing research on Osun. She took a notebook and a camera wherever she went. I, who could not sit still the way Matthew and his fellow Nigerians did, had a book with me, as usual. My greatest fear, as the days slipped by, was that I had not brought enough reading material to last for our whole two weeks.

As Jean and I approached our destination, we heard the bleating of doomed goats along with the usual street sounds: children playing, a radio blaring *fuji* music, cars struggling with the unevenness of the terrain, a rooster or two. "I don't know if I can handle this," I said as we sat down on the bench waiting to be summoned. "The goats here are so adorable, the little ones especially." Goats were even more prevalent than children. They crossed the roads at their leisure and ate whatever appealed to them. Without them the garbage would probably be more plentiful, but they didn't get rid of it all.

"You mean the sacrifice part?"

"Yeah, that mostly."

"You know that the Yoruba idea of death is very different from ours, don't you? The dead don't go away. They're still around, but in another form."

"I'll try to keep it in mind."

Jean went in to Ifayemi first, and I started in on Basil Davidson's *The Black Man's Burden*. Davidson is the same age as my father. They both fought in Europe in World War II and saw atrocities committed in the name of nationalism. The book came out in 1992, and the parallels it draws with Eastern Europe are even starker now than they were then. For me it was helpful to begin with the idea that "ancient ethnic hatreds," the phrase so often invoked to explain the horrors of the former Yugoslavia, were neither "a black thing" nor "a white thing." There was no single, easily labeled place on which to plant blame.

When Jean reappeared an hour later, she sat down and opened her notebook with barely a nod to me. I took off my shoes and went into the same room from which she had emerged; it was cluttered with covered dishes whose uses I could not imagine. This was where Ifayemi had told us what would be needed. Now he sat with a half dozen young male assistants lined up against the walls. I offered him the requested two hundred *naira*. Ifayemi intoned something over it. Then he asked me to press my forehead to it. "Now say your prayer," he said.

"My prayer?"

"What you want."

"I should say it aloud to you?"

"If you wish. Or not."

I closed my eyes and lowered my head. Over the past year, I had tried to turn my experience of being shot into a novel, and I asked for success in that effort. When I was finished I looked up. "May I ask the *orisas* a question?"

"If you wish."

"Can I find out if I'll get married again in this lifetime?" I was surprised to hear my own words. "Women looking for husbands" had been denigrated at many points in my life—in graduate school, of course, and by feminists—but before that, by my famously handsome father, who had always let me and my two sisters know that he could spot 'em a mile away by the obvious way they dressed and moved and giggled. Daddy had no use for them—on the ski slopes, on the golf course, or in any of the places where he spent time with "his girls," one of whom was, of course, our mother. Women "like that" were not serious about their golf or skiing. They were there for "something else" and deserved our contempt.

Ifayemi looked directly into my eyes, and I felt exposed under his intense gaze. Perhaps that was why I had been so concerned about what to wear. Then, wordlessly, he threw down a chain with eight beads on it and drew a series of lines in the powder that was sprinkled over the round divination tray, edged in elaborate carving, that lay between us. He repeated this process until the tray was covered with lines. Then he began to chant, and the assistants repeated a refrain that changed each time someone snapped his fingers.

Next, the sacrificial animals from my list were brought in by two of the assistants. "Hold each one of them against your forehead," Ifayemi said, "and let them know your prayer." This was the part of the ceremony I had most dreaded, but when it happened I felt an unexpected connection to each animal. The pigeons seemed resigned to their fate. The goat looked like a drawing I remembered of the Three Billy Goats Gruff. The chicken had russet feathers like the Little Red Hen whom no one would help and who finally did it herself. I felt their soft exteriors and their beating hearts. They wanted me to have a happy life.

As the assistants took the animals away, leaving behind a few feathers and a clump of fur in the bowl in front of me, I thought of St. Francis seeing God in animals as well as in people. Would all of them really be killed—or any of them? I listened during the rest of the procedure for bleating or squawking, and there was plenty of that. But I didn't see any dead bodies while I was there, and I didn't ask where my creatures had gone.

What I prayed for was not the things I had said I wanted. Instead I used a version of St. Francis's prayer: *Lord, make me an instrument of thy peace, a channel for what you would have me do.* In order to connect what was happening around me to the beliefs I already had, in order not to be a tourist, in other words, I needed to will myself to go beyond everything I knew and understood. And as I prayed I felt that something *would* come, something I had been unable to attract up to that point.

In the final part of the ceremony, Ifayemi broke a coconut with a hammer and collected the milk. He then told me to take a piece and hand the rest around to him and his assistants. When we had all eaten a few ceremonial bites, he poured the coconut milk over my head. It trickled through my hair, down my neck and over my breasts and back. It wasn't cold exactly, but it certainly was sticky, especially after it started to dry. Then I was told to take the dish with the feathers and fur, to follow the youngest assistant, and to leave the dish behind the house with what looked like garbage waiting to be burned.

"Is that it?" I asked when I came back, soggy with congealing coconut milk.

"Yes. You are finished." We both paused and then he added, "Very good. It looks very good."

"Does that mean I will get what I asked for?"

"There's no problem," said Ifayemi.

"You mean with any of it?" How could there be no problem? What about my novel? Ifayemi probably didn't even know what a novel was, and perhaps the *orisas* were equally ignorant. Should I offer a two-minute lecture on the origins of the genre? Not now. Jean was waiting and we needed to call Matthew.

On the way home, Jean and I spoke very little. I had asked her that morning whether her expectations about coming to Africa had been met. Now that question was hovering over my own head as well. My expectations had certainly been vague at best. But the confusion, disappointment, and irrational joy swirling through me as we lurched along the rutted roads toward home was so unfamiliar I could not have begun to put them into words. I had stepped outside of my own system of beliefs. What could be waiting for me there?

4

Beside Nike's house, a narrow, red-dirt road branches off the highway. I knew it went up toward a village with a mosque and a church because at certain hours I heard bells or the wail of a muezzin in the distance. That evening, unnoticed and covered with mosquito repellent, I decided to slip out through the gate. The sun was going down, and the air throbbed with the invisible activity of insects. A rattling car or a sputtering motorcycle passed from time to time as I walked, kicking up a reddish dust that I stepped off the road to avoid.

Two women carrying baskets on their heads exchanged the evening greeting, "*E kurole,*" with me. A man asked, "How are things?"—the stilted translation of the general salutation "*Bawo ni?*" How far away from the streets of New York was this world where everyone greeted everyone! A rusty sign told me that the pair of long, low buildings, painted yellow, with no glass in their windows, was an Anglican school. Once or twice, my chin thrust up toward the crisscrossed vault of a towering palm tree, I had a sense for the first time since leaving the States of being alone with a continent around me.

Then the houses became more frequent. Most were low, cinderblock buildings with half-naked children gathered on the porch under a corrugated, rust-reddened roof or playing on the swept dirt out in front. There were also a few pastel, two-story structures that I could imagine myself living in, with cut-out balconies and square, shuttered windows, their tiny panes edged in wood. Children ran up to me, giggling and shouting the "*Oyibo! Oyibo!*" that I was getting used to. I held my hand out and they slapped their small palms against my larger one before dashing away.

Finally, I reached a small, sun-bleached church with rose and yellow gothic windows and a free-standing bell tower beside it. The front door was open, so I peered into the turquoise interior under a vaulted, wood ceiling. The chancel at the far end, painted strawberry pink, enclosed a bare altar. Rows of heavy pews looked permanent and old. Behind a raised, hexagonal pulpit like the one in my church in New York, a quartz wall clock told me it was ten after five. From a nearby building I could hear children's voices singing in Yoruba. A bulletin board near the door let me know that Sunday services started at ten.

The next morning I found Nike sitting on the porch when I went out to collect my sandals; we had all learned to leave our shoes by the front door. "You're up early," she said. I told her about my visit to the church and my plan to retrace my steps while the day was still cool. "Let me come with you," she said. "It's a lovely little town up there, and I know that minister."

At first we walked in silence, but then she began to ask me about myself. How did I like Nigeria? Of course I told her I liked it fine so far, but I wanted to steer the conversation toward her. How long had she been living in her house? "Almost ten years," she said. We were walking side by side on the two ruts of the road, the dew from the grass wetting the hems of our *boubous*. A woman with a baby on her back came toward us, and she and Nike had a short conversation.

"Excuse me," Nike said, when the two of them parted, "that woman has started a little stall to sell fruit down this way. I gave her some money to set it up and she tells me she's doing very well." We stepped to the side of the road as an old car with two people in it sputtered past. Nike exchanged greetings with them too; she seemed to know everyone in the neighborhood. I wanted to ask about her absent husband—her second, Felicia had told me—and about the police commissioner who came sometimes at dinnertime in his own Mercedes but did not, as far as I could tell, spend the night. Instead Nike asked me if I was married.

"Not anymore. I have a son who's twenty-six now, but I've been separated from his father for twenty years."

"My son Olabayo is twenty-three," she said, and we walked in silence again for a while. "But you haven't thought of remarrying?"

"Well, I haven't done it, at any rate."

"That's too bad," she said. We were now in front of a group of houses near the church, Nike greeting each person who came out to look at us. *Too bad.* I'd thought many things about my extended state of off-and-on singleness but I'd never thought of its being too bad. The phrase implied that I was a marriageable person who was depriving herself—and even some man—of something good. "I now like being independent," she went on. "With David away so much, I've become used to being on my own. So I might not marry again even if the commissioner asked me." She looked at me as if testing my reaction.

So that was where things were, at least on her side. "I like being independent too," I said. "I guess that's why I've been that way for such a long time." As we approached the church, the minister, wearing his black cassock and a white smock, came out and began ringing the bell in the tower. Its reverberations spread over the sounds of a Nigerian morning: a crying infant, a rooster crowing, a motorcycle putt-putting up the road. When he was finished, we all shook hands and Nike introduced me to the minister. "I'll come to your service next Sunday," I told him.

"We will be very happy to see you," he said.

That afternoon, we were driven to Nike's art school to see a traditional masquerade and to shop in the small gallery attached to it where the student artists' works were sold. For someone who had not planned to shop, I'd already spent almost half of my money on batiked T-shirts and long, flowing *boubous* for myself and my new daughter-in-law. Even so, I climbed a narrow wooden staircase and found myself in a room full of carvings of all sizes. My favorites were two tall pieces done in a dark wood with many human figures in intricate designs. I had never felt connected with African art, but I wanted to know who had made these pieces.

I was joined in my admiration by Whitney, the other white person in our group. She made her living as a textile artist in New York and had already done one piece of batik. "I'd like to try carving too," she said, picking up one of the smaller pieces. "I think I know who did these. There's a family of woodcarvers here. I'll point them out to you when we get downstairs."

Summoned for the performance, we arranged ourselves along the length of the school's porch, facing into a cement courtyard bordered on three sides by a decorated wall. To our left, a circular hut with a grass roof served as a backstage to which the actors retired to change their elaborate costumes. On the other side of the courtyard a row of musicians had been drumming sporadically since we arrived. The students handed out bottles of Fanta and Bitter Lemon, and then Nike walked into the middle of the courtyard and formally welcomed us.

The masqueraders were a family that passed its skills on from one generation to the next. The oldest, and the main masquerader, was the father, but my favorite was his smallest daughter, no more than four years old, who wore a beaded headdress above her tiny wrapper and blouse and rotated her pelvis and her elbows with breathtaking speed. She was skillful on the ground—but something more happened when she was thrown up to the top of a human pyramid, standing on the shoulders of one of her brothers, who was balanced on his father's. She was completely self-possessed, gyrating above us like a coiled spring.

Her performance was part of a series of skits in which men transformed themselves: changed sex, reversed their costumes to become crocodiles or wide-winged birds, and staggered around as old people tripping and falling in pursuit of a member of the opposite sex who was in actuality another man. It reminded me of clown acts I'd seen at the circus and, like Queen Victoria, I was "not amused" by some of it. What was so funny about the sexuality of women and old people? It was the pure acrobatics that most thrilled me: the sinuous pyramid of father, son, and youngest daughter, or the two sons holding waists and ankles and doing spectacular flips across the courtyard.

After the performance, people started dancing. It seemed rude not to join in, but in spite of my having been a modern dancer for several years in New York, I felt self-conscious. I had rejoiced when "I Wanna Hold Your Hand" became a hit, free at last from horrendous memories of learning—and doing—the box step as taught by Arthur Murray on Yonge Street in Toronto. More recently, my relationship with Felicia included an African dance class taught by a friend of hers who paid as much attention to the two or three white people who took her classes as she did to those who shared her "roots."

But dancing in Africa was something else. I *knew* I looked silly wiggling my hips and waving my arms in a doomed attempt to look "like one of them." I also knew that this was the way we unable-to-have-fun white people are supposed to feel around *the real thing*. From time to time a male art student came up and led me into the center of the impromptu circle. But of course he was just being polite, and I was eager to let him know, as quickly as I could, that he had fulfilled his obligation. Our three American teenagers, having no such inhibitions, impressed the Nigerians, as they had impressed me in New York, with the spectacular moves they had picked up from MTV.

I honestly can't remember if it was the same student each time who pulled me in. All I know is that I gave him my best smile, did the shoulder and hip rotations I had learned from Felicia's friend in Harlem, plus a few moves from the glory days of rock and roll with perhaps even a few Martha Graham contractions thrown in. By the third or fourth time, I even forgot to be self-conscious and moved back into my place in the circle feeling that I had successfully avoided making a complete fool of myself.

The next morning I was the last of the first shift to arrive for breakfast. The conversation already in progress concerned which of the young men we had seen at the art school were cute, which were shy, which were the best dancers, which of them liked which of us. I poured my tea over three lumps of sugar, more deliberately than usual, saying to myself as I did so, *This too shall pass, just breathe in and then out,* as I recalled similar discussions with other girls when I was a teenager who was always ignored by the boys at the prep schools linked with mine.

Jean, who was seated across from me and who was the nearest to me in temperament, looked to be taking in this banter with as much discomfort as I was. I noticed that we were both wearing traditional hand-dyed indigo outfits that we had bought the day before, but neither of us made eye contact. All of a sudden Nike looked over at me and announced, "I know which one likes you!" drawing the o-o-o out to emphasize her glee.

"Let's hear! Let's hear!" came from Whitney at the foot of the table.

"I think you know which one I'm talking about, Kate." When I looked up blankly, she almost shouted, "The carver! He was dancing with you yesterday."

"I know who you mean," offered Whitney. "Kate's been admiring his carvings already, upstairs in the gallery."

"Folorunso!" squealed Nike. "We call him Foley. He's my best carver. A talented boy. His family are all carvers. The father—the grandfather is very famous. The brothers, all of them, learned to carve when they were children. I have some of his work here, too, that I bought. I'll show it to you."

"Can we go to the gallery today?" asked Jean's daughter Alix. "I want to buy another wrapper."

"I think you are supposed to go into town to see the king of Osogbo," said Nike. "Where's Max? I'm sure you can stop on the way home if you want."

I tried to look pleased, but the suspicion that everyone was making fun of me, the oldest woman in the group, kept me from looking forward to a return to the scene of the dancing. When we did not stop by that day, I was simply relieved. But when Whitney led me, the next day, to the sun-drenched area behind the gallery where half a dozen carvers plied their hammers and chisels, the best-looking one of them, bare from the waist up, looked unmistakably pleased to see me.

Whitney and I sat down in the doorway and watched him and his mates as they worked and chatted, so obviously enjoying what they were doing. What was the source of the happiness on Foley's face, and could he pass some on to me if I got to know him? Good things didn't come my way all that often, at least in the area of romance, and when they did, I often found ways to lose them or push them away.

We did not go back to the school for several days but my morning walks with Nike along the red-dirt road behind her house became a regular part of that first trip to Nigeria. We talked mostly about men, with me revisiting my own marriage as Nike contemplated ending her second. In truth, Nike had been a wife for most of her life, whereas I'd been mostly alone. Her marriages had each lasted about fifteen years, which put her in her mid-forties. She didn't have a line on her face to show for it.

"You're a professor, aren't you?" she said one morning.

"I teach English literature" I said. "I suppose that's why I read so much."

"But I've seen you writing, too, on your computer."

"That's just a journal, but as a teacher at a university I do have to write. I've written one book, and I'm supposed to be writing another."

"Perhaps you would like to write something about *adire,* our traditional indigo cloth that you like so much. You know, the history of it, how it's done, with photographs and so forth."

"That sounds like fun." And then, I'm not sure why, I said, "You know, I'm eligible for a paid leave. Maybe I could come here for some of that time." Nike was delighted. I would be welcome whenever I could come. The idea of returning to learn about her world, and perhaps to contribute to it, shone a warm light in my heart. We could continue our morning walks, go to other places as well. She wanted me to see Ogidi, her native village—and Chinua Achebe's village, too, it said on the back jacket of *Things Fall Apart,* a book that was part of my arsenal of reading material. If I had any suspicions about Nike's motives for attaching one of her artists to an American with a solid bank account, I let them go whenever I saw her waiting for me on the porch.

She seemed to think the world of Foley and wove him gracefully into each conversation. I have since learned that a traditional Nigerian courtship relies heavily on an *alarina* or "go-between," chosen by the man—who is of course *doing* the courting. But the *alarina,* a friend of the man, is also close enough to the woman to be the sender and receiver of messages between them because it's improper for either courting party to express any feelings directly to the other. I've often wished that our "modern" ideas about courtship as a private matter had not displaced this role for well-wishing friends, who might begin by telling the women, "I know who likes you—oo—oo!" Well, if this was what Nike and Foley were up to, they made a great team.

With the first week of our trip now behind us, Whitney and I struck out on our own one morning. We took a cab to the art school, where we heard that the carvers had gone to the bush to get wood. Whitney re-trieved the round divination tray she had started carving and took it out to the back courtyard to work on it. I took *No Longer At Ease,* the sequel to *Things Fall Apart,* into a tiny office where there was a TV. The absence of "print culture" around me only made me aware of the degree to which I can't *not* read—the extent to which I feel anxious, in fact, when I'm not accumulating (from the printed page) mental capital for later use.

I was about to take a break and see how Whitney was doing, when my alleged suitor appeared at the door. "I have been looking for you," he said rather shyly. "I wish to ask you a question."

"Fire ahead—I mean—please do."

"I would like you to go out with me." It sounded as if the phrase "go out with" was one that had been supplied to him for use on this occa-sion, three English words he had probably never used in that order be-fore. "Would you like to go out with me?"

"Sure," I said with a smile. "Where do you go out when you go out with someone in Osogbo?"

"We can go to a bar, if you would like that."

"And how would we get there?"

"I will carry us in a car. I think Whitney will come, too, and my brother Emmanuel."

And so we went, the four of us, in a car that Foley (as I came to call him) borrowed from a friend. I knew that "to carry" and "to bring" are synonyms in French, and I liked the substitution. It was my first taste of pidgin, a language I have had to learn to make myself clear. No one un-derstands "car," only "moto" or "vehicle," and no one says "gas," only "fuel," pronounced as you would if you were singing "Good King Wenceslas," with two syllables. Things don't get broken, they "have fault." They're not left over, they "remain." People are never out or away, they "have traveled," and "minerals," not "soda pop," is what one drinks.

When Foley pulled up in front of the school in the car he had borrowed to carry us in, Whitney and Emmanuel, already a voluble pair, got in the back. I hoped that the four of us would remain in a group once we got to our destination. But as we settled into our seats at the bar, the other couple seemed to have decided, perhaps in advance, to engage in a one-on-one conversation just out of earshot. A fuzzy black-and-white picture vibrated from a TV set forty-five degrees above our line of vision. "Can you follow that?" I asked, indicating the soccer game unfolding indistinctly over our heads.

"Yes," said Foley with a serene smile. "I understand it very well." He made no further comment.

There was no way *I* could ask *him* what was going on. My former pro-football-player father was always so afraid I would ask my date a stupid sports question that he had drilled me in the rules of the game—but only in his own sport of football. A commentator spoke in a clipped, if barely audible English, but I had no idea who was playing, let alone who was winning. Foley watched the game intently, though. After a while he asked me how I liked Nigeria, and I was no more helpful to him than he had been to me. "You don't understand our language," he said without judgment. No, I sure didn't. "Would you like me to teach you?" he persisted.

"I understand it's a very difficult language."

"I will teach you," he said with utter confidence.

From time to time I tried to catch Whitney's eye, but she wasn't cooperating. Finally she and Emmanuel, laughing from some recently shared joke, suggested that we move on to an auditorium in town where a celebration for Osun's husband Sango was taking place. Inside the auditorium someone handed us paper plates topped with *amala*, a purplish-brown fermented substance I've never learned to like, with a peppery sauce over it and a knot of blackened meat on top. I caught sight of Felicia, Jean, and their respective daughters, and we found seats right behind them. In the car, we'd arranged ourselves in pairs, but here

Emmanuel moved in beside Foley, with Whitney next to him and then me.

From the front of the auditorium a man in traditional clothing was speaking in Yoruba over a crackling public address system. I stared at him, completely miserable. My "first date" had been an utter disaster, and I wasn't even sitting next to the guy. Finally I leaned across the intervening pairs of knees and handed Foley my plate of food. "It's too hot," I said plaintively. "You have it."

I was starting to feel hungry, nevertheless, but the man with the microphone showed no signs of winding down. The auditorium, with its sloping cement floor, hard seats, and dim lights overhead, reminded me of the inner-city high schools where I had gone with Felicia and other volunteers. But at least in my country people complain about the neglect such dreariness announces. Here they were having a celebration and no one seemed to mind the ugliness of its setting. Luckily, Felicia, who was sitting directly in front of me, stood up to leave just as I was sliding from massive self-pity to irritation. I took my cue from her; the rest joined me, and we followed her out.

Once outside, Whitney gave me a knowing smile and skipped ahead, followed by Emmanuel. Foley walked over and took my hand, holding it all the way down a flight of steps and over to the car. Perhaps I'd "caught" the feeling of confidence with which he told me he could teach me his language, because a current of strength flowed into me from his steady grip, and I said to myself: I want this hand in mine along the long road of life.

In the car I sat next to him in the front seat till he dropped Whitney and me at Nike's house. "I will see you soon," he said, leaving me elated and jittery from hunger—but also baffled. What was the basis for my feeling as we walked down the steps? What was the source of its certainty? Why this man? Why now? And why here, of all places?

For the next few days, Nike was "not around," a noncommittal phrase that is irritatingly common in Nigeria. It doesn't tell you where the person is or when they will be back, but my suspicion was that Nike had gone to spend some time with her new man away from the curious eyes of her children and her guests. I said nothing about Foley to anyone, and even Whitney seemed to understand my need for silence. Then one morning, a few days before we were due to depart, Nike reappeared on the porch.

"You haven't been to the gallery to see your carver," she said as we slipped into our shoes and headed toward the gate. "He is waiting to show you his small pieces."

"How do you know that?"

"We talk very often," she said. "He's one of my best artists. You know, he was living with a senior brother, up in the north, and that brother came to see my friend Segun and brought some pieces of Foley's to sell. I told him I would buy one if he would bring the carver to see me. So when I met Foley I asked him to come and carve at the school. That senior brother was selling his work and paying him hardly anything. That's how they do it here. Everything is for the older ones."

"If I want to buy anything more," I said hesitantly, "I may need to borrow some money."

"Your credit is good here, my dear," she said. "And I've been thinking about what you said about coming back next year. Are you really serious about it?"

"Sure." I wondered, as we kept walking, the late afternoon sun white behind a bank of trees, what she had said about me in the frequent exchanges she and Foley had. And what, if anything, had he said about me?

The following morning our group went to the grove that lines the banks of the Osun River. This area is now a national shrine, restored in the fifties and sixties after years of neglect and desecration, by a European artist who immersed herself in Yoruba culture and married a much younger Yoruba man. At the grove, half a dozen of her immense sculptures were pointed out by a guide. We had to "dash," or tip, the guide, who then turned around and demanded that Jean pay him an even larger sum because she had her video camera and intended to take pictures.

Jean put away her camera, quite angry. I won't say the excursion was ruined for me, but I remembered *my* vision of Osun's abundant waters, based on the words on the back of the brochure: "That this invitation has arrived in your hand is no accident. Consider it a call to come and deepen your connection and understanding of African ancestral traditions." How did this incessant demand for "dash" from us Americans fit into these traditions? Perhaps the lesson of this trip would be one about expectations. In Nigeria it certainly seemed a good idea not to hold onto them too tightly.

As we drove past the art school, I asked if we could stop there, but the others wanted to get home and I was too timid to insist. Foley might not be there, after all, and I had not yet mastered the skill of catching a taxi, which involves calling out your destination to a passing driver who stops only if he and his numerous passengers are already going that way.

The next morning Max took off early for the Transamerica office in Lagos to confirm, he said, our return tickets. I wondered why such a long trip was necessary, and that night I found out. The FAA in the States had apparently issued an ultimatum that planes could not land in American airports if anti-terrorist equipment had not been installed at the point of departure. The Nigerian government had given the FAA the finger, as it were. While we were in Nigeria, the deadline for installing the devices had passed, so our charter carrier would not be taking us back to the States. Max had apparently known nothing of this before we had embarked two weeks earlier.

Now the struggle was to get our paid-for return tickets accepted by another airline. Regular airlines have agreements to honor each other's tickets, but a charter company has no such arrangement. Varig, the Brazilian airline, had been willing to make the exchange, Max told us that night, but it wanted a forty-dollar upgrade from each of us. Did we each have that much? I had asked Nike that morning for a loan of a hundred dollars, so I was covered. But our three teenagers, who had brought substantially less spending money than I had, looked aghast.

Felicia then led us in a round of applause to Max for his valiant effort so far, but I was beginning to dissent. This man had brought, to a very unreliable country, two children, three inner-city teenagers, and five adults. And he had no insurance, no credit card, no cash reserve—nothing to take care of an emergency.

With this cloud over our heads, we attended the Osun Festival, the high point of our trip, according to Max's brochure. Everyone from the Nike Centre wore traditional *adire* fabric, dark and light indigo blue. Other groups and families were also dressed in common fabrics, which made staying together easier. I was looking around for Foley, when one of the other male students took my hand firmly as we half-walked and mostly ran, amid much pushing and shoving and beating of drums, through the crowd-lined streets of the town and then along a dirt road that took us, under high-arching trees, to the Osun River.

From time to time a honking car would force us off the road. Sometimes it was a Mercedes filled with dignitaries, but, just as often, it was a humbler but no less assertive vehicle. We also had to avoid the men and boys running beside us, who were lashing each other with switches and leaping back and forth to avoid the blows. What did it mean? It was a traditional festival thing to do, my companion said. But why the rush? He shrugged his shoulders. We had to keep up with the rest of our group, did we not?

The focal point of the procession, which begins in front of the king's palace and ends as close to the river bank as you can get, is a virginal young woman who is borne along above the crowd on a chair. She carries on her head an immense calabash of sacrificial offerings to be poured into the river. We got only as far as the clearing where the royal household was set up to acknowledge the successive groups of performers as they danced and drummed and the men did their full down-to-the ground bows. Then our turn came. Right after Nike's students had performed, Darlene, the largest member of our group, did a spectacular shimmy that drew applause there in the grove and then again in Nike's living room, where we watched ourselves on video after dinner.

That night I was in my room finishing *No Longer at Ease,* when Nike knocked on my door and announced, "Someone wants to see you." I walked into the living room wearing my white Victorian nightgown.

"You need to go out on the porch," said Felicia, and there was Foley with a smile I could feel as well as see. We sat in the dark on the steps, and he asked if I had enjoyed the Osun Festival.

"I don't know. It was sort of like the Fourth of July that we have in America."

"You have festivals in America?"

"Yes, but this one isn't religious. It's about the founding of the country." I was trying to tell him I was disappointed in the Osun Festival, but that would have needed a common framework that I didn't have even with my fellow visitors. What had I been expecting? A wading in the waters? A sense of the *sacred*? Some sign of the presence of a power beyond our own? But perhaps the sacred is an experience that eludes transportation from one culture to another.

"What are you reading?" he asked, and I noticed that my Achebe novel, *No Longer at Ease*, was still in my hand.

"I'm always reading."

"I know. Will you read tomorrow?"

"We're going to the University of Ibadan," I said. "I need to go to their bookstore." I was, in fact, on my last book and dreaded making the trip back to the States empty-handed.

"You will be gone all day?"

"I don't think so. When we get back, maybe I'll come to the school and you can show me which carvings are yours. I would like to buy a small one if it's not too expensive."

"Thank you. I will look for you tomorrow." He stood up and brushed his hand across my forehead. "*Odaro*. You know what that means?"

"'Good-bye'? Isn't that *odabo*?"

"*Odabo* means 'good-bye.' *Odaro* means 'till tomorrow.'"

Because of a growing shortage of fuel, we made a very late start for the university and got back only in time for dinner. The next day was Sunday, our last full day. Jean and I went to the Anglican service, which we tried to record on the tape recorder she kept hidden inside her bag— and therefore, as we found out when we got home, away from the sound waves we were so eager to preserve. We spent a desultory afternoon packing, since nobody believed that we would all get on the Varig flight that left the next day. Our hope was to get a few of us onto it and to book seats for the rest on the next Varig flight, which left a week later. Since my semester didn't start for two more weeks I felt no pressure to hurry home and a growing desire to stretch out the visit for as long as Nike would have us.

I was disappointed that Foley did not come to Nike's that night to say good-bye to me. By then I had told him I had a guest room in my apartment and he could stay there if he came to the States. Beyond that, I felt wary. A visit to the Soviet Union had taught me that men can be drawn to American women for reasons that have little to do with their inner qualities—or even their outer qualities, for that matter! When Foley had ventured, the next time I saw him after our strange "date," that he would miss me when I left Nigeria, I was pleased but not wholly convinced.

I was therefore delighted when he appeared the next morning to drive us to the airport in the van. I saw Darlene, the member of the group with whom I got along the least well, climb into the front seat next to him. She had been at the breakfast table when Nike made her first declaration about Foley's interest in me, so I felt able to ask her if she would mind moving. I don't know what she would have said if Felicia had not intervened, urging Darlene to ride in the Peugeot that was coming with us and our added baggage.

Foley and I had only a brief conversation in which he asked me if I would set up some workshops for him in New York. "I'll do what I can," I told him. "I've never done anything like that before, but I know people I could call." It was a money conversation that we had, in other words, not a romance conversation. For most of the three-hour drive we sat in silence while the others in the van dozed off. Yet for the whole ride I felt a sense of utter peace, an immersion in the fullness of the present moment, just from being in his presence.

At the airport, Foley stayed with the others while Felicia, Max, and I went into Lagos proper to negotiate with Varig. There are no phone lines connecting the airport and the city, so we had to drive through heavy traffic, midday heat, and surges of children assailing us with items to buy. Varig told us that its flight was now filled, so there was nowhere for Max to vent his frustration except at the crowded office of our now dysfunctional charter carrier a few blocks away.

"You're a business!" he kept shouting. "And the way that works in my country is that you give a customer the service he paid for, or you give him his money back!" But to all intents and purposes, Transamerica was not a business anymore. Not in this town anyway.

Max had taken me along to Lagos because he wanted me to claim that the tour was mine, that the people on it were my students, and that I, a white professor, had to get them back to the States quickly. "Nigerians are as racist as anyone else," he had said to me as we were waiting in the Varig line at the airport before going into Lagos. "They don't give a damn about African-Americans, but they jump when white people snap their fingers." His comment reminded me of one of Felicio's from an earlier, happier moment. "I sometimes wonder," she said, "if the ancestors of some of these people were the ones who put my ancestors on a boat."

By the end of the day nothing had worked. We rehearsed the lines that I never got to deliver, and I'd even offered to put the cost of our Varig upgrade, now raised to eighty dollars apiece, on my credit card if everyone would promise to pay me back when we got back to the States. If only we could have gotten off that cheaply!

As we made our way back to the airport where the others were still waiting, Max took another tack. "I don't think you really want us to get on this plane, Kate. Looks to me like you'd be happy spending another week here. You weren't aligned with my intention to get us out of here today, and when there's no alignment, there's no results." I was sure he was actually berating himself for having been fooled once again by a white person. When would he learn that you couldn't trust any of them, even the ones who appeared to be nice?

It was getting dark, and I felt sorry for silent Matthew, who had driven us into Lagos, for having to spend so much time, after such a long day, in traffic that moved so slowly and emitted so much carbon monoxide. Cars broke down and blocked others. On both sides of the road piles of pipes, bags of cement, concrete blocks, and coils of rusting wire cable seemed to have been abandoned. Was all of this caused by *my* people?

"That's right, Kate," said Felicia. "You always want to do things your way rather than aligning with someone else. And look what a powerful person you are!"

"This is bullshit, both of you. I've spent the whole damn day in these offices with you, and I offered the use of my credit card just because you didn't have the foresight to take care of our upgrades when they were only forty dollars. It's your fault we're not on that Varig plane. You're a business just like Transamerica, and we're your customers."

So it was after many miserable hours of inhaled carbon monoxide and escalating bitterness that I saw Foley again. We four pulled into the crowded airport parking lot and, after wearily explaining what had and had not happened, Max disappeared again into the terminal to negotiate with Air Afrique, our next best hope. I sat down next to Darlene in the doorway of the van, but she immediately got up and walked in the direction Max had gone.

"What's up with you, Darlene?" I called out toward her departing back, and she turned around.

"I've just about had it with you, Kate. For the whole time you've been here you've been acting like nobody's feelings matter but yours."

"When did I act like that?"

"When did you not? That's the trouble with people like you. You don't have a clue how you appear to others."

"Ya can't take 'em anywhere," Whitney piped up gleefully. "Even in the depths of Africa they act like Scarlet O'Hara."

"Yeah, *you* defend her," said Darlene. "What a pair!" She turned and followed Max's path into the terminal.

"What do you think got into her?" I asked Whitney.

"She's mad because you made her go to the "back of the bus" this morning. But she's mad at me too. Go figure."

"I think she's mad," said Warren, my favorite of the three teenagers, "because you're both so skinny."

"Come on, Warren, that's mean," said Whitney, who is even more elongated than I am. "Let's talk about how we want to spend our extra week here now that we've got it."

"I wanna get stoned," said Darryl, our other male teenager.

"Stoned? They have stuff to get stoned with here? I asked.

"The best," said Darryl. "*Ganja!*" He and Warren exchanged raised eyebrows. "I didn't know you indulged, Kate."

"I don't much anymore. But I used to."

"Yeah, back in the sixties," said Warren, looking at me as though I were an artifact from an extinct civilization.

"You know, they were accusing me of not wanting to leave," I said to Whitney. "But now I'm not really looking forward to another week with them." In fact, Darlene's outburst made me realize how misguided I had been in thinking of our group as "one big happy family"—the Brady Bunch, as Warren kept calling us. I was hurt, too, and perhaps that's why I chose that moment to overcome my reluctance to publicly single Foley out. I climbed up beside him on the hood of the car and put my arm around his shoulder. "You okay?"

"Very fine."

"Me too."

We Americans spent the night sleeping on metal airport benches while Matthew and Foley slept in the car and the van. The next morning, in a state of collective exhaustion, we drove back to Nike's welcoming home. I let Darlene sit beside Foley, but I sat behind him and watched him handle the scary moments of a blowout on the highway. The van rocked precariously, but he brought it slowly to a stop. Jean waved a red towel to warn approaching cars that we were pulled over to the side. Max spread branches over the road behind us. Broken-down cars are a common sight, and with no shoulders on the highway, these signals seem to be standard practices. Inside this fragile protection, Foley changed our tire with presence and dispatch and I found myself pulled, unresistingly, toward adoration.

5

Our exit from the Murtala Mohammed airport that day was at least a partial triumph. Max had, in his hand, tickets issued by Air Afrique that would allow all of us to depart in a week. Air Afrique had required payment of seventy dollars apiece for the upgrade—in cash only. We pooled our money, but we were still a hundred dollars short until Felicia spied two white men who looked to be well clear of the problems we were having. She sent Whitney, a glamorous woman by any standards, to solicit from them the cash we needed. Five minutes later Whitney sauntered back with a crisp hundred-dollar bill and a business card from a Shell Oil executive. Max went over to the men and followed this up, explaining the situation and promising to repay the money the minute we reached the States. I don't think he ever did.

Back at Nike's that night we were watching a video of the Osun Festival in which our grinning faces fitfully appeared, when Foley showed up on the porch. Nike had asked him to drive into town to buy her some beer, and he invited me to go with him. I was certainly happy to get away from my group for a while. We drove without saying much, Foley, continuing to exhibit his mastery at avoiding potholes, me, enjoying being in a moving vehicle with fewer than half a dozen people in it. After delivering the beer to the kitchen, we sat on the back porch, with the sounds of cleanup in the kitchen behind us and chirping insects well-ing up in the darkness around the house. I wanted to figure out a time to meet at the school to look at his pieces.

"What will you do tomorrow?" he asked me.

"I have no idea. I assume we have a free day. A free week, actually. I'm up for anything you've got."

"I would like to spend the day with you," he said. "And then," he paused for a moment, "I would like to spend the night with you." He paused again. "Do you understand me?"

Had I heard him right? Had he taken what I had just said too literally? Surely he meant "the evening." I had learned the different greetings for "good evening" and "good night," but perhaps the distinction was a formal one only.

"Well, we can certainly spend the day together. And as far as the evening goes, I'll have to check with my group."

"Perhaps I will come and carry you."

"If you can," I said, knowing he didn't have a car of his own. "If someone from here is going to the gallery I'll go with them, but if not, I'll expect you."

"I will come," he said. "*Odaro*."

"*Odaro*." I felt as if I had spoken a password into an inner realm of Nigerian life where no one from our group had stepped but me. They only knew *odabo*.

That night I slept very little. At around three, I thought about taking one of the sleeping pills I was saving for the trip home, but that seemed excessive. Really, it was silly to be so agitated.

The next morning Foley did not appear, and I was quite shaken. If he *really* wanted to be with me, he would surely come to get me. If I had not said, "I'll expect you," perhaps I would not have minded so much. And if I had not wanted to keep my expectations a secret, having them would not have been so fraught. As it was, I sat on Nike's front porch, my computer open on my lap, from after breakfast till around noon, with only a short break to take a quick hot shower in the bathroom off Nike's bedroom, the one place where hot water for showering was available, if only briefly.

It was then that I saw Matthew backing a Mercedes toward the open gate and asked him where he was going. "To town," he said. "You want to come?"

"Could you take me as far as the school?"

"Sure. Are you going to see Foley?"

How did you know? I wanted to ask, but I simply nodded and got into the car beside him, not a bit certain what would be waiting for me when I got there.

As I walked in the gate I saw Foley and Emmanuel talking animatedly. Foley immediately came toward me and took my book out of my hand. "I am happy to see you," he said, and he clearly was. Why had he not come? I was learning to recognize that in Nigeria the most useful answer when things do not turn out as you expected is: *I don't know.*

"Have you had lunch?" That was something we could *do.*

"I have eaten," he said. "But if you are hungry I will get you something. Do you like rice?"

"Sure. Rice and beans, maybe. Is there somewhere we can go and get that?"

"I will bring them here. Manuel!" He practically snapped his fingers. And the next thing I knew Emmanuel was on his way out the gate and across the paved road in front of the school, an empty covered dish in his hands. Foley and I sat by the back door facing the courtyard where several other students were chopping away. "After you eat, I will show you my carvings."

Five minutes later Emmanuel reappeared. Under the cover of his dish were rice, beans, and a piece of some sort of meat. He went inside and came back with a spoon.

"Here," I said to Foley. "You can have this meat if you want it. Rice and beans is fine with me." I found it easy to be a vegetarian in Nigeria. The meat is tough, even when it comes from familiar animals like goats, cows, and chickens. Foley ate the meat and, I think, even the bone. Then we went upstairs, and he showed me the pieces I'd liked when Nike had showed them to me before I'd even met him. I picked out one that was about twelve inches high: a man and a woman riding a mule, facing in opposite directions but definitely a pair, he with a sword in his hand, she with a calabash on her head. "How much for this one?"

"A thousand *naira*. Thirty dollars, okay?"

"A thousand *naira* is thirty-four dollars," I said.

"Thirty dollars for you."

"You've made a sale. I'm going to pay Nike and she will pay you, okay?"

"Is fine." I held it in my hands as if it were a holograph of the culture that had formed him. He also gave me a business card with the address of the school on it. FIFTH GENERATION WOOD CARVER, it announced under his name.

I went out to the front porch. Foley said he would be back in just a minute. When he reappeared, he had a folded but rumpled sheet and a pillow under his arm. "Would you like to come with me?"

"Where are we going?"

"I will show you."

"Okay." We crossed the main road and turned up another that had deep puddles in several places that he crossed first, his hand firmly holding mine. Then, after walking through some tall grass, we reached a clearing where a house stood. He took out a key and opened the front door. Inside he opened another door to a room that had a small window and an iron bed with a bare mattress. We walked in and he locked the door, putting the key back into his pocket. I watched him spread the sheet across the bed, and then I spoke.

"Look, Foley, I did understand what you meant last night, but that doesn't mean I want to spend the night with you. This isn't even night, for goodness sakes." He sat down on the bed, and I joined him. "I'm too far from home, and besides, I barely know you. I get the impression that people here think that every American woman is fair game for every African man, but not this one. I meant it when I said you would be welcome to stay in my apartment if you come to New York. But I'm not an easy lay, and when I say no, I mean it."

He put his arm around me. I reluctantly took it off. He looked puzzled but not determined. "Anyway, you would think I was a slut if I let you have your way, wouldn't you?" I noticed even as I said it what quaint language I had fallen into: *He had his way with her and alas, she was ruined.* In truth, I never for a moment thought he would force me to do anything I didn't want to do, the locked door and deserted surroundings notwithstanding.

"You know, we all made a promise to Felicia and Max before we left that we would set a good example for the teenagers in our group by not sleeping with anyone here."

We had done no such thing, of course, but it was a line I was willing to draw even as I continued to lean my body into his as we sat. What I really wanted was for us both to loosen up a bit, get the feel of each another's bodies, get out of the fast lane of goal-oriented sex into a more playful mode. And it worked! The neckline of my dress was wide enough for him to reach under my breasts and across my nipples. He got undressed down to his underwear—I was surprised to see that he was wearing some since I was not. I let my hands, and his too, go where they wanted to. Knowing that this touching was all there would be made it all the more arousing.

Rolling across the rumpled bed like kittens at play, our arms and legs reaching around each other from every imaginable angle, we had a wonderful time for an hour or two. We even took a nap for a while. I kept my dress on and my knees more or less together. By the time we stood up, my resolve had all but vanished. Nevertheless, as clearly as I knew my own name, I knew that it would be a mistake to take my foot off the brake and let myself roll down that slope.

It was dark out by the time we got back to the school, where we ran into Felicia and Max. Trying not to put disapproving thoughts into their heads, I asked them how they were getting back to Nike's. They pointed to one of her cars, and I got into the front seat next to Matthew. "Isn't this nice," I said. "My lucky day, huh?" I did not say "See you tomorrow," and neither did Foley.

Meanwhile, new guests had arrived at Nike's, three women from the New York dance troupe Urban Bushwomen. Deborah, Patricia, and Jawole wanted to learn the Nigerian dance moves I found so difficult to imitate, so a daily dance class, which we were invited to join, took place on the upper floor of Nike's house. Jean and I also decided to try our hand at batik, so Yetunde bought us each candles, dye, and a piece of a fabric called guinea brocade. Yetunde showed me what to do, but it was soon quite obvious which sections of my fabric were done by her and which by me.

It was Jawole who rescued me from the condition that had struck fear into me when I saw that we would not be leaving on schedule: the absence of something to read. She offered the loan of a five-hundred-page Booker Prize–winning novel by Ben Okri called *The Famished Road*. Its vision of Nigerian life as a vivid, round-the-clock nightmare was difficult to read, but at least the act of reading, itself, relieved me of a major anxiety. I was only halfway through the book when I gave it to Yetunde at the airport, just as we left. But I had begun to see Foley's country—the things about it that disturb me, anyway—through Ben Okri's penetrating eyes.

For the first few days of our extra week in Nike's home, I had no organized activity to take me out of the house; and since hailing taxis was still beyond my domain of confidence, I stayed there for the first few days, reading, taking the dance class, and working on my batik. Foley came once to visit me, but he acted as if he did not belong there, and I was beginning to feel the same way. The only solution, I realized, was to overcome my fear of hailing cabs and go by myself to the school, book in hand. Perhaps I would see Foley there and we could talk more comfortably.

When I finally acted on this realization, I learned of a general strike, planned to begin the day we were supposed to leave Nigeria, to protest the jailing of Mosood Abiola, the Yoruba millionaire who had won the presidential election in June. I've been told that the reason for this high-handed action by the supposedly outgoing dictator was that the Hausa, the largest but least wealthy or educated of the three main tribes, would never give up power to a Yoruba man. Protest rallies had been held in Lagos. People were being shot and killed.

As our departure day drew nearer, I voiced my concern about this strike to Max. Should he not try to find out if the airport would be open and if foreign airlines would be honoring the strike? Everyone who didn't live in Nigeria was already rushing to get out of the country. That was why the seats on Varig had gone so quickly. "That's just the kind of thinking we ought to avoid," Max replied. "All sorts of things *can* happen, but we only mess ourselves up trying to second-guess the situation. What good will that do us except to get us caught up in negative thinking, focusing on what we don't want to happen? I say we need to focus on what we do want and align on having that be what happens. Are you willing to do that?"

"Sure, why not?" I said with a defeated shrug of my shoulders, and went back to *The Famished Road*.

The following day I again caught Matthew about to leave for town and asked him if he would take me to the school, where I tried to shake off my anger at Max. The office where Foley had asked me for a date was packed with students listening to their still-ruling dictator on a fluttering, almost imageless TV. Not understanding a word, I waited to see if Foley would show up. Then I went home and decided that I was too old for him. This was just an adolescent episode, a way of healing the part of me that had not received attention like this at a more appropriate age. Foley's age was a mystery to me, but I knew there was a large gap between his and mine.

The next day was Friday, our last day in Osogbo. I went for my usual walk with Nike, and when we got back, Foley was waiting in front of the open gate. Nike looked pleased to see him, and they exchanged a few words in Yoruba at the end of which he said, "I will come again soon." This promise made me immensely content. But by four he was still nowhere in sight, though Whitney, more adventurous than I when it came to cabs, brought a message from the school that he was on his way. Feeling like Penelope at her loom, I kept reading. After dinner I asked Whitney, who had gone back to the school after giving me the message, if she had seen Foley. "He must have a really hard time with good-byes" was her only comment.

I passed another sleepless night, though I could not believe that I wouldn't see him before I left. I told myself that I simply didn't know why he had not come, but then my need for the sense of control that certainty brings was too great. So I made up reasons drawn from my background, most of them psychological like Whitney's, having their origins in *how he felt about me*. The words "I don't know" still do not come easily out of my mouth. I make my living gathering and transmitting knowledge.

The next morning I got up to go for my final walk with Nike. "I'm going to miss doing this," she said before we were joined by Jean and Whitney, who had asked the night before if they could come along. Jean walked with Nike up ahead and I let out my anguish to Whitney.

"Maybe we should ask Nike," she said. "I'm completely out of answers."

"Would you ask her for me? I feel too embarrassed."

"Sure. If I were you, I'd find out from her where he lives and just go and get him." In fact, that *was* what Whitney would do, and I tried to appropriate her courage. On the return portion of the walk, I joined Jean so that Whitney would have Nike to herself. As we approached the house, Whitney announced her findings. "Nike thinks that Segun may have asked Foley to line up for some fuel for him last night."

"You know," Nike said to all of us, "Foley is younger than Segun and lives in his house. So he has to do what Segun tells him to do." We approached the gate, and it was Segun who opened it for us. Nike spoke to him in Yoruba and then Segun turned to me. "I am sorry to have inconvenienced you," he said, bending forward in a traditional gesture of respect to an older person. But I only felt reproached for my ignorance of Nigerian ways. Could there be, in a Nigerian courtship, an *anti-alarina,* someone who, for whatever reason, does not want the liaison to proceed?

Then I looked up and Foley was waving to me from the balcony. "I will wait here," he called down to me, so I went inside to have breakfast and finish packing. My idea was to stretch out with him on one of the mattresses up there and just hold him. But that didn't work out either. Men and women don't touch in public in Nigeria. Instead we sat on the top step of the balcony, and I told him about Nike's idea that she and I do a book together. "So I might come back here in the spring."

"Thank you," was his obviously pleased response.

"Do you know when you'll be coming to New York?"

"Maybe November," he said.

"And how long would you stay?"

"Maybe three months."

"Well, good. Maybe I'll come back with you then."

"Good," he said with a smile I was going to miss.

"We want everyone's suitcases on the front porch," came Max's voice from below, so I went down to take care of that. When I came back, about fifteen minutes before we were supposed to take off, Michael told me that Foley had gone to the school. So I sat inside the house next to my packed suitcase and my computer, staring at my book, and concerned only that we would take off before he showed up. Matthew kept assuring me that Foley would be back soon.

I'm still not sure what the delay was about, but when the van that would take us to the airport finally pulled up, Foley climbed out from behind the wheel. As I went to get my suitcase, I saw Nike summon him and figured that he would be driving the van as he had done the last time and that Darlene would go in the seven-seater Peugeot. Then Nike called me over to the car. Foley was sitting in the back seat. Max tried to order me back to the van but Nike insisted I sit beside Foley.

This time we used the drive to feel each other up in every way that two people can when they are fully clothed and in a car filled with people. By the time we got to the airport I felt quite elated. Even my physical hunger for him was somewhat assuaged. I knew I would miss him a lot more now than I would have, had we left on the previous Monday or Tuesday. I also knew that actually having sex and then leaving so soon afterward would have made the break much harder and more complicated.

When we walked into the airport building it was almost deserted. The Air Afrique office was closed. The strike was on in earnest. A British Airways flight was in the final stages of boarding, its seats all taken. It was Max's turn to feel betrayed, and he did. "We'll stay here till we get on a plane," he said, and we circled our wagons around our suitcases. He was so rattled that he couldn't find our list of art items, including Foley's small carving, with their values attested to by an official person in Osogbo. If we could not find it, we would have to leave the things behind. Finally it turned up in Felicia's suitcase.

Foley had said he would wait with Matthew and Yetunde till it was certain that we would leave, so I went down to the parking lot to tell him what had happened. That morning I had been prepared to call my department chairman to tell him I was still in Africa, the most politically correct place I could possibly be stranded. Spending the interval in the airport darkened this fantasy slightly, but I would be with Foley and he would take care of everything.

When I got back to the terminal, Felicia had decided that we needed to give up on Air Afrique, which had humiliated her husband so thoroughly. "Who woulda believed," she wailed, "that we could get so fucked over in a place where white people aren't running the show?" I have friends who would tell her that white people *are* running the show, that the folks at Air Afrique, and perhaps even the Nigerian dictator with his millions, were pawns in the hands of the real enemy. Basil Davidson and others speak of indigenous political development curtailed, even deformed, by an economically more powerful Europe. Yet sitting on the hard metal bench surrounded by our luggage, I was glad to hear Felicia say that perhaps all evil did not reside with me and mine.

"Who has a credit card with some room on it?" she asked. I stepped forward and, after an hour's negotiation, got us all onto a Lufthansa flight that would leave Lagos ten hours later. What felt like lifesaving benevolence wrapped in German accents produced a one-way ticket for each of us. I'm not sure what forces let me go several thousand dollars over my credit limit. But because I did, everyone treated me like a hero. I felt, in fact, quite powerful. I had *done something* when nothing seemed possible. Max assured me he would get Air Afrique to give us our refund once we got back to a country run by sane people.

I continued to shuttle back and forth between the airport terminal and the van until Felicia called me back. "Are you crazy, Kate? It's dark out there and you're an obvious target for who knows who."

"I'll go with her," said Jean.

"What a zoo, huh?" I said to her as soon as we got outside. "I'm so pissed off at Max for being such a fuck-up I need to get some air into my lungs."

"That's why I came out, too," said Jean. Africans approached us asking if we wanted money changed or help of any kind.

"*Ra-ra,*" we said firmly. These were the first Yoruba words that Max had taught us when our yellow van was first assailed by small children with items to sell.

Foley got out of the van as we approached. He put his arm around my shoulder, and the three of us struggled to dispel a rather obvious sense of awkwardness. "Is there anything you would like?" I asked, suddenly wanting this not to be my last sight of him. I'd sensed in him all day a wish to make our time together neat and clean, friendly rather than forlorn, which felt like the best way to me also.

"Some food," he said.

"All right," I replied. "I think we still have time."

As we walked back, Jean asked me a question. "How do you think you'll deal with the antagonism that black women are going to feel toward you for being with a black man?"

"Are you offering yourself as my first test case?"

"I guess I am. There's lots to say about it. I just wondered if I could be straight with you."

"You can. And I'll be straight with you, too." I wanted to talk more right then, but as soon as we arrived we were ushered past a checkpoint where an exit fee of twenty dollars was collected for each of us. (This charge had been included in the cost of the trip, and Max had kept it aside.) Then, along with Jawole's book, I gave Yetunde my last hundred *naira* to buy something for Foley. We had said good-bye while it was still light outside, and it had been a nice farewell. When I had asked when I would see him again, the words evoking a pop song from the seventies, he said, without knowing he was referring to another song, "Maybe I will see you in September."

The high point of the trip home was a long stopover in Frankfurt, where the bathrooms were spotless and the toilet paper abundant. We were served a free buffet breakfast there because our plane, the last to take off before the Lagos airport was closed down, had been forced to leave without the requisite two fat-and-protein-rich meals that Lufthansa served. Working my way through customs, producing my passport and green card, I felt optimistic about Foley's parting statement. This belief persisted as I squeezed into a taxi with Max, Felicia, and their daughter,

Marie, and reconnected with my country's wide, well-marked roads and late-afternoon traffic patterns.

Now I know that Foley's hopeful words at the airport were an example of a Nigerian trait I have had to struggle with: he tells me what he thinks I want to hear. In a centrifugal culture like mine, confrontation, or telling someone something you know they don't want to hear, may keep a misunderstanding from expanding into the stratosphere. Full self-expression is a duty as well as a right, a form of freedom of speech. But in a land as crowded as Foley's, saying your piece is not the beginning of wisdom. Silence is the only way to gain privacy, while confrontation threatens a peace more necessary for survival in small communities like his than in huge, impersonal New York. Could Foley and I really build a bridge between these two extremes and find a meeting point somewhere along it?

I was not yet moving to the New York rhythm around me when a notice arrived in my mailbox telling me that my credit card had been canceled, though not, as I foolishly hoped for a moment, the debt that had brought this about. The amount had not yet been posted, but I needed to let Max know that my debt was about to start accumulating interest that I wanted him to pay. Thus began a three-month altercation between us about who should pay me back for the Lufthansa plane tickets.

"The cancellation of those charter tickets was a circumstance I couldn't foresee or control," he insisted over the phone. "My responsibility can't possibly extend to a situation like that. You lent the money to the individuals you said you would pay for."

"No, I lent it to you," I said. "To your company. You know, the folks who put out that nice brochure that just happened to come into my hands calling me to 'deepen your connection and understanding of African ancestral traditions.'" *And you left a preposition out of that sentence, buddy,* I wanted to add, ever the English professor. Had *this* been there all along, this nastiness in both of us, ready to jump into action as soon as we had each regained the security of our own home terrain? Was this the same Max who had urged me to do an *ebo?* Was I the same person who had done it, the one who was so proud of making that leap?

"I've written a letter to Air Afrique," came Max's voice into the receiver. "I say we're going to get repaid, so you need to keep your negativity out of my space. That's all I have to say to you." He hung up before I could, and we barely spoke after that, though I told Jean and Whitney that I intended to take him to court. Even if I won, there was no guarantee that I'd ever see any money, a lawyer friend warned me, but I didn't care.

To make matters worse, Felicia had told me, months before the trip came up, that she and her board of directors had decided to give me an award for having been a volunteer for a decade. I had been with her organization almost since its beginning and was certainly proud of all the money I'd raised and all the kids from rough high schools with whom I had made connections. We took a group of these kids and spent a week at a nearby campsite and guided them through a difficult ropes course, then met with them weekly, one-on-one, for six months to a year afterward. I'm still in touch with three of "my" young people, and they all know where I am if they ever need me.

In the first weeks and months after I'd come out of the hospital following the sexual assault and shooting, I surprised and even annoyed many people by asserting that I had no wish to leave New York. I had no wish even to move out of my eight-room, rent-stabilized apartment, a response that the owner of my Upper West Side building would certainly have welcomed since it would have given him a large space he could sell at top market prices. Well-meaning people also insisted that it would be quite normal for me to develop a fear of black men.

But if anything, my "close encounter" opened up a way to go further into a world I had always been drawn to. Meeting Felicia and working under her direction with black teenagers of both sexes gave me a chance to get to know many people who could have been my assailants. By the time I went to Africa I could sit in the subway, look any young black male in the eye, and be reminded of someone I had taken to the movies, whose mother I had talked to about her son, whose neighborhood had become familiar to me.

For ten years I had been honored to be taken into their lives. Now, newly returned from Africa, the continent to which they have special claim, I dreaded the award ceremony for which I'd bought, in a happier frame of mind, a gorgeous African outfit. I kept hoping to hear from Foley about his promised arrival in the States, sensing that, if he came with me, I would feel less conflicted about the evening. Whitney gave me some photographs she'd taken of him and one picture of the two of us, and we silently agreed that he'd be a prize anyone there would envy. But the phone refused to ring. By then I was going regularly to my neighborhood Episcopal church, and when we came to sing the doxology, "Praise God from whom all blessings flow," I asked that this one flow in my direction.

I prepared for the awards ceremony by treating two of "my" young people to a ticket to the event. Grace had become my goddaughter, and Abby had lived with me for three months after her baby was born. Grace's parents were dead, victims of AIDS, and Abby's mother was dead as well. Her father had been involved with half a dozen women whose children were Abby's brothers and sisters. I'd met him when he came to visit her in the hospital—a very good-looking man.

"My father was very handsome too," I told her, sitting on her hospital bed and telling her she'd be okay even if her baby's father never showed up. I couldn't help thinking of my father's affairs, which I now understood to have been numerous. "It makes things hard for a daughter sometimes."

The night of the event I put on my outfit, a four-piece, hand-woven ensemble in brown and cream that set me back more than the entire amount I had taken to Nigeria. Knowing that some African-Americans take offense when a white person wears African clothing, I wore a coat and carried the head tie until I was inside the hotel. In Nigeria, everyone loves to see white people wearing African outfits, which they consider an embrace of their culture. "You look so African!" they'd say to me, with no thought that I was appropriating one more thing that is *theirs*.

At the dinner, Max and Felicia avoided me. Or perhaps I avoided them—I'm not sure which it was. But no one else knew that anything was going on that had not been going on before I left. I'd had run-ins with Felicia in the past because it seemed to me that you always had to agree with her, something I was not about to do unconditionally. Our disagreements were always coded in terms of race—in my mind as well as in hers. But until we went to Nigeria together, the good in the relationship always outweighed the bad. She was, until Foley came into my life, my point of connection with an African-American world to which I am drawn for reasons I understand no better than she does.

Our relationship ended two months after the awards ceremony, when I let Grace and some of her friends get high in my apartment and then actually told Felicia that I had done this. Of course she asked me to leave the organization immediately, and when I came to my senses, I could understand why. Grace and her friends were furious with Felicia, but we got together again around my dining room table and agreed that marijuana was not a useful way to cope with our social nervousness. I never told anyone this, but the social nervousness I was feeling stemmed from the fact that Foley, a man I barely knew, had arrived a week before and was now installed in my apartment and my bedroom.

What made the whole thing even more ridiculous was that Foley confessed to me—after I'd explained as best I could what had gone down between Felicia, Max and me—that he did not inhale. "I don't like what it does to me," he said, at which point I started to laugh uncontrollably.

"You wouldn't understand," I said when he asked what was so funny. "It's an American joke."

Well, Air Afrique finally did repay us, though not till the beginning of December, and only after many letters from Max and a meeting, he said, with their people in New York. I went up to his house on 137th Street and spoke to him in person for the first time—except for our brief, task-oriented exchange in the airport—since our cab had dropped him and his family off three months earlier. He handed me a check, which I cashed at once. Foley had been in New York for a month at that point, and we were planning to go back to Nigeria together when my semester off at two-thirds of my salary began in January. I knew I could live more cheaply in Nigeria than in New York, but I needed a plane ticket to get there.

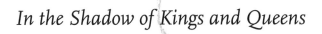

In the Shadow of Kings and Queens

6

Six weeks after Felicia's event, two long-distance phone calls came on the same night. The first was from my sister Ellen in Toronto, telling me that our mother had died and that the funeral was the following Saturday afternoon. "You can get a bereavement rate on the plane," she said, "but only if you tell them the name of the funeral home, so here it is." She was speaking as coolly as I was feeling. Our mother had been on the most advanced-care floor of an elegant nursing home in midtown Toronto for two years, not interacting with anyone. She was barely in our lives by then, at best a vague irritation, at worst a troubling reminder of much greater irritations that we could now, perhaps, finally put aside.

"How did she die?"

"They told me at the Belmont that she forgot how to eat. You know, learning to chew and swallow is one of the first things babies do. She must have regressed all the way back, and I'd told them no heroic interventions, so I guess they just let things take their course. A natural death, you could say."

"When did it happen?"

"Last night. They called me this morning at work."

"So where is this place?" I had turned on the light by this time. The Roman-numeral–faced clock on the wall said eleven-thirty. I'd fallen asleep earlier than usual.

"Just a funeral home on Avenue Road. You know Mum had no religion, really. There won't even be all that many people there, though we have to round some up for Dad's sake."

"How is he?"

"Who knows. It's bound to be difficult, though."

Our father was the more alert one when the two of them had moved to the Belmont, after an anxious two years on a waiting list. The end of their life together was infinitely worse than anything I could have wished on them in my angriest moments growing up. The man who had once done well as a football player and an amateur heavyweight boxer came back, as his physical power diminished, to vent his rage against his now-incontinent wife. Yet who but a saint would not want to strike out at Mummy, a chain-smoker by day and now a bed wetter by night after downing her generous "ration" of Scotch and doggedly demanding more?

Daddy was simply not used to being ignored. Everywhere he went, people had been charmed by his Errol Flynn good looks, his elegant, tailor-made suits, his way with a joke. For sixty years he had effortlessly captured the spotlight. Now even yelling didn't work, and the visiting social workers noticed Mummy's bruises. Alzheimer's was the label they used. How many years of maybe a bottle a day? Well, it was over.

"I'll try to come up on Friday morning," I said. "It's a day I don't teach. Can I stay with you?"

"I'll have a full house," Ellen said, "with Janet and Liam and my kids. But when I spoke to the Graysons they said you could spend the weekend with them. They're still living in our old place, you know."

"Yeah. It should be interesting. Maybe I can even sleep in my old room."

The second phone call, four hours later, came from Nigeria. In a voice that echoed under the Atlantic, the words I'd been waiting to hear finally came: he would arrive at Kennedy via Swissair on "Sunday next," the very day I was due to return from the funeral, if I understood him correctly. I had to shout to make myself heard, and only then realized that Foley's not "keeping in touch" until he had some definite news had something to do with how difficult, how unsatisfactory, and in fact—for him—how expensive it is to make a long-distance call in Nigeria. I was once again sleepless at this sudden turn of events, though I decided I could take a bus to Kennedy from LaGuardia on my way back from Toronto on Sunday. If I was sure which Sunday he meant by "next," that is.

The next morning I spoke to Mrs. Grayson—Alice, as she asked me to call her, though it had been so drilled into us girls never to call grown-ups by their first names that it was difficult, with these old family friends, to make the switch and greet them as fellow adults. "I'm arriving in the afternoon on Friday, if that's okay with you. Maybe we'll have some time to talk a bit."

"I'm sure we will," came the crisp voice from the other end of the line, and I tried to picture which room she was in. "What is it you would like to talk about?"

"Well, Mum, I guess." Alice and my mother had been each other's closest friends for almost seventy years. They had met on the brink of adolescence at the boarding school in Ottawa where I had also been sent.

"Well, I don't want to drag up old stuff," she said. "There'd be no point in that now, would there?"

"I suppose not. . . . Okay, I'll see you Friday."

"Are you all right, dear?"

"I'm fine," I said. And I was. Much too fine, in fact. Face to face with a question that had worried me ever since I was a teenager leaving Toronto, I was utterly calm. Back then, as now, I wondered what sort of person would I be if I felt no grief when my mother died. Would it be a sign that I was missing an essential human capacity? Yet perhaps the proximity of the two phone calls was more than a coincidence. Perhaps I could finally look at marriage through eyes that were no longer my mother's.

In this calm state, I booked my ticket and began seeing my apartment as I imagined Foley would see it. He had to be an extremely visual person and fond of wood, so he would like my early American pieces: some good things that I got when my parents moved to the Belmont, plus a hutch and dining room table bought with wedding present money, as well as flea market finds and a few treasures from the sidewalk. He'd probably like my two roommates too—my attempt at communal living. It's a way of life that enrages my co-op board, who insists it is illegal. I warned my roommates, Sean and Dennis, that Foley was coming with one or two of his friends, hoping they wouldn't mind my turning the fourth bedroom into a guest room for Nigerians. "Let's see how it works," they said.

As I packed—putting a nightgown, a black dress, a pile of student papers, and the novel I'd be teaching the following week into my brown leather backpack—I kept waiting to be gripped by a sense of loss. Later, standing in line in the Toronto airport, passport in hand, I wondered if perhaps my mother had felt this same apathy when her mother died. When I was thirteen, my one surviving grandmother had suffered a fatal heart attack on the street near our house, and as far as I could see no one in the family had cried but me.

Yet everyone knew I hated my grandmother, whose lap was never a haven despite her fondness for Elizabeth Arden Blue Grass soap, hand lotion, and cologne, and who never tired of reminding you to fold the tiny embroidered towels she had put out for you in her immaculate bathroom after you'd washed your hands with a bar of her turquoise soap. Folded towels were her passion—a trait I have since picked up along with a certain anxiety, while cooking, for instance, about keeping my hands clean. I still don't know why I cried so hard back then. I can only think that this woman—who never seemed to laugh—was my one shot at a grandparent, and I had blown it for lack of the charitable heart she knew I didn't have.

My father's mother had died of appendicitis when he was twelve. His handsome father was thrown from a horse while hunting six years later. My mother's father, the member of the provincial legislature from northern Ontario, where Mummy grew up, died before I was born. Nobody ever spoke of him, which makes me wonder if my mother's attraction to alcohol came from him. In any case, everyone thought my tears for my grandmother were fake, and part of me agreed. Would you cry for someone to whom you had to be forced to be polite? Perhaps I'd done it *just to get attention.* This was the motive everyone in our household—nannies and maids included—ascribed to just about everything I did, certainly to any visible expression of feeling. Showy emotion was lower-class, something to avoid. Well, I wasn't about to offend in that direction now.

When I got to Toronto I took a bus to the justly praised Toronto subway system with its stations in various pastel shades: "bathroom colors," Margaret Atwood calls them. People in Toronto don't push, don't fight with a door that a conductor is trying to close. The ads on the trains are similarly low-key: "I really do think you'd like . . ." or "Why not try . . ." When I first left the city, I had no use for the pallor of politeness I saw enveloping every aspect of Canadian life. Now I treasure every demonstration of terminal mild-manneredness.

The three-block walk to my old house took me past a series of monuments to the legacy I'd tried to escape. I walked past the Granite Club, where I'd learned to make figure eight's in a satin-lined, corduroy "skating skirt" like the one on my Barbara Ann Scott doll. My father swam there every day when he was home, which was less and less often as I got older. The Badminton Club and Fran's Restaurant were still there too. These were the places you went—if your parents moved in the same circles as mine—to hang out over the holidays, drink Coke, play badminton, and eat lunch with your chums (later on with a beau, and finally with your husband). Fran's was the place to go at one o'clock in the morning after one of those "formals," given by parents who had been through all these routines themselves, where each girl wore a dance program on her wrist.

Walking up the flagstone path to the front door now and ringing its small, melodious bell, I was surrounded again by the disappointments that had sent me into the strangeness of New York almost four decades ago. This was the path I had walked after someone had driven me home from a formal. Above me were the windows to my room with its French Provincial dresser and bed, skirted and covered in chintz that matched the curtains, where I would tear up my almost empty program card, the only evidence of how the evening had really gone, and wonder how I could learn the secret of popularity on which all good things seemed to depend.

Alice, as I now struggled to think of her, opened the door herself, though a maid soon came in and asked if we wanted tea. We went into the library, where the mantel over the fireplace was now covered with silver-framed photographs of five generations of this prolific Catholic family. The Graysons are the only friends of my parents who actually have a religion, except for my Aunt Dorrie, a staunch Anglican, and their one Jewish friend, a man who remained a bachelor until well into my teenage years and who would have been defined by his religion even if he'd never gone near a synagogue.

Two chintz-covered love seats and a roomy armchair looked equally welcoming, so I chose the armchair while Alice took the love seat behind the table where our tea things were soon brought, all gold-rimmed and matching. "Now tell me, dear," she said, "which room was yours. I know we're sleeping in your Mum and Dad's old room, but I don't know which of you girls slept where."

"Mine was the one in the front of the house, the farthest on the right when you get to the top of the stairs."

"Good. That's our official guest room, and since you're an official guest, you may as well sleep there."

"Thank you." We began with small talk as my eye was drawn from her to the photographs, then to a pastel drawing on the wall of a pair of small boys, a year or so apart in age. They were blond and blue-eyed and wore matching short pants and shirts with sailor collars. "Who are those?" I finally asked.

"That's Scotty and Ian at five and seven. I have the girls up in our bedroom. I love the artist, don't you?"

"It's beautifully done," I said. "The outfits they're wearing remind me of the uniforms we wore at camp."

"Oh, yes, Camp Oconto," she said. "We've even sent a couple of our third generation there—I hate to think how many years ago that was. All you kids went, didn't you?"

"Oh, sure, all three of us. Ellen's daughter rode her first horse there too. She rides in shows now, you know."

"And how about you? Any grandchildren?"

"Not so far, but Kevin did get married last summer."

You kids. That was my life with Mum and Dad, right there in those two words. We kids accompanied them when they went skiing, never complaining if we fell or got cold, happy to practice our snowplow turns, grab hold of rope tows, and later chairlifts, to whiz past trees on whose needled branches clouds of snow rested peacefully. We kids got to share a double bed while they demanded twin beds for themselves— an item almost unheard of in French Canada back then. We also got used to being called by one another's names, as if we were all the same unit in different sizes.

This business of the beds didn't strike me as strange at the time. "Your father sleeps diagonally," my mother said. What did seem strange to me was how the other kids acted, crying at bedtime for days, even weeks, and who were sometimes sent home if they couldn't stop. *Homesick,* it was called, and it was considered quite normal. *They missed their parents.* That's why they refused a nice cup of cocoa, pushed away the hands that sought to console. But what was it about their parents that they missed? Was it the routines of home, a special kind of food, their own beds? What did their parents do for them, the absence of which created such an inconsolable sense of loss? What need did they have that could not be met, just as well or better, by the counselors or by any one of us?

Most of my school chums (a word that calls up my mother, along with "beaus," both of which she claimed to have had in abundance) spent the greater part of their summers at camp even though their families had summer homes in Georgian Bay or Muskoka. Perhaps all of our parents feared an unstructured summer—"doing nothing," my mother called it, even though at our own vacation home in Cobourg we could ride, swim, and play tennis, take our bicycles to the town beach that skirted Lake Ontario, and work on our tans and our Ping-Pong and our golf games, under the eye of a parent or nanny every day of the week.

At camp we came and went summoned by bells and whistles. We canoed, made key chains and ankle bracelets, passed tests and won merit badges, slept six to a tent or a cabin, and put on an annual Gilbert and Sullivan production. One of my favorite memories has groups of us stifling knowing giggles at our music teacher, who was apparently unaware of the real meaning of these words from the finale of *Iolanthe.*

Up and away, soon as we may
We'll commence our journey airy
Happy are we as you can see
Everyone is now a fairy!

That was the year that I, a tall girl, played Strephon, the male lead. But perhaps even then I would not have enjoyed long stretches of time without schedules or goals. I certainly can't enjoy them now. Like a female Scott of the Antarctic, I need a place to get to, a place that's difficult to reach.

I'd finished my tea and produced a wallet-size picture of Kevin and Mitzi at their wedding before Alice asked me what it was I wanted to talk to her about. "I guess I've been wondering about this for years," I began. "You've known Mummy for longer than anyone else. How come things turned out the way they did for her?"

"I'm not sure I understand you. Her death was sad, but there's really no reason why people die in one way rather than another."

"I'm not talking about that. I'm talking about what a beautiful couple they seemed to be, at least in the pictures we had around the house, two people with money and looks—"

"Are you trying to tell me you think your Mum and Dad weren't happy? That they didn't have a good marriage?"

"That's not what I was saying exactly, but no, I don't think they had a good marriage. Not the kind of marriage I'd want, anyway."

"How do you know?" She set down her empty cup, her voice still polite but with an edge of irritation. "You were hardly ever at home, dear. Didn't you go off to New York right after being a boarder at Elmwood?"

"No, I was here for a couple of years. But I still want to ask you some things." My hand tightened on my own teacup.

"Well, I don't think we should be talking about this. Not now, certainly, and maybe never. What's the point? I didn't invite you here to say unkind things about your mother and father."

"I don't want to say unkind things. I just want to find out what happened."

"What do you mean, what happened? You know, Eric and I have been married now for almost sixty years, and let me tell you, marriage is not always smooth. I think your parents were very happy and I think if you had ever bothered to ask either of them they would say the same. Don't you agree?"

The maid had slipped in quietly for the tea tray. She wore a white apron trimmed with eyelet over a black dress whose hem barely covered her knees. "Wait, Lila. How about some more tea, Cathy? We can easily add hot water to the pot."

I welcomed this solicitous gesture, as well as being called by my old name. The women's movement and my job at Rutgers had begun at around the same time, and I'd changed my name to the feminist-sounding Kate to signal a fresh start. "Do you really think your parents were unhappy?" Alice asked.

"Why would Mummy have become an alcoholic if she were not?" There, I'd said it. Not Alzheimer's. The real *A* word.

"I wouldn't have called it that," she said finally. "Though perhaps, in this case, it is accurate. But I'm still not sure I see the point in dredging up the past. Nothing's going to change now, is it?"

"That's why we can talk about it now. There's no risk of hurting anyone. And God knows, it didn't help anyone *not* to talk about it all this time."

"We come from different generations, dear. Yours talks about everything, I gather."

"I'm not accusing anyone or blaming anyone. There's no point in doing that at this stage of the game. But I've lived in the dark all my life and I'd prefer not to."

"Well, the person you ought to talk to, really, is my husband. He went to Cambridge with your father and they were in the war together, so he knows things that I don't."

"She didn't talk to you?"

"No, she didn't. And I probably knew her better than anyone—except your dad, of course. But we didn't talk about our marriages. You just didn't do that. We didn't, anyway."

"I had no idea it was so—severe. I mean the ban against talking about your husband. I can't imagine living like that."

"Well, you don't have to, do you? Here's our tea. I guess I'll have some more too." This mutuality of pouring and stirring and drinking from identical cups was steadying. We were two women talking, after all, not about husbands but at least about something important.

"I don't want to dishonor Mum or Dad," I said. "But I think she had some rough stuff to deal with. I couldn't talk to either of them, so you're the only resource I have."

"All right, I see what you're getting at. Eric will be out this evening, but perhaps the two of you can talk over breakfast tomorrow. In the meantime, I'll tell you what little I know. Then perhaps we should get you settled. You're having dinner with your sisters, aren't you?"

"Yes, and if you can give me a key, I won't have to bother anyone when I get home." Had she heard that? I had called her house "home."

"All right, I'll get straight to the point. You probably know that many men who promise at the altar to forsake all others don't necessarily do that." I nodded. "Well, most men are, or try to be, at least discreet in these matters, but your father was not. You could almost say he went to the opposite extreme."

"I've heard that, but never with any specifics. I read about the German spy in the papers, but other than that—"

"Oh, that was awful. He almost had to resign from the cabinet, which would have been ridiculous. She wasn't his type at all. I always felt certain about that. And I felt truly sorry for your mother. But we never said a word about it, not to each other, anyway. And you weren't around at that point."

"No, I was as far away as I could get."

The phone rang, and Alice answered it while I turned my attention to the bookshelves on either side of the fireplace. The books were as anonymous as ours had been: a leather-bound set of Victor Hugo, an illustrated history of Toronto, a recent *Britannica* with appendices. "Look, I need to make a few more phone calls," Alice said when she hung up. "And you probably need to get going too. If you have any questions we can talk some more tomorrow."

I retraced my steps to the subway, intending to transfer to a bus that would take me within walking distance of Ellen's house. I heard more languages and saw more Indian, Pakistani, Slavic, and Irish faces than I ever observe in New York. In the Toronto I grew up in, strains of "Rule Britannia, Britannia rules the waves, for Britons never never never shall be slaves!" seemed to be coming from every open window. But post-sixties Toronto is a collection of distinct ethnic neighborhoods, their boundaries marked by different items in the shop windows and different alphabets on the street signs. It has an enormous Caribbean population too. Growing up, I don't remember ever seeing a black person. I'm certain I didn't talk to one.

It was not yet rush hour, so I was able to settle myself in a molded plastic seat on the smoothly running subway and think about what my mother's oldest friend had said. The scene that came to me was a Saturday night in the early fifties. We were at our summer home, the one that my father's father had built just before the Crash of 1929, not long before he died; my mother had been courted there, a time in her life that she liked to talk about. On weekends the house was filled with friends of my parents, mostly couples by that time. The "girls" had stayed in the main house then, the "boys" in the guest house by the tennis court.

During the day, everyone still played golf on the town course or tennis on our court, which was sheltered by a high cedar hedge. Between the house and the hedge, a sloping lawn, kept green with sprinklers, was bordered by beds of flowers that changed with the seasons, from palest pinks, yellows, and blue in the spring to oranges and burgundies in the fall. Behind a wooden bathhouse that was no longer functioning, a row of six tall poplars rustled almost continuously. Their leaves needed regularly to be raked up from the driveway or skimmed from time to time from the clear, light-fractioning surface of the pool.

The scene I remember, as if I were still there, might not have happened every weekend, but it blends so smoothly with our other weekend rituals that it does not stand out at all. Everyone gathers for drinks and dinner. Then some people head off to play Ping-Pong in the small house behind the main one while others sit on the veranda not far from the Scotch, rye, glasses, and ice bucket set out on the wrought-iron caddie. I'm allowed to play Ping-Pong with the grown-ups, and I'm getting good. But now I'm on the veranda and people are splashing about in the pool, screaming, or pushing each other in. My mother and father are not part of this group. My two younger sisters are upstairs by now, supposedly in bed.

"Does anyone want anything?" my father asks loudly from time to time, and from time to time my mother says *yes* and he gives her a refill.

At around ten, my favorite guest stands up and stretches. She's a former fashion model who now comes to our house most weekends with her husband. (She has taught me how to use a sewing machine and is motherly toward me, having two sons but no daughter, as she often remarks.) "All this fresh country air sure makes me sleepy," she says with a yawn. "I'm going to turn in for some shut-eye." Everyone nods, and we hear her feet on the gravel leading to the guest house. Five minutes pass. Then my father says more or less the same thing, and his feet crunch on the gravel—even though his twin bed, like my mother's, is right above the veranda. For a painfully long time nobody speaks. Then my mother refills her glass and asks me what in the world am I doing still up.

Keeping track of the stops we were passing on the long subway ride to Ellen's, I tried to figure out how often I had observed this sequence, and to what extent I have filled in its details now that I understand what was happening. But it fits with other memories I have of my mother when she swallowed behavior I vowed I would never put up with. And if that meant I could never get married, so be it. One of these memories is of a Dior evening dress Mummy bought, in 1953, to wear to the upcoming coronation of Elizabeth, to which my mother and father were invited. The dress was peach satin, heavily beaded, and not very full, since each guest was allowed only eighteen inches of space in a Westminster

Abbey pew. Mummy and Daddy were going to Ascot also, and being a devotee of Elizabeth Taylor in *National Velvet*, I envied my mother her day at the races almost as much as her morning in the Abbey.

Ellen and I were completely caught up in the "Lilibet" craze that year. Pillaging *The Illustrated London News* for photographs, we made scrapbooks of the two little princesses with their corgis, their nannies, the changing guards at Buckingham Palace. On the big day we were up at six and glued to the radio in the maids' sitting room, thrilled as the clanging of bells and the high voices of the Westminster choir rolled out to us across the ocean, *"Vivat Elizabeta! Vivat! Vivat! Vivat!"* But by then my father had decided to run for Parliament in a strongly working-class riding, and he didn't think potential voters would go for him in a top hat with a wife in a Dior dress on his arm. So they were not there but in their room asleep as we listened downstairs.

Mummy put all the coronation clothes away and nothing more was said. But in the same strange way that tears had taken over when my grandmother died, I was seized by a grief I didn't really understand, though by then I'd learned to give vent to it only when I was alone in my room with the door closed. Perhaps my mother had learned the same thing. Today, one can see a gray satin Dior dress just like hers in the Metropolitan Museum's costume collection. The peach "original," along with her mother's tucked, high-necked, summer wedding dress, which I wore in 1965, and a heavier Worth wedding dress passed down to her and then to my sister Janet by one of Mummy's aunts, are displayed behind glass in the Royal Ontario Museum.

My sisters had grown up in this chilly, look-but-don't-touch world, too, so as the subway doors hissed open and closed smoothly, my apprehension about seeing them grew. Ellen, the middle one, has taken on preparing at Christmas the dinner that was once produced for us by a cook and two maids. Her fridge is so full that things fall out when you open the door, and you can always help yourself to whatever you see—the antithesis of our parents' much larger kitchen, where we were not allowed to go because our presence would bother the help.

Ellen was wearing an apron when she let me in, and I could smell her curried chicken casserole bubbling in the oven. Janet, the youngest, was in the living room watching a news program with Liam, her second husband of ten years. They live in Washington, D.C., overlooking Rock Creek Park, and work at the World Bank; they are the closest to our parents in income and size of clothes closets. While I was in New York trying to make myself into a dancer and hiding the origins that made that outcome so unlikely, Janet was Winter Carnival Queen at McGill University and spent her holidays driving around Europe in a Deux Chevaux with her friends. Her Christmas presents to me from Morocco or Indonesia (her present and former World Bank bailiwicks) or from Ireland (where the Bank sends her and Liam on periodic vacations) are always my favorites.

And yet, with all these reasons for warmth and good will, we three were on only the most thinly cordial of speaking terms. No dramatic changes took place, in other words. The two of them talk often on the phone, and, since Ellen's divorce, they take vacations as a trio to Cancún and Club Med. I don't like Club Meds, or resorts, or lying on the beach. I don't even like vacations much. But Ellen and Janet have had this rapport ever since I went away to boarding school. Maybe excluding me is how it began, a shared defense against our unavailable parents that's now so deeply embedded that it can't be removed without damaging what surrounds it.

Now that we're all over fifty with one divorce apiece, we have a long history of not being there for one another. I get news about one of them by asking the other—that Ellen had a hysterectomy or that Janet's job at the Bank would soon be downsized out of existence. I've always assumed that both of them accepted our mother's word when she said there was no need to travel to New York to see me when I got shot. Janet did come by at one point, as she has since reminded me, but I remember wondering at the time if she would have come had she not been in the city on World Bank business—and put up by them, as she always was, at the Helmsley Palace.

But now we had Africa, a continent we'd all spent some time on, to draw us together. In the mid-sixties, when Nigeria was hailed as an example of what could be achieved after colonial rule, a pregnant Ellen went to Ibadan with her physicist husband, who taught for a year or two at the university there. Janet, the most widely traveled member of the family, made her way around the world on her own between her marriages. Since then, as the head of a predominantly male delegation from the Bank, she's worn a *chador* on the streets of Morocco.

I hung up my coat and stood in the doorway to the living room. "What are you watching?"

"A program about Quebec and separatism," said Janet. "That's all that's going on up here, apparently."

"What are they saying?"

"The usual stuff," said Liam. "Everyone wants to be on their own these days." He was an engineer at the Bank whose area of expertise was Nepal, where a huge dam project to which he'd given five years of his life was about to be canceled. "They want electricity," he'd say when I asked the usual questions about the environment. "And who are we to tell them to do without it when we have no intention of doing so ourselves?"

I sat down next to him on the rose sectional couch that goes so well with the room's pink walls and burgundy rug—colors you will not find in my cool blue, purple, and white apartment. An early determination to manifest our differences visibly had to be at work here after so many years of being dressed in matching hand-smocked dresses and double-breasted coats with matching hats and leggings. Even Jan, who wore these items long after Ellen and I had outgrown them, has distinguished herself through decor, filling her beige and lime green apartment with Haitian paintings and Indonesian shadow puppets. We've taken different roles as well. Ellen is our den mother, Janet our paragon of corporate elegance. I guess I'm the "bohemian," if that's still a category. Certainly I'm happy when people tell me I look like I used to be a dancer.

"When did you all arrive?"

"I came up yesterday," said Jan, "to help Ellen with some last-minute arrangements. But you and Liam must have arrived at the same time. What airline were you on?"

"American."

"Air Canada for me," said Liam. "That's too bad. We could have taken a cab together."

"But you came here and I was going to the Graysons."

"Oh, that's right." We all turned our attention to the young blond anchorwoman who was interviewing an expensively suited spokesman for the separatist cause.

"D'ya need any help, Ell?" Janet called toward the kitchen, where a faucet was running and then shut off. "I think we've grasped the essential arguments from both sides."

"Come in whenever you want. We're just about ready to eat if you could give a shout upstairs to Matt." Matthew is her second son, the one who was born while his parents were in Nigeria being a faculty couple.

"I hear you've been to my birthplace" were the first words out of his mouth as he took his seat at the butcher-block kitchen table. "I'm afraid I can't give you any vivid impressions. I left when I was a year old."

"Things were a lot better back then," said Ellen, a pile of plates in her hands.

"That's probably true about most parts of the world," said Liam. "In more places than it's not true, at any rate."

"This is a depressing conversation," said Matthew. "Let's all try to think of something cheerful to talk about."

"We don't have to be cheerful all the time," said Ellen. "Remember, we're here for a funeral." I looked around to see if anyone was willing to continue with this subject, but everyone had their eyes on their plates.

"Is everything all set for tomorrow, then?" offered Liam in his delightful Irish brogue.

"There wasn't much to do," said Ellen. "Wendy, Dad's old secretary, made a lot of the calls, and Eric Grayson wrote the obit for the *Globe and Mail*. He's going to deliver the eulogy tomorrow too. We'll be taking her ashes out to the vault on Sunday afternoon."

"I don't think I can be there for that," I said. "I invited these people from Nigeria to stay with me, and they're coming into Kennedy on Sunday."

"When on Sunday?"

"The plane gets in at five, so I've booked a flight at one-thirty. I didn't know this was going to take two days."

"Well, you'll have to go then," said Ellen.

"Are these people you met on your trip?" asked Janet.

"They're artists who study traditional Nigerian arts at the school where we were staying. You know, batik, wood carving, things like that."

"I've seen batik from Nigeria," said Janet. "What I like even more is their traditional *adire*."

"Maybe some Christmas presents will come out of this," I said to the sister I find the hardest to buy for.

By the time I called a cab to go back to the Graysons', nothing more complicated than this had been said by any of us. None of us had mentioned our mother, and my early departure involved romantic hopes I would have been embarrassed to admit to either of them. Perhaps there really was a danger of unpleasantness if our conversation were to take a personal turn. We each had our grievances, so perhaps it was wiser to detach than try for a solidarity that was not in the cards.

7

And yet, had I ever really been there for my sisters? When we were growing up in Toronto, I was in my own world, imagining a life elsewhere. It started, I guess, in the library of the house where we grew up, a wood-paneled room with a red Persian rug and floor-to-ceiling shelves of leather-bound books that no one ever touched. On an inlaid coffee table in front of the fireplace, I could always find *Harper's Bazaar, The New Yorker, Life*—and my favorite, *The Illustrated London News*, an adult version, it seemed to me, of the world of A. A. Milne in which I felt so at home. So even if none of my nannies ever took me to watch the changing of the guard at Buckingham Palace but only to the Parliament buildings where Mummy's father served long ago, I lived in the shadow of kings and queens.

But I also lived in the shadow of the skyscrapers that lined Fifth Avenue along which one could stroll on one's way to Bonwit's and Best's and Peck & Peck. New Yorkers went to parties in the same kinds of evening clothes my parents had on when they came to kiss their girls goodnight—Ellen and me in one room, and Janet in "the baby's room" on the other side of the upstairs veranda. I wanted to be part of the "we" of *The New Yorker's* "Talk of the Town," meeting people who were lucky enough to be there already. Sometimes my life elsewhere took place in the future. But sometimes that future was happening right then to a *talented creature* known to no one but me.

Her talents would change several times, to be sure, before she found the right vocation. When I saw *National Velvet* I had just learned to ride, and for a while I spent my allowance on movie magazines and waited to be discovered—who knew by whom. But the life of a child movie star must have been too remote from my own for me to sustain. The young actors and actresses I read about had mothers who took their children to Hollywood for screen tests and pleaded with directors for starring roles for their little darlings, things I knew Mummy would never do. When I brought the subject up, she said she hated the kind of mothers who "lived through their children."

So I switched to a fantasy that I must have known would please her. In this one, I lived in New York, in a penthouse where I became a sought-after interior decorator. This was a profession "where a woman is in her glory," said the pages of *House and Garden,* another inhabitant of the library coffee table or sometimes the master bedroom's chaise longue—and how I loved the ring of those two-word phrases, the rich vocabulary of my future profession. "In her glory" meant living in a building with a welcoming doorman. It meant giving lots of parties where conversation bubbled around me—and was often about me. Most of all, it meant not getting married. With so many admirers, why would I need a husband?

I must have borrowed from my mother that vision of happiness as a succession of exquisitely managed parties. It was only during the six years when Daddy was away fighting the Germans that Mummy ate supper with us—and then only on Thursdays, Nanny's day off. Sometimes she would let us pull on a rope that hung inside the dark dumbwaiter to bring our trays up the three flights from the kitchen to the nursery—a feat our nannies never let us perform. My memories of our all-female household are vague, but even with all the rationing and drawn blinds and mock air raids there was a freedom that later disappeared when Daddy resumed his life with us. I loved the barred, gabled windows of our nursery, where a children's encyclopedia and the complete Mother West Wind series were lined up on the shelves at one end behind cribs and matching dressers full of dolls' clothes. Most of all, I loved our cavernous dumbwaiter with its swaying ropes, a place where death awaited me, or perhaps my sister Ellen, if somebody pushed.

Or perhaps I liked it simply because none of the houses I went to for birthday parties had one. These other homes had the same claw-footed furniture that we did, the same lighting fixtures made to look like candles, the same oil paintings of Venice or the French countryside in gilt frames with lights over them. But those houses were new, in Forest Hill Village—where, I was told, many Jews lived—or farther north in the country, where horses grazed behind white wooden fences. Only our house went back to the 1880s, when Daddy's grandfather brought his wife from upstate New York to Toronto. I found his name at the top of the list of births, deaths, and marriages in the family Bible to which, in a childish scrawl, I added my own.

On those special wartime Thursdays, as we cleaned our Beatrix Potter bunny china plates, Mummy delighted us with stories about our future selves. The defining event for these selves was, of course, our weddings, and Mummy's stories were remarkably predictive. Baby Janet, conceived when Daddy came home from the war to take an officer training course, would have one like hers, with many bridesmaids dressed in the same color. Ellen would have a small but lovely wedding that included only one bridesmaid. I would not have a wedding because I would elope with a movie star. Cornel Wilde—"Corny," I would call him—was Mummy's choice of a mate for me.

For the rest of the week we saw very little of her. She was out serving on committees, Nanny said, in a world that was run mostly by women and disdained by men, if my now-decorated father was to be believed. What the people in this world did was raise money, and that meant planning parties to which handsome men and elegant women flocked in full evening dress. I could see from *Harper's Bazaar* that this life went on in New York at an even greater intensity than in dignified, WASP Toronto, where everything but its many bell-ringing churches was closed on Sundays.

I can thank my mother's work on one of these committees for the next location of my imagined life, the one that began when my ballet teacher showed me her pink satin toe shoes and told me that, if I practiced diligently, I might someday have a pair of my own. It seems that my mother had something to do with the Ballets Russes when they came to Toronto. I was taking ballet lessons and developing the beginnings of my away-from-home life, driven by a series of intense imagined friendships with actual people I didn't really talk to—mostly crushes on boarders at the school I went to as a day student. I don't remember the names of any of these girls, or even what they looked like.

I have a photograph of myself at the age of ten holding up a tube of lipstick to my already painted lips as I sit in front of a mirror encircled with lights backstage at the Royal Alexandria Theater. The Ballets Russes is about to perform its famed *Nutcracker* with a cast that includes a local little girl who will sit on a throne at the back of the stage. Wearing a white dress with satin sash and ruffles around the neck, hem, and sleeves, I am surrounded by the smells and sounds of a world where a woman is in her glory in ways that *House and Garden* could never imagine.

Once I had been powdered and "mascara'd" and given "just a touch of rouge," someone took me up an iron staircase to the wings, where dancers were doing pliés and twisting the tips of their satin shoes into a tray of powdery rosin, and where the orchestra could be heard warming up on the other side of a thick, velvet curtain. Alexandra Danilova and her blond partner, Frederick Franklin, shook my hand. Under her false eyelashes, elaborate lines edged Danilova's exotic eyes. On her black hair, parted in the middle, rested a rhinestone crown. The two of them took my hand and we were photographed taking a bow. I assumed this move would be repeated at the end of the performance, but it was not.

Even before that night, I was living a double life. Outwardly, my days were as close to exactly alike as my nannies and teachers could make them. With two bus tickets tucked into my school bag, I set off every morning for my Gothic-style Anglican school, named after Canada's first bishop, Bishop Strachan. There I studied and ate lunch with girls my age, all of us dressed in the school uniform of white sailor middies and navy pleated skirts.

I came home to a house with pillars on either side of a black front door whose two brass knobs and brass mail slot made it look like a face.

I went upstairs with a butter tart or some cookies—whatever the cook had made that day. We kids were not allowed into the kitchen after Daddy came home from the war. We all ate in the dining room, where dinner was not until seven, so each day the cook would have a sweet waiting for us in the pantry. A slam of the front door meant that Daddy had returned from his office. Over dinner, he wanted to know if our school chums liked us. It was the most important thing, he said, so I told him yes, I was popular.

Of course, our mother's Thursday night stories had come to an end. We girls kept our coats and books out of sight, did our homework in our rooms, and learned good manners—whose main rule was not to interrupt when Mummy and Daddy were talking. Postwar North America replaced the "home front" where young men, more unprepared and ill-equipped than anyone would acknowledge at the time, had kissed their brides good-bye and then witnessed horrors they had no vocabulary to speak about, even to one another. Now that they were taking up their former lives, romance had to be rekindled, which meant keeping children out of sight as much as possible.

I must not have looked forward to coming home from school because I regularly managed to lose my return bus ticket. A former nanny whom I liked now worked close to the school, so I spent the afternoon with her and she gave me ticket money that I supposed my parents paid back. Things got more serious when I arrived home one day missing a shoe. My father, who thought that teasing was the best way to cure undesirable behavior, took to doing an imitation of me that I can still see and hear, though I don't remember losing the shoe. The phrase "losing my mind" came to represent a real fear. Could part of it have disappeared along with my shoe?

Perhaps the source of the problem was that the life that went on in my head became even more vivid after my evening with the Ballets Russes. There, already destined for stardom, I inhabited a world of daily dance classes, a world I'd learned about in a book I found in the public library during the war, when our household was composed of women. *Theatre Street* is the autobiography of Tamara Karsavina, one of the three "baby ballerinas" brought to Europe by Sergey Diaghilev, the founder of the Ballets Russes. Karsavina's parents were both dancers at the Maryinsky Theater in St. Petersburg. But it was Tata's mama who persuaded her husband, the Maryinsky's ballet master, to send their daughter to live as a boarder in the theater's school.

It seemed that the life I wanted required parents like these. So my dancer self had no parents. She was simply the fourth "baby ballerina," a phrase that swept aside the problem of my age, who lived and traveled with Tamara and her entourage in a life consumed by classes, rehearsals, and nightly triumphs in glamorous cities. I tried to fall asleep with my toes pointed so that a nanny, pulling off my covers, would discover a "natural" dancer.

I wish I could say that this imaginary life flowed out through my angular body, that my ballet teacher recognized a budding genius standing at the barre, her outer arm extended at shoulder height and curved just so. But no. I probably just acted remote and preoccupied. My sisters called me stuck up, a sign that you think you're better than others, the worst sin a child of wealthy parents can commit. And Ellen and I got into fights that led not only to tears but to more enduring damage too, like bruises and scratches—fights brought on by nothing more serious than that in the posed photographs taken in our drawing room, she, the baby, is so much prettier than me. Perhaps I just wanted to tear her apart to find out what made her so lovable.

But in fact I knew. Mummy liked to tell me I was a huge baby and that I talked in sentences before I could sit up. Though she didn't mention being ashamed of my bulk, my inertness, my lack of appeal to strangers who loved babies, I can understand her disappointment. As for my father, I don't think he wanted a boy any more than any other man of his generation. Like all male children from families like his, he spent his early life in boarding school and probably didn't imagine himself spending much time with his children of either sex.

But something had to be done. I bit. I kicked. Ellen was taller than me by the time I was in fifth grade. Daddy teased her relentlessly about her size in the same falsetto voice he used to mock my absentmindedness. "Acres O'Reilly," he called her, after a character in *Dick Tracy*—toughening both of us up, I suppose he would have said, for the brutality of our peers. So Mummy decided to separate us by sending me to her old boarding school in Ottawa. Her memories of the place were happy. Her oldest friendships began there, with Alice and a host of other chums, and I was thrilled to be going. A list of what to bring arrived in the mail, and Mummy and I shopped for the items on it: skirts and sweaters; a taffeta dress for concerts; a dark, wool one for church. Weekdays, I was to wear a green pleated tunic, a beige blouse, stockings, and a green blazer with the school crest on it.

Elmwood is housed in a sprawling Tudor-style building in Rockcliffe Park, the Ottawa suburb of quiet, tree-lined streets where crests hang over doors and unfamiliar flags flap in front of ambassadorial residences. We boarders made up an inner circle of about twenty-five, sleeping in cream-colored metal beds, gathering for evening prayers before dinner as well as morning prayers with the day students, hiding candy in our dresser drawers, and complaining about having to stay outside when the temperature dropped below zero. Every winter, the lower field was turned into a skating rink where some of us showed off our white buckskin skates, acquired at Christmas and very much a sign of status.

It must have worked for a while. The classes were very small, and to my considerable surprise, I had no difficulty getting an A in every subject. This produced no particular response at home. High marks were not a good sign for a girl in those days, and our household was ruled by a man who fervently believed that nothing useful came out of books. Really smart people, he liked to say, learn from being with people, so what mattered most was that people liked you. Reading was something you did in your room, not downstairs where other people would see you. I never saw my mother with anything heavier than a copy of *Time* or a paperback mystery in her hand, though she read those very quickly, in bed or lying on the chaise longue in the master bedroom.

It was as a favor to her, I think, that I was allowed to go into Ottawa for one ballet lesson a week, but only one. "What if everyone wanted to do something like that?" asked Mrs. Buck, the principal who had known my mother as a student. Mrs. Buck was from England, and her origin was reinforced by the small Tudor house she shared with her husband, Clement, who cast a shadowy presence with his drooping black mustache and strands of black hair combed across his bald head.

"But everyone *doesn't* want to do something like that," I kept saying, though perhaps they might follow my example, as Mrs. Buck assured me they would, if I got my way. I would learn in my brief stay at the University of Toronto the name of my enemy, Kant's categorical imperative: "Act as if the maxim from which you act were to become through your will a universal law." It struck me then as a way to keep people from even thinking about what they wanted, and perhaps my own categorical objection to rules began with those sessions in Mrs. Buck's wood-paneled, book-lined office with its lead-paned windows opening out onto the school grounds.

The problem for me was that I liked Mrs. Buck. She never went out without putting on gloves and a hat with a veil, and the view of the world embodied in these gestures is one that appeals to me still, especially when it's expressed in an English accent. Yet every moment of our lives as boarders was shaped by rules. Perhaps this was part of our preparation for life after school, since there was never a time when we had to make a decision about what we wanted to do. Expectations long in place covered every daily move: when and what we ate or studied, how we spent our "free" time.

I started doing things that would get me into trouble during my third year as a boarder. The main transgression I remember was putting a jazz bass to the hymns for morning prayers. I took piano lessons, and though my sight-reading was terrible, I could play any tune I could hum, so my services at morning prayers were in demand, at least until I refused to stick to a proper accompaniment. My infractions made me a popular storyteller, so perhaps that's why I committed them. In the sixties I was, for a while, a phenomenal shoplifter, and I knew even then that my motives had nothing to do with the things I stole, most of which I gave away, and everything to do with telling my friends about my audacious hauls.

Two years away from graduation, I was the school's star student, trying to stave off the dislike I imagined in the minds of my classmates by helping them with their homework after evening study hall. My dance classes were no solace; I was not the star pupil I had hoped to be at the Ottawa School of Ballet. And I was miserable at home during the holidays since my old school friends in Toronto had formed new cliques and alliances that did not include me. I remember going half a dozen times to see Moira Shearer in *The Red Shoes,* eager to hear again and again that I must choose between love and vocation.

I suppose it was inevitable that I would at some point step over a line. The escapade that finally forced Mrs. Buck's hand was a consequence of her announced retirement. She and her husband were going back to England, where their married life had begun. They had no children, and the question of whether or not Edith and Clemmie actually "did it" produced many giggles after lights out. Mrs. Buck's successor was to be our science teacher, Mrs. Murdock. We all suspected that Mrs. Murdock hit the bottle in her room at night. If I could come up with evidence of this without getting caught, then I could save the school from a disastrous future.

The door to Mrs. Murdock's room was the only one in a recessed alcove near the stairs leading down to the school's dark-paneled front hall. I remember the room but not the act of entering it. How thrilling—when we had to undergo rigorous room inspection every day—to see clothes, papers, and books piled everywhere. The blinds were drawn so I couldn't see much, but I did find what I wanted: a row of empty bottles at the foot of the unmade bed.

I don't know who saw me or how Mrs. Buck found out about it. But no one believed me when I explained my motive to a tribunal of teachers, including Mrs. Buck and several others whose favorite I had been. Mlle. Raymond, who at lunch presided over a French-speaking group at the table where I often sat, seemed close to tears, and all of them shook their heads as I walked out of the principal's office and I shut the door behind me. After that, everyone kept their distance, as fellow students learned of my Nancy Drew–like sleuthing. The popularity I'd imagined did not come to pass. I studied harder than ever, but what was the point of all those A's now?

When I went home for Easter recess, my mother told me I would be leaving Elmwood and going back to Bishop Strachan School in the fall. "Your father feels we don't see enough of you," she said. And those were the last words spoken by any of us on the subject.

But the year before my expulsion she gave me a gift whose unintended consequences would be to turn us into adversaries. She may have struggled not to live through her children but, perhaps through her committee work with the ballet, she learned of a dance camp in Bar Harbor, Maine, and arranged for me to go there. It was run by a German modern dancer who had worked under Kurt Joos, the choreographer of a powerful antiwar piece called "The Green Table." My mother and her unmarried sister drove me there from Toronto, a trip that involved two overnight stays in New England bed-and-breakfasts. Before she left me at camp, my mother handed me a plane ticket back to Toronto via New York.

Bar Harbor Island itself was a gothic paradise where dead trees and gutted mansions stood witness to a terrible fire that had swept the island a decade or so before. The dance school consisted of a single gray-shingled building that had once been a regular school in the seaside town of Hull's Cove. Its two dozen students and faculty members were housed in local homes whose flowered wallpaper and carpeted staircases were old enough not to look commercial but new enough not to look run down. I shared a room in one of these with Shirley, who had the enviable lot of attending Manhattan's High School of Performing Arts. Shirley was my mother's unintended gift. And as I ate and slept, pliéed and swam in the ocean with her and the other girls, I, too, became someone whose future lay in the world of dance.

One of the people who was working at the school, not as a dancer because at that point he'd had no training, was Paul Taylor. His job was to drive us students—all girls—into town or to the beach in the director's pale green 1932 Packard touring car, and we all adored him. Paul had been a swimmer in college, and he began taking classes with us, just for fun. Little did we suspect that in a matter of only a few years he would become a member of the Martha Graham company and then a major choreographer with his own troupe.

Our daily classes in ballet were given by Mme. Anna Istomina, a Russian teacher who was there with her husband and baby. The director taught modern dance and choreography. I did not have the wonderful "turnout" that allowed Shirley to shine in our ballet classes, but this woman saw in me an ability that many dancers, she said, did not have: I could create interesting movement that would break new ground for myself and others. "When you finish school," she said, "come to New York and I will help you develop your talent. If I'm still alive, that is." She was in her sixties and she died a few years later, but not before she had set me on the road to the future she saw for me.

Mme. Istomina's Russian name was real, and so was her husband: proof that the song, "Dance, Ballerina, Dance" did not describe the inevitable fate of one who gave herself to ballet. I had thoroughly absorbed *The Red Shoes* at that point, sobbing each time as Moira Shearer threw herself from a bridge in front of an oncoming train, but here was a living woman who had met her mate in a dance class, and whose flawless arabesques he seemed to admire as much as anyone. She would never do her pirouette in rhythm to her aching heart!

Getting ready to go home, Shirley and I discovered that we had tickets on the same flight to New York. She had already invited me to spend a few days with her family, so the transition was a smooth one. When we got off the plane we were hugged, not only by Shirley's parents, but by an uncle and a cousin as well. In this uncle's large, but not very new, car we sped toward the Bronx from the airport that was then called Idlewild. As everyone showered Shirley with compliments and questions, I took in the headstones of the cemetery that edged the expressway, their low- lying outlines imitating the skyscrapers behind them.

We pulled up to a redbrick apartment building on Sheridan Avenue, not far from Yankee Stadium. "Ma, she's never eaten pastrami," Shirley announced, and went on to list ten other foods that had never appeared on our dinner table or in our refrigerator. Everyone looked at me with such astonishment as we piled into the small elevator with metal walls that I didn't dare tell them I'd never been in an apartment building before either. I'd never heard a thump on the ceiling above me or music coming up from below the floor, no voices on the other side of a wall that did not belong to someone I knew. Living so close to so many strangers struck me as exciting rather than confining. One was part of a larger whole simply by being in this city.

Shirley's uncle patted me on the shoulder as he ushered me inside. The two men wore hats with narrow brims. It turned out they were in the hat business. We were greeted by a chorus of relatives and neighbors who hugged me and led me to a seat on the couch. I don't know how or when I figured out that they all were Jewish, or if I ever told Shirley that she was the first Jewish person my age I'd ever talked to.

"They didn't have *any* of this stuff up there," Shirley said as she speared each missed morsel with a plastic fork.

"What do folks eat where you come from?"

My mind went blank. "Roast beef," I finally said.

"We have that," said the now hatless uncle.

The mealtimes of my childhood are not pleasant memories. Perhaps our nannies had grown up in households where there wasn't enough to eat, or perhaps the grim, all-consuming news of the war had truly upset them. But for whatever reason, they were all fanatic about "starving children" and eating everything on your plate. Some even saved for the next meal what was not eaten at the previous one until you ate it, threw up, or did both. It would have been a mistake to tell Mummy, though. She always sided with the difficult-to-keep help as a matter of principle.

It was better when we got to eat with our parents. They sat at the head and foot of a long, mahogany table with two four-armed silver candelabra on either side of a silver biscuit box. Mummy, fresh from a bath, would be wearing one of her long dresses, something with a V neck that zipped up the front, a cross between an evening dress and a dressing gown. A buzzer under Daddy's foot summoned a maid who passed around vegetables in silver dishes, one at a time after Daddy had carved. No one could eat till everyone had been served. If any of us complained, Mummy cut in with one of her favorite phrases: if you can't say something nice, don't say anything. We could talk, but only Daddy could interrupt—a rule I didn't break.

By my second evening at Shirley's, after a trip on the D train to the Empire State Building and Radio City, I'd been taken into another kind of family. Shirley's sister, Lois, had willingly spent the previous night on the Castro convertible in the living room so Shirley and I could share their bedroom, something I could not imagine that my sisters and I would do for one another. The apartment had one other bedroom, where their parents slept, and a kitchen, where we ate, taking our cutlery from a glass jar in the center of the Formica table. I sat across from Shirley's father, a narrow-shouldered man who ate in a sleeveless undershirt. Shirley filled our glasses from a water bottle kept in the refrigerator while, from the stove, her mother served slices of pot roast, wearing a housedress whose armholes let you see her bra. I doubt that my parents would have taken in a friend of mine the way Shirley's did me, though I have no memory of ever putting that belief to the test.

"I'm moving to New York as soon as I finish school," I announced as the two of us lay in bed in the dark, the shouts of the street on that hot night letting us know that we were part of a lively community. The next day, Shirley's mother asked me what time my plane to Toronto was leaving. I turned my suitcase inside out, but my ticket was nowhere to be found. Was the hand of God reaching down to strike me? I had to call home to ask for another, knowing that this loss would be added to the story of my elusive shoe.

"She just wants to stay here with us," said Lois, and of course she was right. I wondered if my mother saw it that way, too, and if so, how she felt about it. I don't remember if anyone met me at the Toronto airport, but standing in the marble foyer just inside our majestic front door, I knew I was not glad to be back. I now had another point of view from which to observe my family's habits and attitudes. But such insights can exact a cost, and mine has been a strange "fear of flying." Not just the anticipation of crashing that I assume is common, but a belief which no amount of checking will dispel, that my ticket or some other vital document has leapt into thin air from the place I know I put it.

During my next (and last) year at Elmwood, Shirley wrote to me several times. It was not that I didn't want to reply to her cheery tales of Performing Arts and her wonderful ballet teacher, Robert Joffrey. But the person I had been when I was with her, the much-missed friend addressed in her sloping handwriting, had gone into hiding, inaccessible even to myself. Luckily for me, my mother agreed to send me back to Bar Harbor the following summer. "Why didn't you write?" Shirley wanted to know, and I was speechless with embarrassment. But she was forgiving. She invited me to visit again on my way home, and this time when I got back to Toronto, I did write.

Even so, when I graduated close to the top of my high-school class two years later, the person I had become when I was with her was no match for my desire to fit in and be popular with the people who surrounded me. Consequently, I followed my classmates to the University of Toronto. My parents had met there at a fraternity party and assumed that my future husband would be found in such surroundings. "College is the only place," Daddy said, "where you get treated like an adult and can act like a child."

What sent me back to New York, a place where I knew no one but Shirley and her family, was that all of my friends were planning to be debutantes the spring of our freshman year. To put it simply, I was almost literally paralyzed around boys. Nothing interesting would come out of my mouth at the formal dances at the homes of my parents' friends or at the Badminton Club where I spent my days pretending to have fun during the holidays because hanging around the house was not what we girls were supposed to do.

"Are you home this evening, dear?" my mother would ask on Saturday nights, as I crept up to my room after dinner with a book in my hand. Of course she and my father would be going out somewhere, and my sisters had not yet reached the dreaded age of obligatory dating. I would have given anything to have been able to casually announce a date with a member of one of my classes in philosophy, literature, or European history. Why was this not happening?

I had gone, in fact, to a big welcoming dance for new freshmen the first weekend of the school year. They had a contest for "Miss Freshie" and I won it; my picture was on the front page of all three Toronto papers the next day. I tried to act pleased, but I was horrified—if everyone said I looked the part, how could I insist that I felt no connection to the person they apparently saw? "We're so proud of you, dear," my parents kept saying, certain that lots of dates would assure for me a happy future.

Two weeks later, I got a call from a boy who said he'd been at the party, asking me if I was free the following Saturday night. Perhaps this was the beginning of my new life. I don't remember the date at all, but only his standing on my front steps and giving me a quick kiss before asking for my measurements. "I'm pledging a fraternity," he said, looking away as he spoke, "and this is something I have to do." What upsets me even now is not that he asked, but that I actually gave him my measurements before my shaking hand turned the key in my front door.

A few days later I told my mother I wanted to study dance and choreography in New York. "Do you think you're talented enough to succeed in a big place like New York?" she asked.

"I don't know. But I want to give it a try."

"Well, all right," she said. "I guess if you fail you can always come back here."

After promising to speak to my father, she found out about a place to live that sounded wonderful. The Rehearsal Club was just down the street from the Museum of Modern Art. It had been the setting for a play and for the movie *Stage Door* starring Katharine Hepburn. If my mother had any fears about how I, who had never managed a budget that went much beyond my boarding school "pocket money" of fifty cents a week, would handle life on my own, she didn't mention them.

I don't know how I made the final leap into the magical light of Grand Central Station—"crossroads of the world," as an old radio program called it. I had no real pictures of my new life. I simply numbed myself, hardly daring to imagine another welcome from Shirley and her family. But I had leotards and tights in my suitcase and a check signed by Daddy for a thousand dollars. "Let us know when you need more," he said as we waved good-bye at Toronto's Union Station. I had never seen a check for so much money.

It was not until the train started to move that I allowed myself to feel hopeful. "You were brave," people have said, but I didn't feel a bit brave. I was just acting on instinct, the way people do in a war. I had a lower berth, but the rocking of the wheels below the mattress on which I lay kept me from sleep. In the morning I emerged, groggy and dazed, into the angled light from the windows of Grand Central and the intensity of car horns on Forty-Second Street. Good things would happen here. Things that would make me proud of the life I was going to have.

8

The city into which I walked that morning, the New York of the fifties, has disappeared almost as completely as the layers of Troy that Schliemann discovered on the coast of the Aegean. Some of my city has been physically submerged: the Rehearsal Club, for instance, and the narrow four-story brownstones on either side of it have been devoured by the westward expansion of the Museum of Modern Art. The wrecking of McKim, Mead, and White's Penn Station had not yet begun.

Part of my New York was imaginary, of course, but the imagination that created it was a collective one. My piece of it came first from my parents, especially from my father whose grandfather had hung out with "Diamond Jim" Brady, but also from William Shawn and his staff "here at *The New Yorker*," and from Gordon Jenkins, whose musical tribute, *Manhattan Tower,* begins with a narrator announcing, "It was raining the first time I saw my tower, the first time I saw it in reality. In my dreams I had seen it many times before . . ."

That city, the mecca to which aspiring artists of every variety gravitated in search of lives their hometown would not give them, was partly illusory even then. Leonard Bernstein's *Wonderful Town,* which my mother and I saw in 1953, celebrates her New York of the thirties rather than mine. But as long as rents were cheap, it was possible to show up, as I did, with high hopes and big plans and few marketable skills. The

Rehearsal Club, where I lived for a year and a half, was a shelter for those aspirations and a monument to them.

From there I moved, a year or so later, to the one-bedroom apartment in Hell's Kitchen that I shared with Paula Gibbs and Debbie Jowett, two of the aspiring dancers I met there and still occasionally see. Paula is now an usher at Alice Tully Hall and Debbie is a dance critic for the *Village Voice*. Our rent was $105 a month, which we divided in three, and we took care of one another as people who live in such close quarters must do. Each week, one of us shopped and made a dinner for all to eat when our schedules allowed, while another cleaned, and the third did everyone's laundry. We all lost our virginity during our time together, and the support of my more confident roommates made me believe I could overcome my dismal history.

We took dance classes during the day from different teachers, and Paula helped me get a job as an usher with her at Carnegie Hall. Our block boasted half a dozen French restaurants and a hanging neon cross. GET RIGHT WITH GOD, it commanded, as we walked toward Eighth Avenue, setting out for work just as normal people were going home to food and family. SIN WILL FIND YOU OUT, it told us, as we two trudged homeward after an evening shared not only with Leonard Bernstein or Eugene Ornmandy or George Szell but with other ushers, fellow exiles from the world of dull jobs and dead marriages.

My first lover was an usher and a pianist, a former child prodigy whose career never went much beyond the moment of winning the prestigious Naumberg competition. He lived with five other musicians in a building, now demolished, on East 105th Street, down the block from the old Manhattan School of Music. After following him home on the subway one night, my uniform left behind in the locker for women ushers, I lay on his bed listening to him work on the Beethoven *Appassionata* and decided that the joy I was feeling was one my mother knew nothing about.

On the beige wall above his bed, a centerfold from *Life* in which Michelangelo's God touched Adam's extended finger was held by Scotch tape. My lover's touch did not bring me to life, and he soon left me for another usher. But if my heart could be broken, did that not prove that at least one part of my unresponsive body was normal? In any event, I found other lovers among the ushers and on the benches of Washington Square Park, where I spent my spare time listening to folk music when the weather was nice. With hair reaching to my waist, I didn't look as though I came from WASP Toronto, and my paralysis around men began to disappear behind the newly visible, dancing me.

By that time I had my own place in the West Village, the part of New York that, while outwardly remaining pretty much the same, has changed most. When Thomas Wolfe's lament, "You can't go home again," comes into my head, I don't think of Toronto but of a tree-lined web of streets where molded ceilings and chandeliers can be seen through spotless windows only a block away from huge caverns enclosing carcasses of beef, rows of them lit by fires in oil drums. In the fifties the Village was home to runaways like me—seekers of what E. B. White calls "the gift of loneliness and privacy."

Back then it housed a group that is still sometimes called "starving artists," and I moved there in order to be one of them. Of course I didn't tell a soul that my father's father had married a New Yorker, the heiress of the patent medicine fortune that came from Carter's Little Liver Pills. I was in flight from that world, yet I felt quite at home among the shuttered brick houses that Henry James made famous—living in the shadows of my ancestors.

It is we starving artists who have vanished from these houses that now sell for a million dollars and up. My first apartment, a studio in a narrow building whose back windows faced onto a tree-filled courtyard, cost only $69 a month when I began living there. It had a working fireplace, built-in bookshelves, and a partition separating the kitchen from the rest of the room. I lived in it till I married my first husband, Kevin's father, and though I almost starved myself to death there and was hospitalized for depression, I feel nothing but happiness now as I walk past my old front door—*what a gift that I got to spend part of my life here!*

Soon after I first arrived in New York, I called Shirley from a pay phone at the Rehearsal Club to let her know I had truly arrived. She had graduated from Performing Arts and was taking a ballet class every day with

Bob Joffrey in his studio on Sixth Avenue between Ninth and Tenth Streets. Each morning she worked as a page at the Forty-Second Street Public Library, and since I had a student visa, I had no trouble joining her in that magnificent building: my first real job. The library had six stacks; two or three pages were assigned to each. Call slips came to us through tubes that ran along the ceiling and down the wall next to the automatic dumbwaiter that carried books up to the main reading room. Our fellow pages studied at various city colleges. Shirley and I simply claimed to be their classmates.

After work, we went to the employees' cafeteria until the weather warmed up and we could eat our lunch in Bryant Park behind the library. Shirley introduced me to "a dancer's lunch": half a pint of cottage cheese with a jar of fruit baby food mixed into it. Then we'd hang out till our four o'clock ballet class, listening to records in the music library or window-shopping in the Village. Shirley's ears were pierced, the work of her sister wielding a needle and a piece of ice, so naturally I asked Lois for holes of my own. The day I wore my first pair of pierced earrings felt like an initiation. I pinned up my lengthening hair in elegant knots. I bought a large canvas bag with a shoulder strap to transport my dance clothes. I was becoming a dancer.

There was only one problem. My years of weekly lessons were no match for the daily work that my fellow students had engaged in for years. They extended their friendship to "Shirley's friend from Canada," but I knew I didn't deserve it. Standing at the barre, I did what I could to look like everyone else, but what I could do was not enough. When we moved to the center of the floor, I stayed toward the back, though Bob was always very kind to me, especially after he found out that we had the same birthday, December 24. I would have given my life for a word of praise from him or from Jerry Arpino, his assistant, or from any one of my fellow dancers. In fact, I almost did.

It's easy now to trace the steps by which I decided to surpass in thinness these lucky native New Yorkers who were hopelessly my superiors as dancers. I began by skipping the two meals, breakfast and dinner, that were included as part of my weekly rent at the Rehearsal Club. My roommates there were two Rockettes and great friends. Radio City Music Hall was only three blocks away, but their breaks between shows did not usually coincide with the meal service in the Club's basement cafeteria, and eating with strangers was the last thing I wanted to do. So, I would buy a yogurt or another half-pint of cottage cheese, wash out my leotard and tights, and go to bed early.

I'm not sure exactly when my fear of food set in. Perhaps I'd never stopped being, in some part of my brain, the very large, tough-looking infant of my baby pictures, the one who must have embarrassed my mother. Did she hope, every time she picked me up, that there would be a little less of me? Was she waiting for the day when I'd stand and run around my playpen the way the children of her friends did? Only now that she is dead do I imagine asking her these questions. I have dreams that could have been hers—dreams of living in the pillared house, filled with the ghosts of my father's dead parents, that she took charge of as a bride at twenty-one. But, for a long time after we lived on different sides of an international border, the only way I saw to become someone other than her daughter was to be more vigilant than she about what I ate.

The most tangible reminder of our connection was my checking account at the marble-floored First National City Bank on Fifty-Second Street whose old name, ghostlike, is still visible on the stone above its current snappy, blue-and-white Citibank sign. My paycheck from the library paid for my classes, but money for everything else had to be slipped to me under the brass grate by a teller, and no amount of good management held back the flow. Since mentioning money had been taboo at home, I had no idea how large my family's income was, let alone how much of that might be required to heat a three-story house, pay a living wage to three maids, feed, clothe, and send three girls to school, furbish two cars and a summer home, ski in the Laurentians, and maintain membership at the Golf Club and the Hunt Club and the photogenic Midocean Club in Bermuda.

It was when I took the money slipped under that polished grate, surrounded by men in gray suits who were preoccupied with high finance, that I felt most like my mother. Banks charged extra in those days to give you your balance, and though mine should not have been hard to figure out, it was alien territory for me. My mother had sat at her desk by the window in the library once a month writing checks, but she always ordered me away whenever I got close enough to see the actual amounts. This monthly ritual was the only "wifely duty" about which I ever heard her complain. It did occur to me that perhaps we were rich, but no, she insisted, we were just "comfortably off." Did she know from which streams the money came—not just Daddy's salary from a company started by his grandfather but also her inherited portfolios and his? I doubt it. She probably didn't even keep a running tab.

The speed with which money raced through my hands alarmed me, mainly because I could not control it. I didn't even know if it would be an imposition on my parents to send me another thousand-dollar check, so ignorant was I of what proportion of the whole it would represent. The subway cost fifteen cents then, and my weekly rent at the Rehearsal Club was eighteen dollars. My Rockette roommates got paid $125 every week, a steady stream of money I could not imagine what I would do with.

The problem intensified once I decided to take a modern-dance class each morning at the Martha Graham studio in addition to my four o'clock ballet class. Shirley and her friends had been taking both since they entered Performing Arts, so I had little choice but to do everything I could to catch up. I couldn't eliminate shelter or transportation or daily dance classes, but perhaps I could do without food. I bought apples from the first Balducci's on Sixth and Greenwich, and eating maybe five or six a day, one every few hours, I made a bag of them last two days. Occasionally I was gripped by strange cravings and would devour, for instance, an entire box of pretzels alone in my room, which was by then a single unit on the top floor next to the common bathroom.

As my appetite became an enemy that I could subdue and a gateway to other triumphs, my visits to Shirley's family on weekends became sites of a struggle I did not want them to notice. Of course Shirley was on a diet, and her family accepted this as a defining condition of a dancer's life—one more thing that made her different from them. But I was picking up hints that my ideal family was beginning to find my own behavior strange. I was on the alert for evidence that they no longer wanted me around, but I wanted to hide my suspicion as well as the behavior that might justify it.

Yet Shirley's mother continued to welcome me into their small, crowded apartment with its smells of pot roast and noodle pudding. I didn't pay for the privilege of being there, and more than once, I asked this soft, comforting woman, who seemed so remote from my troubles, if there was anything she wanted me to do. I knew I would feel better if the relationship were less one-sided, if there were a few dishes I could wash, a surface or two I could wipe. Was there a rule I didn't know that governed such situations? Why had the reflexes that people call on for guidance in these matters failed to develop in me?

I remember sitting at one end of their living room couch, watching her pat her warm forehead with a lace-trimmed handkerchief as she dusted and vacuumed. "I don't expect you to do anything," she said when I offered to help. "You're our guest. Just do whatever you feel like doing." Hearing words so unfamiliar made me feel even more anxious about pleasing her. To this day, I'm clearer about what I should be doing than about what I want to do.

Since I had decided, even before I left Toronto, that I would not go home again until I could return "in triumph," I dreaded every trip to the bank that brought closer the day I would have to ask for more money. Even in the fifties, a thousand dollars didn't last forever. I could have looked for a second job, but giving up my dance classes would have destroyed my justification for having left home. The solution could have been working as a waitress at night, but I never even thought of a job that would have put me around so much food.

By the time my first year was out, I was eating almost nothing, limiting myself to spending fifty cents a day. Sometimes I tried to panhandle on Sixth Avenue, moving tentatively toward well-dressed men and women with playbills in their hands, not wanting to see the irritation on their faces. Or I'd gesture to the man who cut the cold meats and cheeses displayed so invitingly behind glass in the deli on Fifty-Fourth Street: could I have the scraps he was about to throw away?

But I'm not good at asking for things, and if neither of these efforts worked, I climbed the three flights of stairs to my room and went to bed *hungry* rather than violate my spending limit. Gradually my resistant body, the one that had kept my true spirit hidden from the world, retreated in defeat till I felt almost transparent. From our daily Bible readings at school I summoned up the command: "Let your light so shine before men that they may see your good works" and knew that my own light was finally shining through its shade. Then there was the children's hymn version, which I'd learned in Sunday school.

Jesus bids us shine with a pure, clear light
Like a little candle burning in the night.

With my stomach growling as I tossed and turned in the dark, trying to make sleep come, I felt connected to the pain of the world.

As long as the money was coming across the border, I was expected to go back to Toronto from time to time. After a year and two months on my own, I flew home for a second Christmas with a sense of triumph at hand, if not yet attained. What I remember most about that trip is my disappointment. I expected my parents to be proud of me. I had conquered the part of me that had compelled me to ask them for things I did not deserve. They had sent me to Bar Harbor, coughed up more plane fare after my visit to Shirley, wasted a semester's tuition at the university. They'd even told me I could come home if I failed. What more could I do to show that I would soon stop being a burden to them?

On that visit home I went with my mother to see my old pediatrician, the familiar, bespectacled, white-haired Dr. Brown, who'd spent his days, serene and jovial, surrounded by children who unfailingly screamed, despite his efforts to distract them from his needle with a punch on the other arm. I watched him shake his head as he moved the lower weight on his standing scale from its hundred-pound notch back to the fifty-pound one. I slipped back into a six-year-old self as he took my blood pressure and pressed his cold stethoscope to my chest and back.

"Now you listen to me," he said back in his office, its walls crowded with the same, framed diplomas and photographs I'd seen many times before. "You weigh eighty-five pounds, which is barely enough to keep a girl your height alive. Keep on going the way you're going now and you'll be dead in three months."

I looked at the side of my mother's face and then back at him. What was he talking about? I'd never been stronger in my life. How could I be dying when my body was so close to being my own? No one in Toronto could see me for who I was. I should have known that and refused to come. As we left the Medical Arts Building, I realized how far my mother was from being proud of me. "How could you let yourself do this?" she asked me in the car.

"Do what?"

"Get to be skin and bones like this."

"But you and Daddy said it was good not to eat too much." My mother always took less than my father, and both of them warned us girls (who had more than most, after all) not to be greedy. What did I expect from her? Had her mother ever given her the kind of full-body embrace I got from Shirley's mother? My grandmother once gave Mummy a prayer book and some hand towels for Christmas. "For clean hands," read the card that went with these things, "and a pure heart." So I doubt it. I myself have no memories of ever being held against Granny's large, corseted body. And no one went to church with her.

Christmas dinner was different from other family meals only in degree. We had to be even more on our guard, because the table with its extra mahogany leaves was covered with a white damask cloth that was older than any of us, and Mummy didn't want to see grease and cranberry stains around anyone's place when the plates were cleared. For me, the past was always vividly present in the dining room with its floor-length, white curtains, its lead-paned windows that faced our driveway, and the French doors that opened onto our backyard. The hunting prints on the walls were an understated memorial to Daddy's handsome, womanizing father, who'd been thrown from his horse and killed while out hunting. The sideboard held a flatware service for twenty-four in boxes lined in velvet.

That Christmas Daddy carved, as always, and made a big point of giving us our choice of light or dark. There were toy crackers to be pulled and paper hats to put on, more vegetables than usual to be passed by our maid and an extra woman who was hired for the day, and flaming plum pudding with ice cream or hard sauce but not both. And more than ever, we were expected to observe the rule: if you can't say something nice, don't say anything. My father's sister, who in her picture hat looked just like their long-dead mother in the painting that hung in the front hall, had joined us, as usual, with her alcoholic husband and their three sons; so enforcing the rule was more difficult but also more necessary.

I have no idea how I got through the holiday, but I know I was in a hurry to get back to New York. My mother got from Dr. Brown the number of a doctor on Park Avenue who dealt with conditions like mine, whatever they were, and no one protested the brevity of my stay. The day before I left, I saw a pillbox with a mosaic top on my mother's dresser, and I asked if I could have it. I was drinking coffee with saccharine by then. It would be perfect for my little white pills.

"No," she said. "It's something I especially like." I didn't steal it from her, but on subsequent visits I took several other items: a small Victorian china clock, a silver hand mirror that had belonged to my grandmother, and a cobalt-blue glass that my mother demanded I return when she discovered its absence. I did send it back, but it broke in transit. After that, I gave up stealing from her, waiting till the sixties to hone my shoplifting skills in Jensens, Bonwit's, and other landmarks in a part of the world I still consider my mother's territory, imagining how impressed my father would be with my skill at stretching his money.

Once back in New York, I moved out of the Rehearsal Club and into the Hell's Kitchen flat. Because I didn't want to stop living, I took seriously what Dr. Brown had said and tried to figure out what it would mean to eat "normally." The regimen that Debbie, Paula, and I had developed was a help. Our schedules were such that we all ate alone and usually standing up. I made sure I ate less of our shared supplies and dinners than either of my roommates—while going to great lengths, when it was my turn to cook, to produce interesting casseroles and other low-budget fare with the limited money we spent on food.

It was difficult to figure out what "normal" eating might be, because I realized I had never really enjoyed it. Food at Elmwood, though a far cry from what Jane Eyre ate at Lowood, was gray, overcooked, and doused with gravy or on the soggy French toast I most remember eating there (a favorite of all of us at the time) maple syrup. I learned that an inability to start eating is the twin of an inability to stop, and I alternated for a while between starving and gorging, all in the service of gaining just enough weight to prevent the fate Dr. Brown had predicted, but without blowing up—a constant fear of anyone with an eating disorder.

The "Park Avenue man" my doctor recommended had a name—Dr. Kugelmass—that conjured up pictures of sinister characters in German children's stories. His office was in the east Eighties, so I walked about thirty north-south blocks and six horizontal ones to my scheduled appointments. In the windows of the elegant stores I passed on Madison Avenue were items that reminded me of home: Queen Anne desks, period chairs, and fire screens; tea sets by Spode and Meissen just like the ones, passed down through both sides of my family, now resting on the top shelves of our pantry; a doll's hospital with teddy bears and china dolls like those that had once lived in our third-floor nursery; dresses and shoes and handbags identical to the ones in my mother's walk-in closet.

I took my time in both directions, sometimes unable to tear myself away from the plenitude that was so close yet so out of reach. If only my family could have lived in one of these buildings whose lobbies enclosed fountains and mirrors guarded by doormen who would have greeted me by name. How different I might be if I had slept between sheets trimmed with ruffles from one of these linens-and-comforter shops, bought my cosmetics from a drugstore with colored globes in its windows, gone to school with some of these girls in their gray and navy blue uniforms, stopped at the very preppy Prexy's for "the hamburger with the college education." From Harvard, perhaps, or Princeton, or Yale, all of them male-only schools back then.

When I got to my destination, the dark, carpeted waiting room was always filled with people of all ages with metabolic abnormalities, since no one had yet put the words *eating* and *disorder* together in a single diagnosis. People of all ages with thick necks and squat bodies rocked on carved, upholstered chairs. Gaunt men and woman whose hair needed combing looked about with fear in their eyes. Some made noises, others repeated words. It was as if I had arrived in an underground kingdom out of *Fantasia*, the Hall of the Mountain King. In the flesh, Dr. Kugelmaas was not as scary as I had expected. He was a balding man wearing a white coat and silver-rimmed glasses, just like hundreds of other doctors. On my first visit he gave me a shot and a prescription and told me to come back in a week for another injection.

I did go back faithfully for several months, walking each way and taking in all the items along my route that called up memories of home. Protected behind glass, the items were free to stir up a longing that was disconnected from my actual past. Though I kept my appointments, I was so terrified of what the weekly shot would do to my defenseless body—what ravenous energies and obscene swellings it might set in motion—that I never filled the mysterious prescriptions I was given. Of course I assured the nurse that I had.

It was around this time that I dropped ballet and began another modern-dance class. My new teachers were former members of the Graham company, May O'Donnell and Gertrude Schurr, who were, I was told, lovers. Paula, Debbie, and I had known several gay couples, and living in the Village, I was glad to be surrounded by fellow exiles from the family circle. But in Gertrude and May I saw something more. They supported each other quite openly and were always clearly delighted to see the other one walk in the door.

The next few years of my life are very indistinct, but for a while it looked like this switch from ballet to a less competitive environment was helping me to come to terms with my need for food and for money from my parents, at least as long as I stayed on my own terrain. Though I swung back and forth between bingeing and abstaining, somehow I managed to summon enough strength and enjoyment to stay with my schedule of classes and ushering at Carnegie Hall. But the next time I visited my parents, I fainted on the street and was taken in an ambulance to the hospital, suffering from the usual symptoms of severe food deprivation: a racing heart, low blood pressure, and incoherence. This was in Ottawa, where my parents had moved, now that all their children were out of the house. My father was still a popular member of Parliament, but he now represented the area where we spent our summers. He held a number of cabinet posts in the course of a long, much-photographed career in which he never lost an election.

My collapse happened the day before I had planned to go back to New York, and my mother and father were scheduled to leave for Italy the next day. Perhaps it was a political trip and he got to take her for free. Perhaps it was pleasure, but in any case they left instructions with the doctor in charge to keep me for as long as necessary—and took off. This, I found out from the nurse in charge. "How could they leave me?" I asked, but of course she had no idea how to answer.

But by this time, I had my own doctor in New York, a wonderful man with an office in the Village. A student at May and Gertrude's had told me about him. "I don't think you need that kind of treatment," she said when I described my visits to Dr. Kugelmaas. "Or that kind of doctor. I'll give you the number of mine. He understands the kinds of things that are happening to you."

Dr. Wadro was famous among dancers for understanding things almost no one understood in those days. I had stopped having my period, but I trusted the medication he prescribed to bring it back. When I told him I had lost my virginity he gave me a hug and told me he was proud of me. "I know what this means to you," he said, and he was right. When I told him, six months afterward, that I was pregnant, he performed an abortion for me. In the years before Roe v. Wade, this could be done legally *only if* he asserted that I was a threat to my own life and to order round-the-clock nurses, who must have been told that I was dangerous.

I'm not sure if they really believed this or not, but I thought I had to act the part convincingly, so I refused to say a word or look directly at anyone for the required length of my stay. It was expensive, so I had to tell my mother, who was cool but not angry. "Nice people have to do things like this sometimes," she said over the phone. I wondered how she knew.

From the hospital in Ottawa, I called Dr. Wadro and told him how frightened I was at being attached to an IV tube with no sense of when I would be able to leave. "They can't legally keep you there," he said. "If you feel you can do it, just tell them you're leaving. Do you have enough money to get to the airport?"

"I think so. And I have an aunt here who likes me. I think she would loan me the money if I don't have it." This was Aunt Dorrie, my favorite family member and the only one who had any real interest in what I was up to. She came to visit me in the hospital and was almost as disturbed as I was that Mum and Daddy had left. She paid for my cab to the airport. I flew back to New York, and the incident might as well never have happened.

I wish I could call up more details of my life after that, but the first half of the sixties involved more drugs than I like to think of, and I know they took their toll. The only binge-and-purge episode I can remember occurred when I was invited to spend Thanksgiving with some cousins of my father's who lived in a large Tudor house in Bronxville, an expensive suburb just to the north of New York City. I saw a box filled with crescent rolls, two dozen at least, being put back into the fridge after dinner, its contents hardly touched. In the early hours of the morning I crept downstairs into the kitchen and ate every one of them. Then I went into the bathroom and stuck my fingers down my throat. I must have hidden the empty box, perhaps in the dancer's bag I took with me the next morning. No one mentioned the rolls but I never heard from my cousins again.

Perhaps there was a connection between my visit to these wealthy cousins and my choice of food as the medium through which to express my realization that most of the world's population is not "comfortably off," as these Bronxville relatives surely were. In a secondhand bookstore in the Village, one of several in my neighborhood that stayed open till midnight, catering to solitary souls like me, I "found" Simone Weil, who had died because she refused to eat more than the ration given to people in concentration camps.

I carried her *Notebooks* around with me and copied her thoughts into my own. Near the end of her life, a friend spoke of "being in the presence of an absolutely transparent soul that was ready to be reabsorbed into the original light," a thought that seemed to me to define exactly the struggle I was waging through my daily dance classes and minimal eating: not thinness as a goal in itself but as the gateway to a life of perfect expressivity, a channel for the peace of God.

I've heard that anorexia never stops, that its mentality remains, like traces of a city now submerged, even if one's behavior is somehow released from it. In the years following, I turned to "better living through chemicals" in order to escape the limitations of life in a body. Methedrine, usually called "speed," was easy to get then; and after I left the dance world—in disgrace, I would have said then—with its demand for more and more lightness, I returned to college and became a star performer through the use of my high-flying mind. It was the right move for me and led me to where I am now. And yet, forty years after I began to starve myself, my idea of "a good day" is still one in which I've eaten less than I think others have.

My father while at Royal Military College, Kingston, Ontario. My mother loved a man in uniform.

My parents' wedding, June 1934.

My mother and her daughters riding bicycles during the war, when gasoline was rationed. At our summer home in Cobourg, Canada.

Shortly after the war, my mother, my sisters, and I posed for a photographer in our drawing room in Toronto.

Prima ballerina Alexandra Danilova and me in her dressing room, before my walk-on in the Ballets Russes performance of The Nutcracker *at Toronto's Royal Alexandra Theater, 1947.*

My first husband and me at our wedding reception, Pleasantville, New York, May 29, 1965.

Foley and me during my first visit to Nigeria, August 1993.

Foley and me at our wedding in Osogbo, August 18, 1995.

More wedding photographs.

Foley and me dancing at a party at the Nike Gallery, Osogbo, January 1997.

9

Dance is a vocation that promises to take everything out of you. And perhaps what I most wanted from it was a chance to take it up on that promise. "A condition of complete simplicity," is how T. S. Eliot puts it, "costing not less than everything." The dawn of the sixties found me looking into the mirror that covered a wall in Merce Cunningham's studio on Fourteenth Street to find a person I could believe in. At night, I worked in the box office and then ushered at the Living Theater, which occupied the same building. Shirley had left the world of dance, with its relentless demand for rigorous dieting, to marry a man who owned a hardware store in Worcester, Massachusetts. She'd met him while vacationing with her parents in Florida and had no regrets, she said.

My own life then took place along a circuit that extended from Ninth to Fourteenth Streets and from Sixth Avenue to my apartment near the Hudson River. It was exhausting, it was unvarying, it required determination to stay with it day after day. What filled the spaces was reading: I went in for long books like Dostoevsky's *The Idiot* and Thomas Wolfe's *The Web and the Rock*. I saw myself in Virginia Woolf's edited diaries, and everything by Camus became dog-eared in my dance bag. I also carried with me always a stenographic notebook into which I poured thoughts about a life in art interspersed with lines from Rilke, the Bible, Leonie Adams, and Edna St. Vincent Millay.

After work, I sometimes went home with one of the actors from the

Living Theater, doing it more out of curiosity—to find out what it would really be like to go to bed with this person so different from the men on whom I'd been taught to set my sights—than by anything I would identify as desire. I thought of my body as something to remake through daily training, and sleeping with men who wanted to help with that was part of it. Orgasm, like turnout, could not be forced but with enough determination it could be achieved even if it did not come "naturally." I was practicing, and the more you practiced the better you got.

But practicing is never about the present. You live in a future that may never come and will arrive only if you work at it. When I heard myself described once by the gay stage manager as "an easy lay," I was taken aback. Nevertheless, I knew that those hip, cool, pot-smoking men for whom I pulled out the other half of my trundle bed—and the hippest and coolest of these were black—were means to an end they would not be part of: myself as a fully developed, self-expressive artist.

Insinuated into this rigorous program was Freud, who insisted that my inability to achieve orgasms was the result—the inevitable result—of my unfeminine refusal to renounce a masculine desire for public recognition. Dance put a woman "in her glory" but it was an empty glory, one that would leave me doing my pirouette in rhythm to my aching heart. I visited Shirley and her husband one weekend and listened to them making love, joyfully and noisily, on the other side of the living room wall. Their obvious happiness looked like evidence that Freud was on the mark, though Merce's leading dancer was married to a composer, so the law could not be universal.

It was after I was accepted into the dance company of James Waring, whose choreography was deeply influenced by Merce, that I had what was then called a "nervous breakdown." Having achieved my goal of becoming a dancer, I should have felt triumphant. Instead, I became terrified that I would fail my new mentor—that my awkward Toronto self, the one who couldn't even dance with a boy, let alone on a stage, would suddenly reclaim me and punish me for trying to hide her for so many years. My welcome from Shirley's family had brought out these fears. But now I really was a dancer, and members of Merce's company said it was only a matter of time before he would ask me to join. I had just the kind of build he liked, they said, and of course I worshipped him. Given my omnivorous reading, not only of Freud but of Erich Fromm and the controversial Wilhelm Reich, whose writings could be found in the used bookstores in my beloved neighborhood, it was probably inevitable that I would sooner or later find my way to a psychoanalytic couch, which in my case turned out to be a comfortable leather chair in the Riverside Drive office of Dr. Ernest Angel, a precise, gentle man from Germany who had escaped from the camps and begun a new life and a new family here.

I had been going to this office, with its enviable view of the river, twice a week for three months when my new-found support told me he was going to take his month-long vacation early so he could speak at a conference back in his native country. "I don't think I can manage while you're gone," I told him the next time I saw him. "Do you think you could find a place where I could just be—uh—taken care of for a while?" He did not act at all surprised. "You're the only person I really talk to," I told him. But it was more than that. Without him, there would be no one to listen to the story taking shape in my head, the one that was moving toward a resolution, pulling its disparate threads together, making things matter.

"You don't talk to your dancer friends?"

"Not really. Dancers aren't much into talking."

"And the men from the Living Theater?"

"I get the feeling actors are only interested in themselves." He smiled at this, having been involved in Max Reinhardt's theater in Germany. I never asked him why he chose South Oaks for me and only learned afterward that they had pioneered the use of shock treatment. "We still use it sometimes," said a male voice when I called recently to ask for a copy of my medical records. "When were you here?"

"Nineteen-sixty, I think. I stayed about four months."

"That was another era," the man said. "Now our average length of stay is twelve days. Managed care, you know."

The hospital is still in Amityville, and the day I was supposed to show up there the Long Island Railroad went on strike, so the hospital sent a limousine to get me. The driver and the nurse who had come with him rang the bell of my four-flight walk-up on West Twelfth Street. I was packed and waiting for them, my apartment clean and ready for my friend Diana, who was moving out of her family's house in Queens and subletting my tiny but desirable space. I told her I did not know how long I would be gone. It was the beginning of April. The five-member dance company I had just joined would not have any performances until the fall.

"These stairs are terrible. So dark and dirty." The nurse who spoke these words cast a quick, disapproving glance around my apartment as I held the door for her male companion. The other patients where I was going probably started out, I decided, from places with doormen and elevators, perhaps even lawns and driveways. My image of a mental hospital had come from J. D. Salinger and Robert Lowell. I had not been expecting disapproval. My intention was simply to be in a place where people understood that you could be deeply miserable, as Salinger's characters were, even though you could not point to the source of your misery in the ordered world around you.

The driver of the car that would take me to South Oaks walked over to my suitcase. "This all you have?"

"Yes. I hope it will be enough."

"All right then," said the nurse. "Give me your pocketbook."

"Why?"

"That's our rules. The patient needs to hand over everything she's bringing."

"I don't understand. You can look inside if you want to. There's nothing in it that will cause anyone any harm. But I want to keep it with me at least till we get there. Why can't I do that?"

The man put my suitcase down. "Lady, if you're not going to do what we say, we'll just leave you here."

The thought of being abandoned, even by these two strangers, sent such a wave of terror through me that I handed the nurse my pocketbook without another word. In that moment I knew that this was a warning of what was in store for me, but I was too fearful to call the whole thing off. I sat in the back seat with the nurse, and we rode in silence through the Midtown Tunnel and all the way out to Amityville. In the cars around us people were enjoying, or so I imagined, the freedom that car travel gives. They might have thought I was crazy if they had known why I was on the Long Island Expressway with them—but wasn't that precisely what I needed to prove to the people I was on my way to see, people who might or might not believe me when I said I needed their care?

South Oaks has undergone a lot of renovation since my stay, but the main administration building, the one that most resembled the refuge from misery I had hoped to find, is still standing, a white-pillared mansion dating back to a time when Gilded Age New Yorkers could leave their crazy or alcoholic relatives there and visit them on their way to and from the Hamptons. The modern buildings surrounding this main building were more forbidding, but as our car pulled up in front of the fan-lit front door I was relieved to have arrived. "Here we are," said the nurse, speaking for the first time since we had set out from West Twelfth Street.

Inside, the admitting area looked more like a library than an office. The two bookcases had glass doors, and a spider plant hung from the ceiling by the tall open window. The woman behind the mahogany desk looked friendly. But despite this deceptive ambiance and the dehumanizing ride that had preceded it, my only thought was that I might be found unacceptable and sent home. *There's nothing the matter with you*, I kept hearing. *You just want attention. Go home and pull yourself together.* My sister Ellen actually did accuse me of this a year later, from her newly secured beachhead as a married woman. But if nothing was wrong, I would never get away from a life that had grown too heavy to carry alone.

"Are you depressed?" the woman asked in a gentle voice. Yes, I was. She was reading from a list. "Anxious?" That too. She looked up when she came to the question that followed on the list. "And when did this begin?" I looked at her hesitantly. "What age were you when you began feeling this way?"

"I don't know. I think it's always been like this."

I knew I spoke the truth, but I also knew that this was the answer I needed to give if I wanted to stay. Diana would be settling into my apartment and would be annoyed if our arrangement collapsed. Perhaps Jimmy Waring had let me take time off because he, too, saw what a struggle it was for me to hold up my life day in and day out and hoped that, if the burden were lifted, I would be a better member of his company. And in the circle in which I lived, where everyone had read Salinger, going to a mental hospital carried a distinction I would lose if I were rejected. When the admitting woman summoned a nurse to take me over to the B building, along with my suitcase and the pocketbook I was still not allowed to touch, I assumed I had passed my first hurdle.

The B building would be called "medium security" if South Oaks were a jail, to set it off from the hidden world of barred windows, straitjackets, and perhaps even padded cells where the violent and totally dysfunctional patients were kept. In another group of buildings, called "the cottages" because they were, in fact, small houses, lived patients who were either on their way toward being released or else nonviolent but needing a level of care their families could not, or would not, provide.

The nurse showed me to my room in the B building. It was a single but otherwise exactly like the bedrooms at Elmwood: the same metal bed, cream walls, nondescript dresser. "You need name tags on these," said the nurse as she briskly gathered up my clothes. Elmwood had required them too; my mother and I had spent several afternoons with tea and cookies, needles and thread. The nurse also took my toothbrush, hairbrush, and cosmetics. "They keep these in a special closet," she said. "You line up mornings and evenings to get them, but you've got to bring them back."

"What could I do with a hairbrush or a bar of soap?"

"You'll be amazed at what people around here do." On this note she left with most of my possessions, and I sat down on my bed to read until a bell summoned me to dinner.

The dining room was larger than the one at Elmwood, its tables round instead of long. Sharpness and pointedness were avoided at South Oaks. I was shown to a table for the newest girls, as they called us, though the ages in the room ranged from Daylene, who was eleven and became my friend, to women in their sixties. "What are you in here for?" they immediately wanted to know.

I shrugged my shoulders. "Depression, I guess."

"Oh that. Everyone here has that." The girl who spoke looked about my age. Her shoulder-length hair had definitely not been washed for a while. But why would she want to wash it if she, like me, was not expecting any visitors? At Elmwood we'd had contests to see who could go the longest without washing theirs. There were nods of agreement from the rest of the table as our cutlery was handed out by a large nurse tightly buttoned into her uniform. Obviously you had to be strong to work in a place like this—or have a man with you, like the woman who came to pick me up. At the end of the meal, our utensils would always be collected and counted before anyone could leave the room.

"Ever try suicide?" This was from Daylene, whose prominent collarbones and wide, dark-circled eyes could have put her on a poster for any charity you might name.

"Well, yes, if you can call it that. I stopped eating for so long they told me I was going to die if I kept it up. And yeah," I added, picking up that this was no big deal, "I swallowed a whole bunch of pills once." Sensing interest, I knew I had to add that I'd walked over to Bellevue, where my request for something to clean my stomach out had been enough to keep me on a ward there for a week. This incident had happened just before I'd left Carnegie Hall, during a stretch of the summer when the ushers collected unemployment because the Hall, a nonunion workplace, was closed.

"I've tried six times," said Daylene. She seemed to be the gold medalist in that category, at least at our table of six. "My mom won't take me home till they tell her I won't do it anymore."

"What are they doing to stop you?" I asked her apprehensively. Plates of monochromatic, Elmwood-like food arrived and we all dug in, silent except for the sound of silverware striking our plates. It was certainly easy not to eat much.

"Insulin," she said. "But maybe I'll get electro too if that doesn't do what it's supposed to." Insulin, I would soon learn, is a form of shock treatment where, in a darkened room with rows of beds, they strap you down and induce a temporary coma with a shot that knocks out, for several hours, your body's ability to produce insulin.

"Does it hurt?"

"Not really. It's kind of boring till you fall asleep. And you're hungry too, 'cause you have to get it on an empty stomach, so they don't give you any breakfast."

I could handle that, I thought, especially if breakfast was as tasteless as the food we had just eaten. After our plates were cleared away, cigarettes were distributed, the names of those needing them called out by a nurse reading from another list. In the background, we could hear our knives, forks, and spoons being counted. Then I went back to my room and my book. My nightgown, with its new name tag sewed on by machine, was waiting for me on my austere bed, and I climbed in earlier than I'd done since I was a child with a nanny.

There was no shade on my window, and stretching out between stiff, institutional sheets in the still day-lit refuge that would be mine for the next three months, I could hear the wheels of trucks rumbling past my window from the Sunrise Highway beyond the hospital grounds. I wondered if Dr. Angel had left for Germany, but I never called him. Nor had I told my parents where I had gone, though I'd given the admitting woman their address, assuming, I suppose, that the bills for my stay would be sent there. Perhaps Dr. Angel had called to warn them. Perhaps I was afraid they would say no.

The morning routine about which Daylene had warned me was even more like the army than I'd imagined, with nurses shouting our names as we lined up for our cosmetics and toothbrushes, then breakfast, cigarettes, and a walk over a bridge to the building where we would spend the morning doing occupational therapy. The main room in this building had once been a gym; here patients of both sexes sat in groups or alone to work on craft projects under the eye of our attendants. I started with a cross-stitch tablecloth, but by the end of my stay I had sculpted a nude female with her head on her knees. OT was our only activity. After lunch we were marched back for more.

At the end of a week of this, broken up by an EEG and a few other tests, I was informed that I would be spending my mornings with the group on insulin. I was enormously relieved. It meant they were taking me seriously. They had found something the matter. Spending mornings in a coma would also cut in half the time I had to spend in OT, where I was already dying of boredom. I didn't realize until too late—though perhaps there was no time when the realization would have made any difference—that the treatment involved drinking orange juice loaded with sugar to restore one's insulin. My dread of putting on weight intensified, and it was not groundless.

Nevertheless, I went without protest each morning to the room with the rows of beds, allowing myself to be strapped down, and suffering the hunger that Daylene had told me about, until unconsciousness finally took me away from the shouts and moans of those around me as they discharged their own resident evil spirits. But I resisted the orange juice: threw it up, threw it down the toilet, refused to follow orders. "You know you could do a lot of damage to yourself," one of the nurses told me, "if you don't put enough sugar back into your system. You don't want that now, do you?"

"I don't care."

More coercive measures were needed, so I became a candidate for ETC as well—"electro," as Daylene called it. Electro took place, after our sessions with insulin, in the building we called "violent," though my impression of its patients was of a stillness more horrifying than any overt restraint. The sight of these people, for whom hospital gowns had permanently replaced their regular clothes, was a warning, perhaps even intended as such. If you don't cooperate in every way, this is how you will end up: speechless or screaming, immobilized or repetitively pounding, your eyes vacant or constantly filled with tears, your hair bushy or thinning but untouched by a brush or a comb, eating the even more tasteless, pablumlike meals we had to share with them after our morning of hunger.

Electro happened only twice a week, but it was a relief after those lunches to return to the relative cheeriness of OT. I was frightened, of course, by the thought of a powerful jolt of electricity rushing through the body over which I had so little control to begin with. Those of us selected for this special honor waited in a small, windowless room to hear our names called, one at a time, no one speaking or looking at one another. Then I was strapped to a gurney, my head anointed with Vaseline and readied for the electrodes. Someone put a tongue depressor in my mouth. Then a shot in my arm sent my body into free-fall, a back dive off the edge of the world.

But even at the height of my terror, just before the metal door closed behind me, I knew that this ritual made me part of the hospital's elect. There was no psychotherapy to speak of at South Oaks. Dr. Kershaw, the doctor assigned to me, lived in nearby Massepequa. He had a crew cut, wore a bow tie, and drove a red sports car. Every week we would go into a small room adjoining the OT gym, and he would ask, "How's it going?" Our interaction never got much beyond that level. I don't think my interaction with anyone there got much beyond that level.

The closest I came to having a friend my age was a brief bond with Reuben, whose long, pale face and narrow-set eyes reminded me of a Chagall painting at the Museum of Modern Art that I'd come to love when I had lived at the Rehearsal Club. There was a piano in one of the rooms of the OT building, and I started going in there while Reuben played. He remembered only a few Bach preludes, and he lacked the spectacular technique of my first love and fellow usher from Carnegie Hall. But his playing gave me what I was not able to get from anyone else there: a sense of connection to something beyond our shared predicament.

When those in charge found out about this, they forbade me to leave the gym. "You need to be out here with everyone else," they said, as if the presence of people to whom I did not feel drawn was just what I needed. It was not just heterosexual pairing that they opposed. Any incipient clique was broken up immediately, its ringleaders urged to "go sit with someone else." It seems that they wanted us to "get better" without connecting to anyone or anything we might care about, to surrender to them not just our wallets and jewelry and favorite eye shadow along with our "old selves," but one another as well.

It must have been not long after a two-month period of double-barreled treatment that my parents came to visit, one at a time. "We were told that if we came together it would upset you," my mother said later, so they did as they were told. We Canadians are famous for that. I remember nothing of either visit and might never have known that they happened had it not been for a drive with my father, twenty-five years later, from the airport to the Park Plaza Hotel in Toronto where he, my mother, and I were staying over Christmas.

"Do you remember," he said quite out of the blue as we threaded our way through holiday traffic, "a talk that you and I had when I went to visit you down at that place?" He had never mentioned South Oaks before and would never refer to it as anything other than "that place," but after this first time, as he moved toward senility, he started asking me the same question every time we saw each other. He would then repeat, each time dropping a few details till it became very schematic, the story of a conversation he says he never forgot.

The first time, on a winter afternoon in the car, I was very aware of his movie-star profile, his black, Persian lamb hat, his cashmere scarf, and beautiful brown leather gloves on the steering wheel. Everyone always compared my father to Errol Flynn: his mustache and well-trimmed sideburns looked even better gray. His ready smile, endlessly reproduced on posters and leaflets, made him irresistible, apparently, on election day. "I'm glad my father annoys me so much," I once told Debbie and Paula after he had taken the three of us out to dinner at a very expensive restaurant. "Otherwise I'd have a terrible Oedipus complex."

"I don't remember any talk at South Oaks," I answered him hesitantly. "Remind me of what we said."

"Well, you know you were very upset then, very angry at your mother and me."

"I remember that."

"Well, we spent an afternoon together, you and I, walking around on the grounds, and I could just tell that I was not getting through to you at all. No matter what I said, I knew I wasn't making the slightest connection. Do you remember that?"

"Sure," I said. How could I tell him I didn't remember a thing? He'd surely heard of shock treatment, but I had no idea if he knew I'd had it.

"So I kept trying and trying till all of a sudden I said something about failure. And when you heard that word you were furious. How could I possibly talk to you about failure, you said, when everything in my life had always gone so easily? You were truly enraged," he said, "but I knew I was finally onto something."

"What did you say?"

"I'm surprised you don't know. For me it was one of the most amazing moments I can remember. I'm telling you, I was beside myself, didn't know what to say. But when you got mad, I told you I had failed lots of times. Lots of times. And then we really began to talk. It was one of the best afternoons of my life."

"Oh yes, I—I—remember that now, but—"

It was getting dark. A few flakes of snow were starting to swirl against the windshield-wiper blades. I wished I hadn't lied to him about remembering his visit. Now he had no way of knowing that his "best afternoon" was becoming one of my best afternoons only then, so many years later.

Perhaps I've made up what I remember happening next. We had the radio tuned to a country-western station, and Willie Nelson came on singing my favorite song of his. "Little things I could have said and done, I just never took the time. . ." I know that the "you" who "were always on my mind" is supposed to be the man's neglected wife, but whenever I hear it, my father is singing it to me.

At some point, Dr. Kershaw must have considered me improved because I stopped getting both kinds of shock treatment and was moved to one of the cottages, where my roommate was a married woman from Long Island. "How can you be here and be married?" I asked her quite bluntly. I was beginning to imagine a marriage very different from the one my parents had, one to which there would be no real obstacles once I could rid myself of whatever was the matter with me.

"I just had to get away," she said. "I love my husband and my kids but I had to get away." This was her second visit to South Oaks. "I wasn't really cured when I went home the last time," she said. "Maybe I'm never going to be."

We in the cottages cooked our own meals, under strict supervision, of course, and cleaned the house, readying ourselves for a return to the kind of life we had presumably left. My only treatment now was a brief weekly session with Dr. Kershaw. This man refused to believe that I was, or ever could be, a dancer. "Look how clumsily you walk," he said once as I got up to leave after one of our increasingly heated arguments. I suspect that three months in the hospital had taken the spring out of my step, to say the least, but his derision hit a nerve.

As the weeks passed, I began to press him to let me go back to New York. He thought the visits from my parents had been "a step in the right direction," a direction that would take me out of my apartment in the Village and back to Canada. "Normal people don't live in the Village," he said. Normal people didn't live alone, was what he meant. They didn't have delusional ideas of a career as the next generation's Martha Graham. By the time they reached my age, they got married and stopped hating their parents. "Do you want to get married?" he asked and I gave him the normal person's answer he wanted: of course.

He finally did agree that I could leave, though I don't believe he thought for a minute that I would ever be a candidate for the rewards of normal personhood. My medical records say I was discharged into the care of my father, but I don't remember the trip. Learning that I'd had forty insulin treatments and a dozen sessions of ECT, and reading Dr. Kershaw's account of my periodic weeping, disorganized speech, and tenuous, superficial contact with reality, it's clear that I need not have worried that my case would not be seen as "serious." My diagnosis, in capital letters, was "schizophrenia"; my condition upon leaving, "improved"; my exit prognosis, "guarded." I suppose this referred to the fact that I had still not relinquished the delusion that I was a dancer.

But Dr. Angel was back from Germany, and Diana had found her own apartment. Being alone in mine offered me a chance to reconnect with the life I had made for myself since leaving home. My books, my Olivetti typewriter on its round, marble, ice-cream table, the Klimt-like painting by an artist who had committed suicide, the wooden dry sink, and the blue-and-white quilt I'd found in dusty antique stores along Hudson and Bleecker were the physical elements of my first real home.

I called Jimmy Waring, and he sounded glad to hear from me, curious rather than critical. I had gained fifteen pounds, but I assured him I could get it off quickly, and I did.

Did it help, all that shock treatment? I know I believed it would, and that belief was what carried me forward. I told people it did, and the telling replaced the memories it was supposed to represent. The Becks and their Living Theatre troupe regarded insanity as fuel for creative work, so I was even more *one of them* than I had been as a mere dancer. Looking at my chubby self in the mirror of Merce's studio was unbearable at first, since I fell back into my old habit of seeing the image in the mirror, the one I watched and corrected, as my creation, the one who would become the woman I was practicing to be. And yet I was glad I had gone. There had been a problem. I had taken care of it in the only way I knew. I was *someone* I had not been before.

Almost right away we began to rehearse for a New York performance in December. I was enormously grateful to Jimmy for having given me a leave of absence, and I told him the truth when I said I was feeling much better. I was now *someone* in the dance world, a member of a real company. Yet none of this was enough to blot out the fear that he would regret having taken me in and would decide to throw me out of my new family just as I was growing really fond of its other members. For so long dance had held out this promise of a real family. Now I had one, but the happiness at the center of that promise seemed as far away as ever.

There were five of us, including Jimmy, who is now dead, in the James Waring company. Two from the group, David Gordon and Valda Setterfield, now have their own company. I hope the other, Vincent Warren, is still alive. He had been a lover of Frank O'Hara's, so I can still call up his beauty in a group of poems named after him. He took us all to a drag ball dressed as Ruby Keeler in a silver lamé dress with puffed sleeves, thick false eyelashes, and a pair of silver tap shoes. Wearing my favorite mauve dress and amethyst earrings, my face shining under deep purple greasepaint, I wondered if Valda and I were the only women there.

I did not last long in the Waring company, but it was I, not Jimmy, who precipitated my departure by my asking him to excuse me from the classes he gave for us because I was having a problem with my knees. I don't know what I was thinking when I made such a stupid, disloyal request. What I do know for sure is that he did not forgo a first-rate dancer, or even a potentially first-rate one. Dancing was never fun for me, and the body cannot lie about this. To connect with an audience, a performer must, beneath even the best technique or the most ingenious moves of a composer or a choreographer, be having the time of her life. Why that freedom eluded my grasp I'm only beginning to understand now. But elude me it did.

I did not exactly leave the dance. I watched it slip away from me, though perhaps I was only being guided toward more compatible outlets. I had already registered for the summer session at Connecticut College, where all the major modern-dance choreographers were in residence with their companies. I had been there the summer before my sojourn at South Oaks, so I knew the routine. But I wandered through my classes in the various techniques—Graham, Limon, and Cunningham—as if in a trance, not knowing why I was there.

I also had jobs in two after-school programs teaching dance to elementary school children. I loved teaching, and when I learned that anyone who held these jobs needed evidence of two years of college, I went to the board of education to see what I could do. Canada has thirteen years of high school, so my transcript from Bishop Strachan School and the national exam I'd passed at the end of my stay there— first-class honors in every subject—was allowed to stand for one of these two years. My summers at Connecticut College gave me almost enough credits for a second year. I needed only two more classes, for which I enrolled at the New School, three blocks from my apartment.

Another bend in the road came when my sister Ellen got married the following Christmas in Cambridge, England. My parents sent me a round-trip plane ticket, and the family reunited for the first wedding of our generation. Janet was Ellen's only bridesmaid, an office I was happy not to fill since the walls of King's College chapel held within them the chill of a thousand years of no central heating and Janet's dress, like Ellen's, had a low neck and short sleeves. It was a small wedding, just as our mother had predicted.

Mummy gave me my Christmas check and I decided to stay on after everyone else had taken off. This idea came partly from Jamie, a Cambridge student who was also a wedding guest by virtue of being a friend of Ellen's and mine. He had gone to one of the prep schools outside of Toronto that serves as a companion institution to BSS. There was another prep school a few blocks from BSS, and those two schools were the only ones where people like my parents sent their sons. These were the boys who appeared at the formal dances that were a required part of Christmas and Easter holidays for the children of Toronto's "comfortably off."

Jamie had been at my house twice, first at the "formal" my parents gave for me, and then, two years later, at a similar ritual for Ellen. When I mentioned to him that nothing was pulling me back to New York, he said, "I'm having a party tomorrow night at my digs. There's a bunch of us here who can't go home for the holidays. Ex-colonials, you know."

"Sure. I'm one of them."

I was the only person from the States at the party, and people wanted to know what I thought of the newly elected Kennedy. My answers were uninformed to the point of embarrassment. I knew almost nothing about Kennedy and even less about Nixon. Judith and Julian Beck had regularly organized demonstrations against my adopted country's preparations for a nuclear invasion, but I'd never joined them. Politics was Daddy's world and at that point I still wanted nothing to do with it.

My world had consisted of dancers, musicians, and actors, and none of them was in the habit of asking me what I thought. Thought, in fact, was the enemy. It meant that you lived in your head. An artist, particularly a performer, lived in her body. When I'd had difficulty getting a combination in a dance class, someone was sure to tell me I was thinking too much. My too-busy head had also kept me from being popular with Jamie's classmates. Through dance I'd thought I could kill off that mind and connect to a real life outside the one I was born into.

As I sat, a glass of wine in my hand, in a worn upholstered armchair covered with an Indian bedspread—the only woman in the room except for an English girlfriend or two—I saw that womanhood could include being asked, by men who really wanted an answer, what I thought. I was in the company of some of the smartest people my age in the entire world, people who assumed that my thoughts about American politicians would have even greater weight than theirs. Where in my life back in the States could I get more of this? The answer, of course, was school. The day before he drove me to Heathrow, Jamie took me to a bookstore where I bought a hardbound *Tom Jones* and a lovely framed botanical print. Then I took off, vowing once again to change my life.

And thus it was that I found my way to Columbia's School of General Studies, admission to which required nothing more complicated than taking a computerized exam and submitting the transcripts I had used for the board of education. Of course I could not transfer my dance credits toward a B.A. But after a semester and a summer going part-time, and after trying on several majors as a full-time student—psychology, then French and finally English—I graduated summa cum laude in two-and-a-half years, winning a Phi Beta Kappa key and the department's English prize. Graduate school would be the place, I firmly believed, where I could put my lack of popularity with those prep school boys behind me.

10

On the morning of my mother's funeral, I woke up in a room where I'd spent too many Saturday nights, torn up too many program cards before telling my parents I'd had the wonderful evening they expected of a daughter of theirs. This was the same room where, four decades ago, I had sensed myself slowly disappearing into the safety of its pale green walls, the room behind whose door I'd planned my first border crossing. Now I listened for footsteps on the carpeted stairs before making my way past the Graysons' closed door to the brightly wallpapered bathroom. The mirror over the sink looked like the same one that once held a line-free face I'd been too young to appreciate. The cabinet behind it was now empty and splattered with rust.

After a quick shower, I put on my slightly wrinkled black dress and went down to the dining room where Eric Grayson, who'd known my father for as long as Alice had known Mummy, was seated at the far end of a long mahogany table in front of two eggs on whole wheat toast, a tall glass of orange juice, and a cup of black coffee. He strained to get up as I came in, and planted a quick paternal kiss on my offered cheek.

"So sorry I wasn't here when you arrived, Cathy," he said, pressing on the arms of his chair to sit back down. I was glad he and Alice were not bothering with my new name. Cathy called up the unproblematic world of Lawrence Welk, Daddy's favorite TV show. "But I'm delighted you could stay with us," he went on. "Gosh, how long has it been?"

"I don't know." I took the place setting that was nearest the swinging kitchen door. "I was up here for Mum and Dad's fiftieth, so maybe not since then." The Graysons had replaced our dining room table, our silver candlesticks, our hunting prints with a tiny light over each frame, our dark mahogany sideboard, even our Persian rug and full-length curtains with almost identical items of their own.

"My God, has it been that long? Alice and I are gearing for our sixtieth. So how are you, dear? I'm afraid I've forgotten where it is you teach." I reminded him of my place of employment, caught him up on Kevin, and mentioned my recent travels. "You're quite a girl," he said between bites, sounding so much like Daddy. "You always were. Now what would you like for breakfast?"

"Tea and toast is fine, thanks," I told him, remembering how Daddy used to run his "manners Olympics" from the head of the table, how forgetting to say "thank you" or "may I please have" could lose you a lot of points. Eric rang a little glass bell rather than the buzzer Daddy used to press with his foot, and the maid brought in another cup that matched his, from a different set than the one I'd used the day before. Soon a silver toast caddy appeared too, with four buttered slices standing vertically in it, cut-side down.

"Well now, Alice tells me you want to ask some things about your mother. You know I've known her almost as long as Alice has." He paused. "She really was a wonderful woman."

"I think so too," I said quickly. "But I gather she had a pretty rough life, and I think I would understand her better if I knew more about it."

From the slight lift of his eyebrows, I sensed that he had talked about this with Alice, and I wondered if she had persuaded him to continue their silence. "Well, you know I'm giving the eulogy at the funeral, and I do think she was an extraordinary person who did extraordinarily well." He ran a corner of toast across the last egg yolk on his plate. "Where to begin? Well now, your dad and I came home from England at the same time, and I assure you it was quite an adjustment. People who haven't been through a war just can't imagine what it's like."

"What do you mean?" I was thinking of the Vietnam vets whose stories I had read omnivorously after my shooting.

"Well, we were in our early twenties when we were sent overseas," he said, the faintest of smiles crinkling the corners of his eyes, "and you can't imagine what it was like being a bachelor all over again. Here we were in our uniforms, thinking the world of ourselves, and it seemed like there were women everywhere. Then to come home to the family you had started before you left—I'm telling you, it wasn't easy. We each dealt with it in our own way, of course, and I guess your father's way was to keep on being the way he'd been. We were sent back and forth between England and the coast of Europe, and God, you have to understand what fun London was, even with a war on."

"Do you think he was like that before he left?"

"You mean, after he was married?"

"Yes. He always talked about the war as the happiest time of his life. But I wouldn't imagine it changed his personality." The reason I was asking about the timing was that, late one night when my mother was very drunk, she told me my father had once announced that he wanted to leave her. Everyone else was asleep, and she was attempting to join them by pouring the rest of a bottle of Scotch into a glass of skim milk—good, she said, for her ulcer. "Let's not talk about it for six months," she told me she had said to him. "And then if you still want to leave after that, go ahead."

A year or so after that conversation, I was struggling to get over the most painful end of a love affair I've ever survived. So, I wrote to my mother to ask how old she was when this had happened, thinking I might be following the pattern of her life as some therapists think we do. I was also interested in how old I was when Daddy had dropped the bombshell on her. Her handwritten letter back assured me that no such thing had ever happened. "I even asked your father," she wrote. "And gentleman that he is, he told me he had never even had such a thought. Not even once."

"You know, my memory is not as good as it once was," Eric said, looking up with a small laugh as Alice came into the room. "That's so, isn't it, darling?"

"I think your memory is perfectly fine." Alice was elegantly dressed for the funeral in a black wool suit trimmed with braid, probably from

Creed's or Holt Renfrew's, where Mum had done her shopping too. She pulled out the empty chair to her husband's left and sat down as he rang the bell. "It's not how much you remember," she said. "It's what."

"Cathy's been asking me about George's women, and I must say I didn't keep track of them all that well. There were two main ones, though." He turned toward me. "You probably remember both of them."

I did. Besides the fashion model there was another, equally blond, equally glamorous woman who drank a lot and eventually committed suicide. "Oh, sure. But I'm interested in figuring out how early it all started."

"Honestly, I can't help you there," he said, and I decided to quit while I was as far ahead as I was going to get.

Later, walking out to the waiting car, I asked Alice if I could ask her one more question.

"I don't promise to answer," she said. "But go ahead."

"Did you convert to Catholicism in order to marry Eric?"

"Yes. I mean, he didn't force me to, but it made his family very happy that I did."

I tried to think who had told me that Mummy and Eric had been an item while they were both a part of the Toronto debutante set and wondered if religion had ever come up between them. "And are you happy that you did it?"

"Every day of my life," she said as we got in the car. I've remembered those words, especially since she'd made such a point of saying that even the best marriages go through rough times. These two were the same age as Mum and Dad. How come they had done—and were still doing—so much better?

There were forty or fifty people in the funeral home when we got there, most of them quite old. My aunt Dorrie was the first person I recognized, and she came right over to me. "I'm just so glad you girls all got here," she said. "We're going to have a bit of lunch at my house afterward. Just family and a few old friends. Ellen's been a trooper, hasn't she, taking care of everything."

"How did she find this place?"

"It's pretty well known among the people we know," said my aunt. "Just look at your father. He looks absolutely devastated, doesn't he?"

I saw that he did look dazed, even though he was the center of attention, a position he used to occupy almost all the time. His idea of conversation always involved telling stories about himself: about the war especially but also about his exploits at Cambridge, where, as the son of an affluent colonial, he was welcome to spend a year during the Depression even if he was no academic. He could learn, his tutor told him, "about our people," and throw himself into sports. Cambridge had him to thank, that year, for winning the heavyweight boxing title against Oxford. He was an orphan by then, and a rich one.

At the Belmont, he and Mum had eaten separately, since she needed more care than he did. Ellen told me that the ladies whose table he joined in the dining room had complained that he dominated the conversation and wouldn't let them talk. The matron, "an awfully nice girl," Daddy called her, tried a few different tables until she found two women who ate in silence. I'm sure Daddy wasn't happy about the move, but he must have understood, at some level, that it was pointless to ask for livelier companions.

What a ghastly end to a life so filled with success as we define that word for men! Handsome and rich, Daddy had gone into politics, with the motives of service Americans associate with the Kennedys, and never lost an election. "Politics is a drug," he used to say, meaning, perhaps, that he'd do anything to keep it in his life. But being accustomed to being listened to had taken away much of the need, and so the habit, of paying close attention to what people said. Like so many men, he saw all discussions of problems as requests that he fix them. And fix he did, at least for his constituents. But he'd filtered out everything else, and now he couldn't fix anything.

Now, though everyone's eyes were on him, he was not in charge. Men in striped pants and morning coats were quietly moving us along because we mourners would soon be replaced, on a strict schedule, by other mourners for other dead. "You girls need to sit up in front," said Dorrie. I put myself between Ellen and Liam.

Then, one of the men in charge walked to the front and turned to face us. He had heard many wonderful things about the woman whose life we were gathered here to remember. She had been a devoted wife to her husband and a wonderful mother to her three daughters. He glanced over at us to be reassured that he'd gotten it right. She would long be remembered by her many friends, whose lives she had immeasurably enriched. And when we returned to the hustle and bustle of our day-to-day lives, our memories of her many acts of kindness and generosity might bring a smile to our lips and perhaps inspire us to follow her example.

A packaged funeral, certainly, but a Canadian one. Just like the ads on the subway. We might be inspired, but then perhaps we might not be. No pushing and shoving. Then Eric walked forward and took in the assembled faces before he began to speak. The tremulous quality of his voice made me remember that most of the people there had been very fond of Mum, might even have said they had loved her. What about me? As Eric walked back to sit in the pew behind us, I saw Janet open her purse and pull out a Kleenex. No one else was crying, as far as I could tell, but I was sitting in the front and couldn't actually turn around. Daddy was staring straight ahead as if he were walking in his sleep and might be startled if someone touched him too suddenly.

There was a short reception afterward in an upstairs room furnished very much like our old living room: pale peach walls with a gilt-edged mirror here and a pair of ornate sconces there giving just the right amount of light, beige wall-to-wall carpeting, and brocade-covered furniture that was neither comfortable nor uncomfortable. In my first few years on my own in New York, I'd sometimes wondered, in a vengeful mood, how my mother would feel if I died. Now I thought I knew. She would feel more or less the way I felt about her. Even suicide would have been a wasted gesture.

Outside, I asked Jan what had brought on her tears. "It could have been so different," she said. "I couldn't help thinking about that."

The next morning I called a cab and headed to the airport and on to the rendezvous whose possibilities I had not confided to anyone. "Don't brood over what I told you," Eric said when I thanked them for their hospitality. "Your parents were a fine pair."

"Who produced fine offspring," Alice chimed in, and as the door slammed behind me, I was glad to be heading to a place where I didn't have to talk like that. I was nervous, too, but relieved to be feeling something after two days of minimal emotional functioning, vigilantly maintained. However it turned out between us, I told myself, seeing Foley again would be fun—assuming he actually was on the aircraft I was on my way to meet.

I found two groups of people waiting for the arriving Swissair plane. The largest consisted of white people waiting for passengers from Geneva. But as more and more passengers laden with well-made luggage filed past the barrier behind which we waited for "our" person, the most reassuring faces were the very dark ones, who continued to wait patiently in flamboyant African or more somber American clothing as the crowd thinned out. Gathered in twos and threes, they looked hopeful as they watched the Plexiglas doors that swished as they automatically opened and closed.

Perhaps Foley had changed his mind, or perhaps I had misheard him. His "next" could mean next Sunday. But the others, still waiting, seemed perfectly calm. Perhaps they already knew it would be whites first, blacks second, that the Europeans with neatly matching luggage would glide through customs while the Africans would have every battered suitcase and flimsy cardboard box pawed through suspiciously. "I'm one of you!" I wanted to shout, not that they would have believed me.

Foley was almost the last to appear, but he was easy to spot. He was wearing a full ceremonial outfit—*agbada*, shirt, trousers and hat—in lavender shot with silver and embroidered with more silver. "Oh my God," was my first thought, "every gay man within fifty miles is going to be following him to my house!" When he saw me he ran over to the barrier and hugged me. "How are you! Nice to see you!" he said, drawing out the "o-o-o."

I say he was almost the last because, behind him, were ten more artists from the gallery, some familiar faces, some not. They were followed by a porter pushing a big luggage cart; and after I greeted this unexpectedly large group, the porter told me that someone owed him a dollar for each of the bags. "How many are there?" I asked.

"There's thirty."

I now noticed Max and Marie at the back of the waiting area. They must have known that it takes at least an hour for a Nigerian to get from the plane to the place where he can meet his party. Perhaps Nike had called him to warn us that we should be expecting eleven people. I looked in my wallet: several Canadian bills, each with Elizabeth's face on it, and two American twenties, which I gave to the man. He handed me ten singles.

Max was now standing next to me. "This sure is something else, huh? What does Nike think we're going to do with all these people?" I must admit I forgot to be mad at him as memories of our better days swirled around me, and I wondered if the same thing was happening to him.

"We're not all coming to New York," said a man named Waheed. I remembered his face, and from the nonplused way he was dealing with the surrounding chaos, I could tell that this was not his first time in the States. "Kasali and I will go to Detroit and those two are going to Cleveland. We will take a bus to the bus station in New York. I've done this before," he added, giving me a smile that reminded me why I'd decided to open my house to Nigerians.

"Do you think they have an ATM machine in this building?" I asked Max.

"I'm sure they do," he said, and he was right. It was on the second floor. When I came back down the escalator, I had a hundred dollars plus my ten singles.

"I can take two of you plus bags," said Max, "if you don't mind sitting on someone's lap, Marie." Of course she didn't mind. I'd gotten very fond of Marie on the trip; she'd taught me some of her clapping games, and we did them together while waiting to find out what was happening next. "That leaves five of you plus Kate. Too many for a cab." We went out to the taxi area and Max found a man with a van who would take six people and their luggage for eighty dollars.

"That had better include the tip," I said, but the Nigerians were already loading their enormous suitcases into his vehicle. I climbed in last, next to Foley, and pointed out the skyline when it came into view through the rather dirty front windshield.

"I've been to the States once before, you know" Foley said, his arm around my shoulder. "But not to New York."

I leaned back into him. "You're going to love it here."

The van double-parked in front of my building and I gave the driver the fare. "You must have a big house?" he said.

"I do, but three of us live in it already. I don't know what I'm going to do with all these folks."

What I did was invite everyone for dinner, including Felicia, Max, Marie, and the two Nigerians staying with them. Once in the lobby, I introduced everyone to the doorman, who helped us to get everything into the elevator in two or three trips. We put all the bags in the dining room, and then four of the visitors flopped down onto the living room couch and the floor to watch TV. Foley and I went out to buy groceries, hugging each other apprehensively in the relative privacy of the empty elevator. Then I cooked spaghetti and poured soda, gave out all the blankets and pillows I had, and taped a warning note for Sean and Dennis on the outside of the door.

In all of this, Foley took charge of his compatriots. He helped me with the cooking while they stretched out, waiting to be served; then he handed out the forks and squares of paper towels that let them know they would be eating "American style," not with their hands, as in Nigeria. He was already washing the dishes when I walked into the kitchen with my plate. If taking on one another's burdens is what people do when they get married, we were already moving along that road.

"So where do you want to sleep?" I asked Foley when everyone else had left or settled down for the night.

"With you, *abi?*" he said without a moment's hesitation. I must not have followed suit, because he took my hand and I remembered the sense of complete confidence that had flowed up my arm and all through me as we walked, hand in hand, down the steps outside the auditorium the night of our dreadful "first date." *Abi* is a useful Yoruba word that means "okay?" or "you know?" or "right?" You could use it where Canadians might use their famous "eh?" or where an African-American might ask, "You know what I'm saying?"

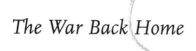

The War Back Home

11

This is a test, this is only a test. But of course I had no more idea, as I kissed Foley good-bye and took off for Nigeria without him, of what lay ahead than I had when I first boarded the train from Toronto to New York. The tests thrown at me on this, my second Nigerian trip, seemed to pile up quickly, though. First, as if to warn me of what lay ahead, I fell into one of the cement drainage ditches that run between the houses and the road in Nigerian villages and towns. The brilliant purple bruise that appeared a day later amazed my hosts as a phenomenon only white people can produce. Then came the car accident, confirming the warnings of my American friends about Nigeria's position as the world's leader in traffic fatalities. Then there were the fuel shortages, the mosquito bites, the difficulty getting food. What would be next?

I got my answer a month before Foley reappeared in Nigeria when my computer began to malfunction. I found a computer school whose charming proprietor spoke very good English; she would be able to recommend, I hoped, a repair place. She was "not around" when I arrived, and since no one in Nigeria has much control over when things happen, one learns to sit and simply wait. I remembered, from my first trip to this country, that Nigerians like the phrase "not around," since it carries no commitment to a future return.

This happened to be the morning of Nelson Mandela's inauguration, and as I waited on the wooden steps leading up to the empty computer school, I picked up scraps of the broadcast from South Africa, interrupted by the nearby voices of children chanting their lessons, from an invisible radio with erratic reception. The woman I was waiting to see eventually arrived and directed me to a computer repair person who was also "not around" when I got there. The young girl who *was* around told me to leave the machine with her. Well, if Mandela could wait twenty-seven years to resume his life as a political leader, I could certainly wait for a few hours, or even a few days, to know if my computer was going to live or die.

Meanwhile, back at home, Nike had arrived with David, her British engineer husband, the one I knew she was planning to ditch. She must have announced to him that I, a professor of English from America, was in favor of this move, because from the moment David set foot in the house, I was aware of his hostility. He forbade the two small daughters he had fathered with Nike, who were now also part of this tense household, to talk to me, and he tried to make life as unbearable for me as his own surely was at that point. It was a prohibition they broke, to my great delight, whenever he left the house—drawn as they were to my straight hair, my computer, my digestive biscuits, and my lap.

When he heard that I had left my computer in the hands of an unknown Nigerian repair person, he was delighted. "You'll never see that computer again," he crowed. "I've been here fifteen years, and if you trust a single one of them, they know you for a fool. They even steal from Nike when they get a chance. We had one girl a few years ago who made off with a dozen of her dresses. That's why we don't let them into the front of the house anymore."

Just like the plantation, I thought, remembering how uncomfortable Foley had been when he came to see me on my trip with Felicia and Max. But how would I survive four more months in Nigeria with no computer? It had become a necessary part of my arsenal against David, whose malevolence, and my reactions to it, went into my journal every day. All my past writing would be gone too, since I had forgotten to remove the backup disk when I'd surrendered my most valuable possession to this alleged criminal I had not yet seen. What would I tell my colleagues at Rutgers, who were no doubt spending the summer more productively?

Even worse than the actual loss and the money and time it represented was the realization that Africa had defeated me. Even if the computer was not destroyed, what would I do all day if it could not be repaired? It was not a major malfunction that had prompted me to seek professional help; one of the keys kept repeating when I hit it. Perhaps I could have kept going by avoiding that key. But suppose the disease had spread to others? In any case, the message was clear: I was my own worst enemy and always would be. Even my anger at David and several stolen glasses of Night Train could not keep back my tears that night.

The next day I went back to the repair place, located at the end of a craggy dirt road. The repair man was there, but he told me he would have to take what, at this point, felt like my entire life-support system, to his main shop in Ilorin two hours away. I should come back in a week.

"A week? Why so long?"

"I only come here for one or two days a week," he said. "I'll bring it back when I come next."

"This is Tuesday, right? So next Tuesday?"

"I think so," he said. "Try back then."

He was not there the following Tuesday or Wednesday, but by the end of that week, I had my computer back, working just fine. David had been proven wrong, thank God, and now one more of my fears had been faced and surmounted. The whole business cost me no more than fifteen dollars including the taxis.

Foley arrived in Nigeria at the end of May, and he rescued me from my constant jousting with David, not a moment too soon. We took up residence, as an official *iyawo* and *oko*, in the building called "the studio," a free dormitory for students too poor to pay Nigeria's rents of five dollars a month for a small room with a shared toilet, shower, and kitchen. I suppose we could have arranged a three-month rental somewhere else, but Nike made the offer, and I suppose I thought it best that I, too, maintain the appearance of friendship. We shared these living quarters with about fifteen students, who were packed in three and four to a room: girls in the back of the house, boys in the front. I felt like I was back in boarding school or summer camp—the places that had given me my happiest early memories.

But not quite. The beds at those places might have been hard and the food institutional, but it cost a lot of money to go there, and we campers and students knew it. Here the conditions were well below those at the boarding school or even of the housing projects where the young people in Felicia's program lived. Someone swept the main room every day, and a few wooden chairs and a bare table were its only furniture. The other rooms were small and dark, piled to the ceiling with the possessions of their occupants. The toilet flushed only if you poured water into the back of it yourself. I did not want to separate myself from the life of the people around me, but I sometimes wondered what my friends back home would think if they could see the setting for my international romance.

What would they think, for instance, of the T-shirt Foley brought me that said: WHAT MAKES US DIFFERENT IS NOT AS IMPORTANT AS WHAT MAKES US THE SAME." We took turns wearing it and I loved it even though I didn't always agree with it, until it disappeared one day, only to reappear at our engagement ceremony on the body of one of Foley's younger male relatives. Africans returning from a trip abroad are expected to bring something for everyone in their extended families, so it wasn't surprising that a pair of sweatpants that Foley and I both wore and a J. Peterman shirt I'd given him for Christmas met a similar fate. "But I gave that shirt to *you*," I complained, only to be told—and not for the last time: *When you give a dash, you don't control what the person does with it.*

Now that Foley and I were on the same continent, I expected him to take me to the market and we would then cook and eat together like any normal couple. To say that this issue of dinner was *the big test* sounds absurd given the severity of some of the others. For one, my wrist hadn't healed properly and would need to be rebroken and reset when I got back to New York. Then there was David, who continued his war with me through Mr. Ben, the manager of the art school and a former employee of his engineering company. Mr. Ben was well situated to spy on me and in particular to read my views of David, since I left my computer (until I found this out) in the school's office, where I spent my days. But these were mild and temporary shocks compared with what I went through when Foley showed up late for dinner.

Some of this difficulty was simply a collision of cultures. Where I come from, the evening meal is saturated with images of *Father Knows Best*. The fact that we never saw a single episode of this program notwithstanding, my family had conformed to its pattern. Though some of my relief at going away to boarding school was that I escaped from it for most of the year, it was the tradition I had learned. Nigerians place no such value on simultaneous eating. I learned this one night after Foley had left to visit his family's village, a two-hour drive from Osogbo, assuring me in his usual fashion that he would be back "very soon."

I had no way of knowing what "very soon" might mean. I assumed that he was presenting himself to his father and his father's wives, to the aunts, uncles, and cousins, and to whichever of the thirty-some brothers and sisters still lived where their father and grandfather had practiced their trade as traditional carvers. He must have sent them a message that he had arrived back on their shores, but how? There were no phones in Osi. When I tried to imagine their response to this news, I had no pictures on which to draw except those that came from *National Geographic*.

Four days later, I was waiting nervously on the front porch of the school with three of Nike's male students. It was early evening and I was hungry, so I suggested that the four of us eat dinner together. Receiving lukewarm enthusiasm, I offered to cook, and took off without further ado to the closest roadside market in search of ingredients for a dish that I could, with help, pull together quickly.

When I got back, everyone had disappeared but one named Bola. Undaunted, I asked him if he had a stove, and he suggested that we look for his girlfriend and use hers. I followed him down the rutted, uneven road, lit only by moonlight, to the kitchen area where those who lived in the "studio" prepared their peppers on a grinding stone and cooked for themselves on kerosene stoves under a single, small lightbulb. Kehinde,

Bola's girlfriend, offered to turn my purchases into an omelette, which I assumed she would share with Bola and me.

Bola and I waited on a bench in front of the house while she used some of her own oil to make our supper. After a few minutes, Bola went inside and brought me my plate, then walked me to the door of my room. I let myself in, assuming he would get his own plate and join me. Instead, he closed the door and disappeared. With mounting irritation, I ate my eggs and then went to look for him. "He has gone out," Kehinde said, as if nothing was wrong. How could he do that? I wondered. And what should I do now? But I was too baffled and hurt to ask.

It was too early to sleep, but I stayed in my room asking myself why I was being treated with a rudeness that would be inexcusable at home. If I'd wanted to eat alone I could have gone to the roadside stand whose owner was by now used to serving me ten *naira* worth of rice and beans at lunchtime. What sort of place was this where people treated each other so horribly? In my anger I felt like the worst kind of explorer stereotype, lost in a mystery no white man could ever penetrate.

The next morning I ran into Soji, one of the two male students who had silently slipped away. "What happened to you last night?" I asked accusingly as he greeted me with his usual smile. "I invited you to eat dinner with me and you disappeared. In fact, everyone disappeared." Just then Bola walked through the gate and into the school's courtyard, waving to both of us with guiltless exuberance. I repeated my question to him, and he and Soji exchanged looks that failed to reveal, even to my suspicious eye, any complicity in a plot to make me feel rejected.

"You know," Bola finally said, "in Nigeria, if someone sees you eating with the *iyawo* of another man, he thinks you are—you know—moving in on his territory."

"You've got to be kidding."

"I am not," said Bola, who understood colloquial English better than the mystified Soji. In the end, I never even mentioned to them the silent diatribes (about them, about Nigerians and their very different culture) that had kept me awake the night before. The idea of the home as "a haven from a heartless world" is ours, not theirs. For Nigerian men, home seems to be more like a pit stop. Certainly it is not a site, given the numbers usually involved, for "family togetherness." I've seen many a Nigerian woman offer a plate of food to her *oko* with no sense at all that she should be eating *with* him. And she would never hold dinner for everyone till he walked through the door. Given how accustomed I had become, as a single woman, to eating alone in the States, I was surprised at how upsetting was the thought that Foley might not be eager to come home to me as soon as the sun went down.

I was learning that, for him, unwinding after work happens not at dinnertime with his *iwayo* but in the time he gets to *play* (a word that lacks our connotations of frivolity) with his male friends. Some, but not all, of this time would be taken up by a soccer game between members of the school and a local team. But what he did, where he went, or with whom, from the time it got too dark for soccer at about eight until he showed up at home, an hour or two later (always glad to see me—but why should he not be?) was information I could never elicit from anyone. Fears of a conspiracy began to crop up.

Naturally my immediate suspicion was that there was another woman—a wife, a family—in his life, a deception that several Americans who knew Nigerians assured me was quite likely. *Everyone knows but me,* I kept telling myself. In my most panicked moments, I thought of my mother telling me, late at night with a drink in her hand, what a wonderful marriage she had with my father. What damage to mind and body had been necessary for her to keep herself from knowing that, when she worried about where my father was, he probably *was* with another woman? "You have no idea what it's like," her shaking hand had announced to me, to which I now replied, "Maybe I do."

Perhaps the only people who could be bearers of light into this darkness were two of the women I lived with: Kehinde and Yinka. Would I like to go shopping with them rather than wait for Foley, they asked one night. Saying "yes" was one of the best things I ever did for myself in Nigeria, where men and women tend in any case to socialize separately. From my reading as a feminist, I already understood that most cultures are less couple-driven than ours, and to that I say, most of the time, thank God.

So Yinka, Kehinde, and I started going to the roadside markets every day to buy our basics: tomatoes, oil, onions, peppers, rice or yams, and Maggi bouillon cubes. To these items, we added fish, eggs, or perhaps *egusi,* a kind of ground melon seed, or *tété,* a green vegetable that women sell from baskets on their heads for two or three *naira* a bunch. Of course I bought enough to feed them, too, and we three would cook and eat when I got hungry, which was usually around eight. We'd save half of what we cooked—more than half actually—for Foley, his brother Emmanuel, and Bola, who showed up whenever they felt like it.

I could do this and also feed myself—tea and Digestive biscuits for breakfast, rice and beans for lunch—for about a dollar a day. As the summer progressed, I found myself retreating into my anorectic habits, struck by the fact that the people around me were not eating three squares a day. Nigerian food is normally spiced with hot pepper to a degree beyond what my Canadian stomach will ever be able to tolerate. The meat is tough, the cassava-based starches heavy and unappealing. So it was better not to get *too* hungry. As a result, my stomach shrank, I never went over budget, and I lost about ten pounds—not a good move in a country where "you've gained weight" is said as a compliment. Later, in the States, I gained it back, but only there.

Nevertheless this cooking arrangement solved many problems. I made friends with some Nigerian women, I learned to cook, and I moved in the direction of doing something *their* way rather than having to have it my way. Observing Kehinde was helpful since her reaction to Bola's absence was so different from mine to Foley's. She was sometimes vocally annoyed with him but did not, as far as I could tell, feel abandoned. "Foley will come," she would tell me each night with such calm certainty that I knew my anxiety-driven scenarios would only puzzle her. I was his *iyawo.* What did it matter where he went?

There seemed to be no way for me to direct the shared future that everyone had decided was ours, since neither of us had ever actually proposed to the other. The closest we had come was a conversation we'd had just before we fell asleep not long before I left for Nigeria. "You know I can't marry anyone now," he said into the darkness above the bed.

"Why not?"

"Because of you." He was certainly being cryptic.

"Does that mean you've been thinking about marrying me?"

"Yes." This felt like a postcoital statement of fact rather than a signal for violins to start playing. Then there was the time we were eating barbecued chicken in my kitchen, and I handed him the last piece, saying, "This one's for you."

"No, for you," he said, and we went back and forth a few times until he took the piece, saying, "What's for me is for you." Well, I could work with that.

So either there was a conspiracy of enormous proportions or else there really was, as people kept saying, "no problem," nothing for me to do but buy a smashing traditional outfit to wear to the engagement ceremony (to be held in the village of Osi) whose date had been set for a week before I left for the States! In a traditional culture like Foley's, your friends and family—and beyond them, your ancestors and theirs—know more than you, a single individual, can possibly know. And that being so, why would not they, rather than you, a foreigner, be the best source of guidance when making important decisions?

The week before the ceremony, my left knee went out. My knees have always been a weak part of my body—a harness caught in a rope tow on one of our family skiing expeditions took part of my cartilage, and a car accident ten years later had required the removal of more. Perhaps the behavior of this knee was only a delayed reaction to my head-on collision. But perhaps not. "Things like that happen to my father all the time," said Emmanuel cheerfully. He probably meant it as a kind remark, but their father was an octogenarian.

I saw everything that happened to me that summer in symbolic terms, each event either a warning or a test. Was my body my friend or my adversary? Was it the site of a struggle to be won, as the early missionaries and explorers of Africa had believed? My future in-laws might be willing to look past the differences in income and education between their son and me. They might not even mind my being twenty years older than he and past the age of childbearing. But they surely would not want him marrying someone they saw as a cripple. As the week ad-

vanced I tried to exercise my treacherous limb and to limp as imperceptibly as possible. On the day itself, I apprehensively got up and the knee
magically clicked into place.

Two cars packed with Foley's friends followed us to Osi. We had just
bought a 1970 Datsun Bluebird from a friend of his, and that day it carried not only Emmanuel and several other people in the backseat but
a noisy dog and an even noisier goat in its boot, as Nigerians call the
trunk of a car. I didn't like to think about what would happen to the animals at the end of the ride, but I hoped the two of them were consoling
each other as death approached. The fact that the goat's death bothered
me less than the dog's seems rather arbitrary, but so it was. "The *orisa*
for carvers is Ogun, god of iron," Foley explained patiently. "And the
animal you do for sacrifice to Ogun, god of iron, is dog."

Perhaps Ogun ruled over automobiles as well, and I had him to thank
for my remarkable protection on the road four months before. "How
will you make the sacrifice?" I asked. "Or maybe I don't want to know."

I was wearing a traditional outfit whose indigo dye still rubbed off on
my white body, turning it slightly blue. My hair had been braided by a
hairdresser who had never encountered straight, limp hair like mine
before. I had been warned that it might take her as much as eight hours
to weave in four packages of extensions. But once Foley had told me he
would like it, and that his family would like it, and once I'd seen hair in
the markets of Osogbo that was quite close to my own shade of bottled
light red and learned that the whole process would set me back less
than twenty dollars, how could I not do it? By the end of the makeover
day my whole body hurt and I cried as I trod my homeward way. If my
feminist friends could have seen me then!

Foley demonstrated how the dog's front and back legs would be held,
and how a machete would cut it in half. If the knife did not go straight
through, it meant that Ogun had rejected your sacrifice, and you would
have to do it again. What if Ogun opposed the marriages of carvers to
English professors? "Are you sure you've told everyone enough about
me?" I kept asking. "Are you sure they're fine about it?"

"Yes," said Foley patiently and repeatedly. "They want for me whatever I want."

People often ask me if Nigeria is beautiful. It's a question I don't really know how to answer. My opinion would be shaped by a long history of ideas about "nature" and "beauty" whose manifestations are hard to find in a country as densely populated as Nigeria. Surely, trees should be dense and towering and should speak of sublimity with a minimal evidence of human presence. From time to time I saw what might be described as patches of rain forest out the window of our car, but mostly I saw low-growing "bush" and mud shacks with tin roofs and tried to imagine the thoughts of the people who spent their whole lives there.

Osi is a very old village without tap water, though its one- and two-story houses are in better repair than those I saw beside the two-lane highway on which we had traveled. They are arranged along deeply gullied dirt roads, their tin roofs darkened with rust, their red-brown mud sides decorated with wooden shutters and carved doors. We trooped past the cooking area, where Foley's father's four still-living wives, including Foley's beautiful mother, were boiling yams in giant kettles over an open fire. The largest house belonged to his father, who was waiting to greet us on its pillared porch. As a prospective "junior wife," I'd been practicing a traditional low curtsy to greet my new family. Foley held my hand firmly as I did it, and my knee with a mind of its own did not give out.

A family meeting inside the paternal house happened next—men only, I think. Retreating toward my friends, I sat on the hood of our car and accepted a Bitter Lemon. As I sipped I watched the women transfer the yams into a wooden vat, then consecutively thump them with their long, pestle-shaped pounders. In whatever direction I looked, I saw adorable children running around; later, during the ceremony I had fifty within the sweep of my vision. Continuous drumming rose and fell from somewhere behind their heads. Everyone stared quite openly at me, the only person there who had traveled beyond this village, let alone outside of Africa, I guessed, except for Foley and one or two of his brothers. I was certainly a long way from Toronto.

Foley's brother, Francis, the best English speaker in the family, had been assigned to make me feel welcome. So it was he who came out of the meeting, after maybe forty minutes, to ask me a few questions. The family had only one, he said, and it wasn't the one about children that I'd been dreading. "Foley has told us," he said, sitting down next to me on a wooden bench on the porch, "that he wants only one wife. We have no problem with that. I have only one wife and so do some of my other brothers. But we take this very seriously here, and we understand that this is not always so in the United States. Will you say something to us about that, please?"

I was completely taken aback. *Me* fooling around? I who hadn't met an interesting available man in God knows how long? "You know, I'm just meeting you today, so you have no reason to believe me other than what Foley has told you about me," I said. "But I assure you, I will never knowingly do anything to cause Foley pain. As best as I can do it, I will be the wife he deserves." Francis took that back to the meeting, and when it ended an hour later, Foley's father came out of the house and sat down beside me on the bench, taking my hand in his. Apparently I had passed muster.

The meal was ready now. Our goat had been killed and skinned, cut up, and cooked. The dog was barking somewhere. A group of ten small girls, their heads covered in palm fronds, their thin bodies wrapped in white cloth, danced in a circle. As I held Foley's hand and closed my eyes, the dog was cut in half. Ogun found our sacrifice acceptable— thank God—so I followed Foley into the low-ceilinged shrine at the far end of the courtyard, where we placed our foreheads to the ground. I said my own prayer as the incomprehensible words of a *babalawo* hovered above me: *Let me be able to grow from whatever comes up in this new life.* From the courtyard behind us the beat of drums moved the energy along.

Back out in the glaring sunlight I took in again the hundred or so pairs of eyes focused on me and my intended. How many of them belonged to members of my new family? I knew from a trip to Ogidi with Olabayo that Nigerian weddings do not require formal invitations. Like funerals, they are public festivals, widely announced, and when people hear about them they just show up. But how much of their attention had to do with the fact that I come from a country where wealth is believed to pour down on you without any effort on your part? Had even the children learned that already? Did I know what I was getting myself into?

Then plates of food were passed around, and some people danced while others ate. Along with pounded yams and a very hot sauce, people other than me ate the dog. I sat next to Foley's *baba* while my husband—or husband-to-be, the distinction didn't seem to matter much here—circulated among family and old schoolmates; he knew everyone there and was obviously enjoying himself. The women serving the food were family members who had never left the village: sisters, spouses of brothers—and, of course, Foley's father's four still-living wives. In my country, I would have offered to help, but here as an outsider there was nothing to do but smile and respond with a nod and a thank-you to all the greetings and congratulations. "*Ase,*" I said in our barely common language. "*Ase pupo.*"

My favorite part of the ceremony was the last, when the women took me into a room and welcomed me into the family. They gave me African names: Foley's mother's and her eldest daughter's and my own special name, Abike, which means "she who is taken care of." "So when you need anything," these gracefully coiffed and head-tied women assured me, "just ask us for it." It was almost too powerful a welcome. Nothing in my past could have prepared me for it.

Visiting Osi, with its light from kerosene lamps and water drawn from wells, I began to understand how Foley had become a person so different from me. It doesn't matter what time it is in Osi. Since the past does not disappear, one need not hang on to it. Perhaps this is why he lets things go so much more easily than I do. If an angry thought about him, or about Nigeria, rushes out of my mouth, I worry about it long after the moment has gone. If I mention it to him later, he looks puzzled. For better or worse, he lives fully in the present.

Before we left I asked him where one went in this town if one wanted to pee. We walked away from the others and turned a corner into a small, deserted alley. "So? What now?" Foley spread his legs to demonstrate my next move. "But," I protested, I have underpants on."

"I can't help you," he said, smiling and lowering his trunk into a good second-position *plié.* "Just—*abi?*"

I loosened my wrapper, which I had pinned and tied in place, and dealt with my underwear as best I could. Perhaps a deeper *plié* would have helped, but having not yet learned the trick of tilting my pelvis up and back, I was not able to keep my feet and the insides of my legs from getting wet. "I think," Foley said with a smile as we made our way back toward the dispersing crowd, "you are now a real African woman."

12

Five days after our engagement ceremony I was due to fly back to New York. After such a long stay in Nigeria, I was looking forward, I have to say, to a stopover in London and a few days with friends there. Yet before I left, a shadow of uncertainty was thrown across the warmth of the ritual that had made me part of Foley's family. It appeared in the short interval between the scary two-hour drive back to Osogbo from Osi, with Foley behind the wheel, and the only slightly calmer four-hour drive, a few days later, along the now-familiar route to the Lagos airport and an awaiting British Airways plane.

Most of my panic in the car driving back from Osi must have been triggered by my body's memory of the collision four months earlier, a memory that my mind still could not call up. With seven or eight people packed into the car, three of us in the front seat, I screamed or grabbed the thin arms of Foley's cousin Aderonke each time Foley rounded a corner or passed a car on a hill. "I don't want to kill you," he kept insisting. "I don't want to kill myself." But I could not relax and trust him, and I think he understood why.

I spent my last few days in Osogbo saying good-bye to people and promising to bring them things when I came back to Nigeria. In the midst of all this, I had a conversation with an American woman named Zoe, who had arrived in Nigeria from New York a week before the ceremony but whom I had not invited to it. Zoe had a studio in the same

Brooklyn building as an American carver friend of Foley's named Tom; that's how she met Foley and me. Then, through "my Foley" she met "Tall Foley," one of the five Nigerians I took home from the airport, and had come to Osogbo to pursue him, displaying plenty of bare thigh and midriff and apparently relishing the knowledge that everyone was apprised of her reason for coming into their midst. Naturally this set every fiber of my Canadian-bred being on edge. There was no group with whom I wanted less to be associated than American women like her.

"You know that Foley is married," I remember her saying. "Don't you? He told me so in New York."

"Your Foley or mine?"

"Yours," she said with a smile, happy, I'm sure, to hear the object of her pursuit referred to as hers. "I'm sorry. I thought you knew."

"Well, no. I know he is married on paper." Any Nigerian male under fifty has to be married on paper or the American embassy won't let him into the country. "All of them are married like that. Your Foley too."

"I think we are talking about more than documents," she said as she turned on her heel and walked away.

The next time I saw Foley I brought up this conversation. His smiling response was not what I expected. "Yes, I told her I had a wife," he said. "She said she wanted to marry black, so I said that."

"Did you say you were married to me?"

"No." But then why would he, since at that point we were not even "engaged." He could see I was still upset, so he said just what a worrier does not want to hear. "Don't worry about that Zoe."

While we were having this talk, standing on the art school's front porch, Foley's friends kept walking up and greeting us, expecting to be greeted in turn as if there were no such thing as a private conversation between a man and a woman for whom a dog has recently been sacrificed. "You really think I have another wife?" he asked. There was such disbelief in his voice, it was hard to reply.

"I don't know. Will you swear to me that you don't?"

"Kate, how could I be married? I have brought you to my family. You have met all my friends in Osogbo. What can I do more than that?"

What more, indeed?

I hoped that Zoe would let me out of her life when we both got back to the States. Instead, she called often to ask me for advice about her romance with "Tall Foley," who had a long-term girlfriend in Nigeria. "Can I trust him?" she'd ask.

"Trust him to do what?"

"To leave her like he said he was going to."

"Well, I don't know what to tell you. I just wouldn't put all my eggs in one basket if I were you."

"What makes you say that?"

"It's just my philosophy, I guess."

"Okay, I guess it's a good one. Usually it's mine too. How are things with you? Is Foley coming back to the States?"

"Of course." Did she really think he would not?

"Well, that's great. You know I'm really sorry that I had to be the one to break the bad news to you, but I think it's better in the long run that you know, don't you?"

"I don't know. Let me just ask you one question. Did anyone else tell you that Foley was married?"

"Not over there," she said. "I didn't ask anyone over there. But I know he told Tom the same thing."

I looked up Tom's number and got his girlfriend on the phone. "Sure, he told both of us," she said. "He never said anything about it to you?"

"No."

"God, you must feel really awful. I feel so bad for you. As soon as Tom gets in I'll ask him to call you."

An hour later, Tom was on the phone. Foley had mentioned at some point that the two of them had had a falling out before he left for Nigeria, but he had never said what it was about. "Nigerians are all liars, as far as I'm concerned," said Tom vehemently. "Foley's no worse than the rest, but he's one too."

"About what?"

"About all sorts of things. They're just never straight with you, that's all."

"But how could he have an engagement ceremony with his whole family and everyone in the town if they all knew he had a wife somewhere else?"

"Well, having a person like you in their family, a woman from another country with a professional career, would be a feather in their cap. You'd better keep a lookout for what they expect you to do for them. Like send their kids to Harvard."

"Okay," I said, wanting only to hang up and scream.

What he had said sounded so plausible, especially when it was said in such a sympathetic voice. For a week, I just went through the motions of my life, energy draining out of me every time I stopped to think. I wasn't up to another conversation with Foley over phone lines where the delay made it difficult to get across even simple things. Finally I called Yetunde, who had become a friend during my first visit to Nike's. She was single and older than most of the other students, so if I could trust anyone it would be she.

"Have you ever heard a rumor," I managed to shout at six in the morning, when cheap rates still applied, "that Foley has a Nigerian *iyawo*?"

She got it after several repetitions, and I picked up that she was surprised to hear me asking her such a question. "I've never heard of that," she said. "But I'll speak to Foley."

"Tell him to write me a letter," I said. "Tell him what people here are saying. Nike's coming to the States in a week or so, isn't she? He can give the letter to her."

I met Nike at the home of a friend of hers in Harlem. She handed me the letter with a smile and no sense of the anxiety that rushed out through my fingertips. "Kate, I love only you," it said. "And I will always love only you." I sensed that the small, neat penmanship was Yetunde's, but I wanted to hold the blue-lined document flat against my chest and let its warmth seep in. "You are missing your *oko*," said Nike, resplendent in her heavily embroidered *boubou* and matching head tie.

"Yes, I am."

When Foley did come to New York in October, full of energy and optimism, I couldn't find it in myself to do more than thank him for the letter. He shrugged his shoulders, as if puzzled that a declaration in writing should have been necessary. In the intervening two months I had summoned up the smile in his eighty-five-year-old father's eyes, the sweetness of his mother whose prominent collarbones and high cheekbones were so like mine, the clusters of wide-eyed children threaded between the dignified, attentive faces of their elders whose welcome had felt so unconditional. If I still had doubts about Foley's sincerity, what could dispel them if not that day-long ritual?

Now that we were officially "engaged," the logical next step was that the following summer we would have (by which I understood that I would pay for) a traditional Yoruba wedding with all the trimmings. I knew that Nike was keen to host this event at the school, and while I was not thrilled with the idea of killing another dog, I knew that *something* has to be sacrificed to make sure that the right deities have been notified and asked for a blessing.

But as my New York friends began to meet Foley, I decided I wanted a ceremony for them too. As usual, Foley was happy to agree, so my first call was to Boston where my son was now at MIT. Kevin had been chilly on the phone since my return from Nigeria, answering politely but briefly my questions about his Ph.D. program and his life in general. He'd made it quite clear that, if Foley and I came to visit, the two of us would not be sleeping together on the striped, foldout IKEA couch in his living room.

"You mentioned the M-word, Mother," he said this time.

"Yes, I guess I did. We want to have a ceremony on this side of the Atlantic. When do you think you and Mitzi would have a free weekend?"

"I'd say don't plan it around us, Mom. You know Mitzi usually works weekends at the hospital, and we don't always know that far in advance when she'll be off."

"I *am* planning it around you, sweetie. Let me know when the two of you can come and we'll have it then."

After a long pause he said, "Okay, I'll talk to Mitzi and get back to you." When he did, I set a date in March and sent out invitations.

I knew, of course, why he was digging in his heels. He still blamed me for leaving his father. "You people in the sixties didn't take marriage very seriously," he told me once. "You figured if it didn't work out, you could just blow it off and—you know—try again." I admit that I did at one time have thoughts like that, and I was sure that he never would.

Yet it was at his wedding that I finally saw Rick, who had cut off all contact with me since I'd won custody of our son twenty years before. And this reunion, after so much time, let me see what I needed to know in order to "try again." Rick looked miserable at the wedding and left early. He'd grown plump. His tall person's habit of stooping was even more pronounced. Everything about him exuded defeat. I could have stayed longer, tried harder, done more, but he carries from his child-hood a weight of depression that no one seems to be able to lift. And because of it we could never have revived the happy pair we were in the heady years of the mid-1960s.

When radical politics showed up in my own backyard, I had just about everything I wanted. As an undergraduate, high on Methedrine, I'd sometimes looked enviously at academic marriages. Now I had one of my own. Our Columbia-owned apartment had French windows and floor-to-ceiling bookshelves that Rick had built with tools he borrowed from his dad, one wall for his books, one for mine. We had a two-year-old son whose bursts of cognitive mastery were a daily delight to his eager-to-boast parents, and I was making "satisfactory progress" toward a Ph.D. from one of the country's most prestigious schools.

My conversion began on a rainy Wednesday morning in late April 1968. Before that I'd refused to even read about the world of politics, which I saw as hopelessly tainted by Daddy's quest for popularity. The Civil Rights movement had come and gone without me. I might have turned on my radio—TV sets were strictly for suburbanites—and heard Martin Luther King give voice to his dream back in 1963. But on that rainy morning five years later, with no thought that this day would be different from any other, I left my son with his father, took my um-brella, and walked up to Hamilton Hall to have lunch with my friend Meredith, who was already a teaching assistant.

When I got there, the doors were chained shut and a crowd was packed into the courtyard under open umbrellas listening to a speech bellowed through a bullhorn. A woman in a yellow slicker handed me a rain-soaked leaflet. STOP THE RACIST GYM! it demanded in large, hand-printed letters, and I remembered something in the *Spectator,* Columbia's student newspaper, about the university's plans to build a gym for its students in Morningside Park, a strip of rocky cliff and grass between the campus and Harlem that belonged, the leaflet said, to the community. I was surprised that the student, whose speech ended with everyone around me chanting those words, was black. I had never noticed black students on the campus before.

I showed the leaflet to Rick, and right from the start he took a dim view of the aspirations it expressed. "I hope they haven't closed the library," he said, putting on his London Fog raincoat, a birthday present from me. Rick was studying for his orals. I had taken a year's maternity leave, so I was now behind him, though we'd started out together in September of 1964. My mother was pleased with the new arrangement. It put Rick out ahead where he belonged.

I'd met Rick in Professor Edward Tayler's Wednesday morning seminar in seventeenth-century prose, and immediately he struck me as the kind of man with whom I would like to have children. A shock of dark hair fell down over his hazel eyes when he leaned over his book. His V-necked sweaters over long-sleeved white shirts and the way he took his time speaking to our group of fifteen men and two women made me think of album covers of American composers: Aaron Copeland's *Billy the Kid,* Virgil Thompson's *The Plough That Broke the Plains.* I was almost disappointed to learn that his family lived in Main Line Philadelphia, the kind of birthplace my parents would be happy to visit.

I didn't learn the first name of the other woman in our seminar for over a month, so scrupulously did Professor Tayler avoid the informal mode of address. Vicky Sullivan dashed off after our meetings to feed her daughter, and I envied her having people waiting for her at home. I pictured her discussing the readings with her husband and bringing his encouragement to her classes. Professor Tayler's label of "Miss"—mine exclusively—felt more like a mark of past failure than a sign of future opportunity.

It was November before I was sufficiently free of anxiety about my single status to focus on the men in the class as distinct individuals and to notice that not all of them went off to eat lunch as a unit. I usually ate with either Meredith or Anne, two friends from the School of General Studies whose move into graduate English the year before had inspired me to follow them. It was Anne who had introduced me to the man who became my source of amphetamines, while I think Meredith had no idea I was even taking them, so secretive, yet so seemingly reasonable, was the practice. But if even only a few of my fellow students were entering the upper levels of their minds with the help of chemicals, could I afford not to be one of them?

The day I decided to speak to Rick, the seminar had just begun working on Sir Thomas Browne's *Religio Medici*. "I liked your comment," I said to him as we all walked slowly toward the elevator, "about Browne's use of punning to challenge the finite limitations of language."

"I started out as a math major," he said casually. "So number symbolism is something I enjoy." The elevator was full so we waited in front of the row of darkened doors, each with its pane of "snowflaked" glass and a small nameplate indicating which member of Columbia's distinguished faculty one might, with luck, find inside.

"A math major. Good Lord! You wouldn't believe how badly I did in the math part of the GRE. I didn't even finish, and half of my answers were just guesses."

"I won't ask you your score," he said.

"I'll bet you got over seven hundred."

"Seven ninety," he said, summoning the elevator.

"I'm impressed."

"Good. Would you like to have lunch with me?"

"Sure," I said exuberantly, thinking how lucky I was that Anne was home sick that day. "Where do you go?"

"There's a luncheonette on Amsterdam and 118th," said Rick. "The food is okay, regular diner food."

"Enjoy yourselves, you two," said Professor Tayler on his way to his office. "See you in Milton this afternoon."

You two. So he was giving us his blessing, this man whose role it was to guide our way through academe, "hand in hand," as Milton puts it at the end of *Paradise Lost*, "with wandering steps and slow." I didn't see a fear of people in Rick's solitary dining habits. I saw a man who not only ate lunch alone but admitted proudly to doing so as well. He didn't mind not eating with *them;* he actually chose it.

Sitting in a leatherette booth opposite him, I found other things that set him apart. "I got bored with math and the people in it," he said, ignoring the menu. "So I took a seminar on critical theory with Maurice Blanchot, who is just as famous as Trilling, and decided to switch to English."

"Where was that?"

"Wesleyan." Instinct told me he didn't want to expand on his four years there. A waitress took our orders. With my girlfriends, I ate a green salad at the John Jay dining hall, but this place had only salad platters so I chose a "normal" BLT.

"What do you think of Tayler?" I asked.

"He's all right, I guess. He seems to have a reputation for turning students into groupies. Have you joined the flock?" His choice of words, and the sarcasm with which he delivered them, raised him to a higher plane than everyone else in the program, myself included. He seemed to have no interest in impressing the people who made me feel so inadequate. I knew that he had one of the fellowships that the federal government was giving out in the sixties: four thousand dollars a year for four years. I wondered if he knew that I did not.

"I don't feel like I belong in that group," I admitted. "I guess it's because I went to General Studies here. *They* don't regard that place as a real school."

"Why not?"

"Because *anyone* who passes a computerized exam can get in."

"Well, none of them's as smart as they're pretending to be," said Rick in the offhand tone I already admired. Then sensing, perhaps, my fear of his judgment, he added, "One or two are genuinely smart, but not all by a long shot."

He must have reassured me because I found myself with the courage to ask, "What about me? Am I genuinely smart?"

Rick put down his sandwich and looked at me in a way that said *something's going to happen between us*. "Sometimes you sound confused," he said, "but underneath it all I have the impression that you think in interesting ways."

Arriving at our Milton lecture, I experienced the conspiratorial thrill that became an essential ingredient of this stage of our courtship. I sensed that our fellow male seminarians, at least the ones who came from out of town, saw me as weird because I lived in the Village. But Rick lived downtown as well, a potential ally, so after our classes that day we took the downtown subway to Houston Street, where he lived at his own chosen distance from that imagined circle called "the Columbia community." To me his solitary ways were signs of the loneliness that surrounds superior people.

The exposed brick wall in his apartment was covered with bookshelves. On them were the complete works of several poets of our shared period, their gold-lettered Oxford University Press spines covered with pale blue dust-jackets. After a meal of pork chops and frozen string beans, he poured Courvoisier into two jelly glasses and told me that most of his books had come from Blackwell's, in Oxford. "I have a charge account," he said. "So if you see anything you want in any of these, I can order them for you and you can pay me." The pile of catalogues he handed me were not only for English literature but philosophy and architecture, religion, and history.

"How did you hear about this?" I asked, in awe.

"I guess Blackwell's is part of an elite education," he said, sitting down beside me on his couch, a wine-colored second-hand item with a pattern cut into the fabric and formidable, though scratched, claw feet.

"I'm envious." I picked out several books, and the move into the bedroom from there was enabled, he would later remind me, by my considerably greater sexual experience. But these jabs at my status as an older woman who had lived on her own in the Village came only at the end of the marriage. At the time I found myself telling him things I had wanted to say about Sir Thomas Browne but couldn't in front of my critical fellow students, and we fell into each other's arms with the delight of knowing that what we were doing was not "just sex" but a joining of minds, his clearly superior to mine. Venturing the next morning toward a joint charge account at Blackwell's, we were as good as engaged.

Rick also liked sexual secrecy, so we arrived at our seminar a few minutes apart, sat in different rows in the lectures we shared, and then met at the end of the day at the subway. Almost nothing had changed externally, yet everything was different. I still studied on the weekends, but I studied with him. We did laundry together on Saturday nights. This freedom not to have to go anywhere, to read together with Vivaldi on the turntable, to be, as Jane Eyre says, "at once as free as in solitude, as gay as in company," *this* was the essence of the happy marriage my mother had always claimed to be enjoying.

Yet one difference was critical: Rick saw himself as brilliant but not as sexually irresistible. His lack of masculine confidence let me know that I'd never have to go through what my mother had suffered. Our point of rendezvous was not a fraternity house but the library, on which we converged separately after our classes. There is still no place on earth where I feel more thoroughly my own creation than in Columbia's Butler Library. The thrill of standing in the heart of the stacks, mastering the bibliographical resources of my field, were pleasures my mother had certainly never known. In fact, my father referred to her having slept through most of her lectures as a major accomplishment.

Of course I would never know the thrill of joining a sorority and marrying a football player in the days when going to university rather than a finishing school was a daring move for a girl from my mother's world. But in the library, I had imagined a different sort of woman, one who could be happy even without marrying. Now it looked as though I could have her and marriage too. Sitting with a pile of books and note cards at one of the long oak tables on the fourth floor of Butler, the library with names of great male thinkers of the Western world carved in a line below its roof, knowing that Rick was *there for me* even when nowhere in sight, what could I not make happen?

Our strategies of concealment took the two of us through our separate Christmases and the first half of our second semester, when I found out I was pregnant. This brought to a sudden end my amphetamine habit, though not my nagging fear that the embryo I was carrying might already be damaged. Neither of us seriously considered an abortion, and this in itself was a sign to me that my life was undergoing a major alteration. How right it was that a force beyond my control was finally guiding my almost-too-long-wandering steps toward this stable, self-sufficient, brilliant man who lived and ate apart. And yes, I would surrender to that force.

"You're the third match that's come out of one of my seminars," Professor Tayler gleefully told us when we abandoned our secrecy one Wednesday morning. At subsequent meetings he seemed to call on me more often. He still addressed me as "Miss," but the word had lost its derogatory edge. Even as I struggled with morning sickness and withdrawal from my "medicine," I no longer worried that, in the very act of speaking up, I was undermining my femininity in front of the guys. Now I could ask them about their weekends without fear that they'd think I was angling for a Saturday night date.

Our parents were pleased too. Rick's dad was an engineer whose company had contracts in Vietnam and Thailand. He was also a life member of the National Rifle Association. But for all that, he was a sweet, mild-mannered man with a profile that reminded me of Steve Canyon, the comic strip detective from my childhood. For most of his married life his wife had been agoraphobic, a disability that had set in when Rick was quite small. Communists were looking for her, she believed, because she was a member of the DAR. At least this was how Rick explained it to me. So she stayed inside, letting her husband do the shopping and lighting cigarettes at about the same rate my mother did. She made it through our wedding under heavy sedation.

My mother arrived right after my master's exam in early May to help me assemble a trousseau, a word that called up a person I did not know I was, a creature assembled from the pages of the women's magazines I hadn't read in years, a woman who was thrilled at the thought of a church wedding with cascades of flowers and a vow to "love, honor and obey." She wanted a set of china, too, and enough glasses to serve elegant dinners for eight. She wanted a chafing dish and sheets with embroidery and ruffles. She wanted gloves and hankies and folding cases to keep them in, place mats, salad servers—was there no end to this appetite of hers?

"It's not you who's marrying me for my money," I joked to Rick, who by then was ensconced in my small Village apartment. "It's me marrying you for my money." By then I must have told him that, at the age of twenty-one, I had come into three thousand dollars a year from Daddy's father's will. The first installment had arrived the January before I began therapy, and though it was not enough to live on, it was not that much less than Rick's stipend. I never used the words "trust fund," but I knew other people would if they found out about it.

My premarital shopping orgy brought me to a part of the city that's still my mother's territory, an area that also includes Dr. Kugelmaas's office and the now-demolished Martha Graham School on East Sixty-Third. Some of the places from which I used to shoplift are now gone, and a degree of tackiness has crept into the neighborhood since my mother and I shopped there together—Bugs Bunny on Fifty-Seventh Street and the now garishly gilded statue of General Sherman across from the Plaza. And I know now that the disapproval I feel, gazing at them, is not only mine but hers as well.

All I knew then, as we wandered through Georg Jensen's and Best's, was that this was my one chance to let my mother spend on me with pleasure. Had I remained single, there would have been no reason for me to have silverware that matched or sheets that looked pretty. Yet even as I stocked up on slips and girdles—yes, girdles—there were times when I reverted to my difficult self. When the Plaza's cleaning service told us it would cost $100 to iron my grandmother's wedding dress, with its high collar, leg-o'-mutton sleeves and hundreds of tiny tucks, I announced that I, like the Little Red Hen, would do it myself.

"If you ruin it," my mother replied, icy with rage, "we won't be able to get another dress for you in time for any amount of money." Though I stuck to my guns I was suddenly scared. Why was she so sure I would ruin it? And how could I have been so sure I would not?

My mother adored Rick, however, and he in turn treated her with a chivalry that said "let me take care of that for you," a good instinct in a potential mate. Yet on the last night of Mummy's well-intentioned visit, the monster who once fought so viciously with her sisters that boarding school was needed to restrain her came back untamed. The three of us, Rick, my mother, and I, were in the Oak Room of the Plaza talking after a nice dinner, paid for by her, and many drinks. "I've always believed," she said, "that a bone is stronger after it's broken than it was before anything happened to it. So don't just come running home to mother when the first thing goes wrong."

"Why should I do that?" I said. "I've always known I couldn't come home when things went wrong. There's no reason for me to start now." For a moment it looked as if my mother would cry, and Rick put a tweedy arm around her shoulder.

"Don't," she said, and pushed him away. In the silence I wondered what Rick was thinking. It had mattered a lot that he took my side when I fed him stories about my life in Toronto. "You're mother's a sad woman," he told me later. And he knew about such things since his was in even worse shape.

On the last Saturday in May 1965, I put on the veil from Saks and the well-starched and ironed dress of the grandmother I had never liked, and walked with my father up the aisle of a small Episcopal church in Pleasantville, New York, near the home of Rick's best friend from Wesleyan, whose family offered us their backyard for the reception, complete with two goats. Daddy, who had disappeared until just before the service, made the same speech he had made at my sister's wedding, claiming that the men in the family do all the work at events like these. The band, the tent, the catered food were not my choice, but their presence told me that this was a real marriage. Then Rick and I removed the "just-married" sign from the Corvair he'd borrowed from his brother and drove back home to the Village.

We visited our families that summer of 1965 and heard, from both our fathers, that the bombing of North Vietnam would end the war "in no time flat." I had never wanted to argue with Daddy before. But I'd never heard him speak with such approval about an action that seemed so wrong. "You don't know a thing about military operations, dear," he told me over dinner at our family's summer home in Cobourg, where Rick and I were sleeping in twin beds in the room I'd once shared with my sister Ellen. The house had been built by Daddy's father in 1928, a year before he died. Cobourg was a summer mecca then for families from the States who played polo in a wooden stadium by nearby Lake Ontario and croquet on their own rolling lawns.

Our summer house was built on a hill with a very old woods behind it. The leaves of its giant birch trees were always in motion, stirred by a wind that had drawn me into sleep for as long as I could remember. On that visit I felt lucky for the first time to have been born into the vicinity of that sound. On the weekend, as usual, my parents hosted one of their noisy gatherings where guests got drunk and pushed each other into the pool. But now Rick was there to protect me from scenes that might otherwise have retained the power to tell me who I was.

Though I insisted that being married was not that different from being single, marriage did lift a shadow I'd been living under for so long I'd almost stopped noticing it: my mother's prediction, delivered when my behavior upset her, that no one would marry a selfish girl like me. I wonder now if she saw my earlier "elopement" with Cornel Wilde as a brief fling, like the marriages of all those Hollywood females whose careers drove away one husband after another. Even after I was divorced from Rick, this shadow did not return until I had left New York and was living alone with Kevin in a garden apartment in New Jersey. My immersion in politics kept it at bay by offering me a new kind of family, first as an antiwar protester and then as a feminist at Rutgers, until I realized, well into the seventies, that the revolution was not going to happen.

Three years after the wedding Rick and I were sitting in the living room of our lovely Columbia-owned apartment in front of a console TV set, a present from Rick's parents, watching a replay of cops in full riot gear clearing the campus of strikers and their sympathizers, of which I'd been one until the early hours of that morning. Kevin was peacefully asleep in his room, a reminder that God had not punished my drug habit by sending me a damaged child. I'd breast-fed him for a year and never got down to my previous 110 pounds. But neither did I touch the bottle of green-and-white capsules nestled in our medicine chest behind the A and D ointment and children's aspirin.

The arrival of the cops was no secret maneuver. The strikers had been occupying four buildings for a week following the demonstration I'd happened in on, and the administration's vague threats had finally turned into an ultimatum. The police would not arrive till after dark, the campus radio station said. So I put Kevin to bed before dressing warmly for a long night of symbolic solidarity in front of Fayerweather Hall, the graduate student enclave I'd walked past many times but had not been willing to enter. Under the eerie glare of searchlights on the roof of the Architecture building, about a hundred of us waited nervously as the late spring chill crept under our layers. Then, as the white-helmeted Tactical Patrol Force formed a wedge of hard, glittering plastic in front of us, we linked arms.

Pushing us aside was easy for them compared to breaking down the heavy oak doors. "If you're hurt," someone shouted through a bullhorn, "go to Earl Hall. They have medical facilities there. If you're not hurt, stay and observe. The whole world is watching!"

Plenty of people were still milling around, so I slipped through the wrought-iron Amsterdam Avenue gate just before it was locked in preparation for what the newscasters would call a police riot, where some students and professors—braver than I was—were chased across the South Field, pinned against the locked gates at 114th Street and pummeled with a fury fueled, it was later said, by the TPF's hatred of a bunch of privileged draft-dodgers who'd had the audacity to form an organization called Students for a Democratic Society.

The next day several bandaged professors were interviewed on the network news. "It's a tragedy," said one, speaking through tears. "I've been at Columbia all my life and this is the death of something. It really is."

"Oh, come off it," Rick said when the newscaster switched to another topic. "It's not a tragedy. It's just something stupid that shouldn't have happened." Rick hated the inaccurate use of literary terms.

I was eager to atone for my cowardice the night of the first action, and eagerly offered the use of our apartment to an assistant professor of romantic poetry who wanted to teach "his" poets as part of the Strike Committee's Liberation School, an informal, SDS-inspired counter-university set up during the strike on the lawn in front of the library and in nearby apartments. Rick declined to participate, but I joined the class and got to watch a teacher combine radical politics and pedagogy, a feat I had never seen or even thought possible.

Surrounded by strangers in my own living room, the sun streaming in through the tall windows that opened onto the street, I became, in Rick's absence, the maternal faculty wife I intended to be when we both got jobs. Halfway through the first class, our teacher, who had asked us to call him Simon, stopped for a break, and I quickly produced coffee from the blue-and-white electric coffee pot bought after my first visit with Rick's family. I'd barely spoken to my next-door neighbors before, but I rang their bell and asked if they had any cups I could borrow. Simon's finest moment came the first time Kevin disrupted the class with "unsilenceable" wails from his crib in the next room. We weren't even doing Wordsworth, but without missing a beat Simon called out, giving the wicker swing he always sat in a gentle push:

Thou Child of Joy
Shout round me, let me hear thy shouts, thou
happy Shepherd-boy!

On days when Kevin was awake, he, too, seemed to sense a theatrical opportunity as he wandered among us, letting his diaper fall from his body as if to suggest that this was what Wordsworth really meant by "trailing clouds of glory."

Of course the motto for the class was Wordsworth's:

Bliss was it in that dawn to be alive,
But to be young was very heaven!

Wordsworth was twenty-eight, two years younger than me, when he began working on *The Prelude,* but for him the bliss had already slipped into the past. Not so for us. We were sure that new ways of seeing and reading and connecting with others were waiting to be born: a time when competition, and the loneliness that came with it, would no longer drive our every move and thought. Even marriage, that terrible divider between "haves" and "have-nots," would soon be withering away because we would all have each other.

13

In the aftermath of the violent first "bust," official university functions ground to a halt. Anyone who could get past the security guards checking IDs and onto the campus could feel how much was at stake for both sides. The hopes of the strikers seemed to take visible form in the pale haze of budding leaves that envelops the city's trees at that time of year. A poll in the *Spectator* told us that a majority of students resented the strike, since it interrupted classes just before exam time. This only made it all the more crucial that we, who had always resented the "jocks" who were leading this opposition, should *be there* to witness and defend our infant revolution.

With Kevin to look after, I could not fully connect to the groups of faculty and students who spent the next few weeks caught up in mass meetings and late-night debating sessions, issuing memoranda and open letters, and forming and resolving splits between moderates and hard-liners that left me unable to choose sides. I was opposed to the university building the gym in the park and to its ties to the war machine. And I now saw my need to impress my teachers and peers as part of a larger system of corporate brainwashing that the university carried out on behalf of those whose interests lay in prosecuting the war. Nevertheless, I was not really a radical as Mark Rudd defined that word, a fact I could not have admitted at the time.

One night in the middle of May I ran into Danny. I was on my way home to join Rick, Chet Huntley, David Brinkley, and thousands of others who, in growing numbers, became committed participants in what would later be called "the living room war." Rick and I were also drawn together, of course, by the upcoming oral exam we would both have to ace if we wanted to survive as a couple beyond the discipline of course work.

"Do I have the perfect demonstration for you!" said Danny with a grin. "It's all about the neighborhood. Just the thing for a young mother." Danny had been one of the occupants of the president's office in Low Library, the central switchboard from which the strike had been run. Once when the jocks and their allies tried to prevent food from being passed in through the windows, I joined Professor Tayler and others in an all-night cordon around Low. Both of us were quite proud, I think, as we blew warm breath into our gloves or sat down on the steps waiting for the sun to come up, to know someone inside whose needs we were protecting.

"We're all ears," I said, referring to Kevin, the star "attention getter" when he and I were on the street together.

"Great," Danny said. Come to the sundial tonight. We're trying to take the momentum of the strike into the community so the student movement doesn't get insular. I'm even more excited about this than I was about the first takeover." Danny pulled a leaflet out of his tattered satchel.

"Do you think there'll be another occupation?"

"I don't know. They're talking about one of the apartment buildings where Columbia has cut off services to force the local tenants out. People who've been arrested once can't do it again unless they're prepared for really heavy consequences, so I'll probably split once we get there. You could do it, though." Danny caught my eye and the street light went on the same moment. Had he really said that I should get arrested?

"I'll try to come," was all I answered. I would have to ask Rick, and what would I do if he said no?

On the way home I read the leaflet, pushing Kevin's stroller with my other hand. "Who controls this community? Columbia, its biggest landlord, or the people who live here? You DECIDE! JOIN US! This *was* the perfect demonstration for me. Didn't I sit in Riverside Park every day with a group of mothers? Weren't they more my community than those jocks from Columbia College, younger versions of the guys for whom my father had trained all of his girls to be an ideal date—drilling us in the rules of football so we wouldn't ask stupid questions as we sat cheering beside them in Toronto's Varsity Stadium?

"Well, well, what are we protesting now?" Rick asked as soon as he saw me with the leaflet in my hand.

"Turning Morningside Heights into an all-white enclave. Letting perfectly good apartments stand empty so Columbia can tear a bunch of buildings down and build high-rise housing for their own faculty and students. Things like that."

Rick picked up Kevin and wiped his nose. "Don't you think they need places for faculty and students to live?"

"Yes, but why should it be at the expense of black and Hispanic people? It says here that more than a hundred thousand low-income residents of this neighborhood have been forced out of their homes in the last ten years. How would you feel if you were one of them?"

"Honey, there's only a limited amount of space within a reasonable distance of the campus."

"So people can live elsewhere. Both of us did."

"But they want a community of students and faculty like they have at other schools. We had that at Wesleyan, and I think more of it here would be great. Isn't a university supposed to be a community of learners?"

"But let the community include people who don't go to Columbia."

I got dinner going and Kevin fed before asking Rick if I could go to the rally. "I get the feeling," he said after a minute, "that you're not really here with me. You always want to go somewhere and I'm just an obstacle in your way."

"I'm sorry you feel that way. But this is something that happens only once in a lifetime. We eat dinner together every night." As I said this I wondered if it would always be true. "I just want to be part of it, that's all."

"I wish I knew what it was you wanted to be part of." He was standing in the doorway to the kitchen, holding our son as I cut up tomatoes and cucumbers for a salad.

"I thought when we got married that we would both want to do things—like this. We're both against the war."

"But you were pregnant when we got married. We can't just rush off at the slightest impulse."

"This isn't a slight impulse."

"Maybe not, but that doesn't change the fact that we're both responsible for this little guy. I thought when we got married we'd do things like that together."

"You could go if you wanted to. I'd be happy to stay home and let *you* get arrested."

"I'm happy at home," he said. "And I want my wife to be too. I don't see why I should apologize for that. You used to complain about your dad always trying to get everyone's approval. Looks like you've caught the same disease."

"That's not fair. I was against the war before I met you, and we've always been on the same side. This sit-in is an extension of that. I just want to do something. I'll be home before morning, I promise you."

"Okay, go ahead, then," he said. He sounded so defeated that I had the urge to give up too. But nobody would win, then, and what would be the point of that?

The rally was just breaking up when I got to the campus. It was held, as they all were, in an open area, paved in brick, whose center was marked by a marble and granite sundial—a gift of the class of 1906—six feet in diameter and encircled with the words HORAM EXPECTATA VENIAT—let the awaited hour come—a clear reference, or so it seemed to me, to the future we were bringing into being. And surely, we were also being anticipated in another pronouncement carved on a stone bench in front of Hamilton, the gift of another class from a time when college was the recreation of gentlemen:

THE BRAVE, FAITHFUL AND TRUE, BY PRECEPT AND
EXAMPLE, STAND ALWAYS AND EVERYWHERE FOR
RECTITUDE OF CONDUCT AND RIGHTEOUSNESS OF LIFE.

Yet I have to confess that, even at the height of my anger at Columbia's wealthy trustee fathers, I never quite lost my sense of connection to the world that sponsored these inscriptions and the McKim, Mead, and White buildings that surrounded them. The family I would love to have had might have gone here for generations, and I often wished, as I walked around my adopted city, that I knew more about Daddy's grandparents on his mother's side, the ones who were part of the Gilded Age world that included Stanford White. My class background, I later learned to call it.

As soon as I reached the sundial, I caught sight of Mark Rudd, whose intense, gravelly voice and charismatic way with a bullhorn had a lot to do with why I was there. I was sorry I had missed him speak. A student I didn't recognize was pushing his way through the crowd toward Mark, who broke into a winning grin as he slapped his comrade on the back. "All right now, let's all move on down to our new liberated building," he shouted hoarsely. "This is the first step in a new alliance between Columbia students and their neighbors. So let's go!"

"All right!" came from the crowd around me, and they started moving toward the wrought-iron Broadway gate. Looking around apprehensively, I spotted Danny a few feet behind Mark and edged toward him through the press of bodies. "I'm glad you made it," he said, putting his arm around my shoulder as if I were his personal protégé. "How's the young mother?"

"Out for a night on the town."

"Really? Does that include getting arrested?" he asked eagerly. "I'm going to split soon because I have charges already pending. But you'll be perfect."

"I'm thinking about it. I just wish I knew more people here."

"So here's your big chance to get to know some folks not in the seventeenth century."

"How long do they keep you in jail?"

"We were there overnight," said Danny over the noise of our fellow marchers. "But I think that was only because they didn't have enough people to book us till the next morning."

Out on the street, people were cheering at us from the sidewalks; and as I was swept along, I decided once again to surrender myself to a larger force. You had to let go if you wanted to be included. Buoyed up by the presence of so many vocal bystanders, we followed Mark down Broadway as if he were the Pied Piper leading us out of the city of Hamlin.

"How's your course in the Liberation School?" I asked Danny, happy to have someone to talk to.

"I'm having a ball. I hear you're being quite the hostess to Simon Bartell."

"He's wonderful. Really, for the first time, I'm getting the sense that teaching could be fun."

"So why don't you do a course yourself?"

"On what? I feel like I don't know enough to put together anything that people would come to. I've never read Marx or Marcuse or anyone like that."

"People are doing literature courses," Danny said. "Look at Simon."

"But he has so much to say about his material. Don't you remember how hard it was for me to talk in our seminar?"

"Seemed to me you held your own pretty well."

"Did you really think that?" I eyed this graduate of the Columbia College honors program who had studied with Lionel Trilling. The lower half of his face was shadowed by a several-day growth of dark beard. Voices around us began chanting THE STREETS BELONG TO THE PEOPLE!

"Would I lie to you?" Danny was in better spirits than I'd ever seen him. Apparently the strike had a liberating effect on everyone it touched. "Anyway, you don't know how much you know till you try to put it out there. Isn't Virginia Woolf your favorite writer?"

"She's not exactly bursting with revolutionary fervor."

"It's not the material," said Danny. "It's all in the way you approach it. You don't even have to do a major figure like Woolf. You can do whatever you want."

"I'll give it some thought," I said, trying to picture Rick's response at the same time that I was reviewing babysitting possibilities.

"Why don't you come to my class?" he persisted. "We'll probably stay together over the summer as a reading group."

"I'll try."

"Okay, I'm off. But don't forget what I said about the group. And tell your old man too. He can't spend all his time studying for orals."

The new "liberated zone" was a redbrick five-story, Columbia-owned apartment building on 114th Street between Broadway and Riverside Drive, slated for demolition to make room for a new School of Social Work. "The community" was waiting for us: fifty or sixty of them. Dressed in the same windbreakers and long-sleeved sweatshirts that we marchers wore, they were the very image of how I wanted to look twenty years hence.

"We want this to be a neighborhood action against Columbia," a man with thinning hair and a pale, Brueghelesque forehead announced from the front step. "So we ask that you students remain on the sidewalk and join us in solidarity from there. If you want to get arrested with us, that's your choice. But stay outside the building." An exception to this policy was made, I noticed, for Mark and the other student leaders, who disappeared inside, followed by a group from the steps carrying pails, mops, and brooms.

I looked around. No one else from the English department was part of the crowd, so I started trying to explain in my head to Rick the rationale for what we were doing. An end to Columbia's ties to the Pentagon-funded Institute for Defense Analysis was one of the strike's six demands, but there was a "war back home," too, against "people of color," and Columbia was playing a key role in it. Attacking our common enemy from where we were would weaken it, which would also help the North Vietnamese, who were attacking this same enemy from where *they were*.

I see now how our identification with the most brutalized victims of American imperialism led us to believe that only solutions that changed everything could be valid. We wanted Columbia to be a true alma mater, a benevolent landlady sheltering *all* her children. Looking out from her carved seat on the steps of Low Plaza, robed in the attire of ancient Greece, she should open her arms to all, house them, and set them on the same paths to good jobs that we sons and daughters of the "comfortably off" were presumably treading. We thought that resisting our own economic order put us outside of it, in a place from which we could see everything and go on to create something completely different.

By eleven-thirty there were rumors that cops were somewhere on Broadway, but on 114th Street nothing was happening. A few people went off to get food. "Does anyone have any candles?" a woman with braids wrapped around her head shouted into the crowd.

"I have some," I called out. "I live only a block away." I wanted to get a blanket, too, and a heavy sweater.

When I walked in the door, Rick was watching the news. "Over already?" he asked without looking up. I walked up behind him and put my hand on his shoulder, feeling his angular collarbone under his round-necked T-shirt.

"I'm afraid not," I said. "But it's freezing out there. Can I take that old army blanket your father gave us?" I knew I needed to leave quickly before I relented.

When I got back to the occupied building, the crowd outside had thinned to maybe a hundred. Other candles appeared, and as I handed out mine, their flames transformed the faces of my fellow demonstrators one by one, till we resembled a group of expectant figures found at the edges of stained-glass windows. I must have given out almost two dozen candles; and this small gesture, more than anything else I did during that time, made me feel part of the movement.

Some of us set our flickering candles in a row along the wrought-iron railing that separated the sidewalk from the garbage cans and the steps to the basement apartment. A black man who looked like a minister led us in singing and clapping: "Deep Blue Sea" and "We Are Climbing Jacob's Ladder," along with the obligatory "We Shall Overcome" and a new one, "O When the Revolution Comes," to the tune of "When the

Saints Come Marching In." This singing was the high point of that long night, drawing us together like soldiers around a campfire on the night before a Civil War battle.

When the cops finally came, sometime between one and two in the morning, they matter-of-factly ordered us to disperse. When we refused, they began escorting us into vans waiting on Broadway. I was more impatient than afraid, and ashamed of my eagerness to get the whole thing over and done with. People struggling against real police power had worse things to contend with than a hard sidewalk, a sense of isolation—even in the midst of so many people united by a cause—and an unsympathetic spouse at home.

We walked in an orderly fashion toward our designated patrol wagons, dividing by gender since we would be held in sex-segregated facilities till we could be booked the next morning. Years later, when I was arrested in front of the White House protesting aid to the Nicaraguan Contras, they handcuffed us as if some pretense of unwillingness had to be present for the officers to feel that they were doing their job. But on this night at Columbia we moved quickly in pairs into our assigned vans like pupils in grade school on their way to the gym. It was a very different scene from the first bust, when the students had been dragged down steps and over curbs.

I spent the night with a group of women, most of them from Barnard, Columbia's sister college. We were crowded into a small cinder-block cell somewhere in the Women's House of Detention, high above the peaceful Village. Our cell had only two bunks, so people began taking off jackets and sweaters and spreading them on the concrete floor. The overhead lights were never turned off, and the intermittent orders of the women guards to "quiet down in there" echoed menacingly against the rough walls and high ceilings.

"Does anyone have any food?" came an anguished voice from the middle of the cell.

"Pipe down, girls, you'll get something tomorrow morning," an official voice barked out. Feeling a headache coming on, I shared my anonymous cell mate's panic at the thought of being confined indefinitely with nothing to eat. The pale-skinned young woman sitting next to me threw up later that night on Rick's rough khaki blanket.

The next morning we were driven to the Center Street courthouse, whose crowded hallways were filled with the sort of men I had learned to look down on: wearers of garish ties, loafers with tassels, rings with large stones. My memories of that morning are vague, but I do recall wishing my father were there, speeding things along.

The clothes my father wore were the kind you now see only in Hollywood movies from the thirties: double-breasted suits with a wide, almost invisible pinstripe and cuffed trousers held up by suspenders. Studs attached his shirts to their collars, just as his father's had done. In the top drawer of the dresser in his dressing room he kept a leather box filled with monogrammed cufflinks. His tie rack held a few striped items but mostly ties with white polka dots of imperceptibly different sizes on dark silk backgrounds. I wondered how he would react to the sight of me, so scruffy in the midst of marble floors and wood-paneled hallways.

The next morning we were booked and released. Rick's blanket was damp where I'd washed out the sick student's vomit under a trickle of cold water, but it still smelled horrible. When I got to our front door, I discovered that my keys had fallen out of the pocket of my duffel coat. A sudden wave of panic only intensified my relief at the sound of Rick's "Who is it?" over the intercom. He could have been out, he could have changed the lock or refused to come down and let me in. Instead he said simply, "No more," in a tone that let me know he meant it. "I want you to stay home and start being a responsible wife and mother."

"I can't do it," I said, my legs trembling under me. "I'm sorry but I just can't."

But why not? Aside from the brief exhilaration of handing out candles, I was not swept up into that sense of a larger whole that people in the Civil Rights movement have written about. Had I been willing to drop out of school, as Danny would soon do, I might have felt a keener sense of belonging. Still, we had a common goal and had gathered in one place to bring it about. At the time, I believed absolutely that this would be the future for all of us in a world where power flowed from the bottom up. But perhaps my determination with Rick, as we took the elevator to the fifth floor and resumed our student life together, was intensified by the sense that this unifying commitment to a national cause might not come again in my lifetime.

I was also beginning to suspect that, behind Rick's threatening words, was his fear of my sexual history, of the men from Carnegie Hall and the Living Theater for whom I'd pulled out my trundle bed. My wish for a community of brothers and sisters was one he could not grant and did not share. But I knew, too, that giving in to his fear would validate it, would allow him to turn our home into a place of confinement and me into the "easy lay" I knew I wasn't. Being married meant freedom from worrying about how men saw me. It gave me the reassurance that, however foolish I might look out in the world, there was someone at home for whom I came first. It bothered me that my husband did not understand that.

When the phone on the kitchen wall rang at noon the following day, Rick handed me the receiver without saying a word. I'd been out trying to make up for my recent defection, in an admittedly nonrevolutionary manner, by buying us a new coffeepot. Rick was too smart to be bought off with something obvious like a shirt from the neighborhood preppy men's clothing store, but our wedding-present Chemex coffeemaker now had a crack in its encircling band of wood. A new one might restore our sense of a common struggle

"It's a meeting of all the arrestees," I said, aware of his new need to know who it was whenever I talked on the phone. "Some lawyers are coming to explain to us about being released on your own recognizance. I'll take Kevin with me."

"When is it?" Rick was still in his pajamas and striped bathrobe, holding an open copy of *Road and Track* in his hand. Before the strike, we had moved our bed into a corner of the living room and converted the second bedroom into an air-conditioned study in anticipation of a work-intensive summer. The students who came over to study romantic poetry thought it a neat arrangement. They took turns sitting on the bed, lined up, hip to hip with their shoes off, their backs "up against the wall," as they liked to say.

"Six tonight. I won't stay late, but I can't not go."

"How many more things are there going to be that you can't not do?"

"There's a lot of things I want to do, if that's what you mean. I wish you felt the same way."

"Shit, what do you want? I'm studying for my exams."

"I'm sorry." Perhaps he was making the same silent promise to me that I was making to him: *This will be over soon and then I'll be the person you want.*

"You know I have my interview this afternoon."

"Hey, that's right. How about we all go up there and I'll let Kevin play in the fountains till you're done."

The daily gathering of strollers, mothers, and toddlers around the two splashing fountains of Low Plaza was one of the privileges of membership in the "Columbia community" even in its currently embattled state. Rick would be interviewed for one of the preceptorships (which usually went automatically to students on fellowship the year after they had finished their orals) on the fourth floor of Hamilton Hall, where Meredith and the rest of the Columbia College English faculty had their offices and which had been more or less restored to normal. The job of preceptor (or teacher of composition) at the College was an excellent first step along the road to the kind of job for which Rick was aiming. He saw himself, and I saw him also, at a small, but good, New England school—with a lesser one nearby that would be delighted to have me.

In hindsight, it's disturbing that Rick's interview and my meeting with my fellow arrestees happened on the same day. He walked out of Hamilton Hall without much enthusiasm for what had gone on there. "They seem to want you to act like some sort of performing dog," he said. "You know, show me your tricks."

"I'm sure you did fine," I said quickly, but perhaps without conviction. Rick always said he hated having to talk down to people, and I wondered if he saw teaching as doing just that. He'd discovered Wittgenstein in college and was hoping to work him into his freshman writing course.

"When will they let you know?"

"They say the end of June. They usually do it earlier, but—thanks to your sit-in-loving friends—everything's been put back at least a month." My meeting led me to two women who also had children Kevin's age but whose husbands took politics seriously. As soon as I walked into the church auditorium where we had been told to gather, I recognized the woman with braids around her head whose request for candles had given me such a welcome role to play. From the way her toddler daughter was patting the face of a blond boy sitting on the floor, I could tell that she and the mother of the boy were friends.

The fact that our three were the only children in the room made it easy to connect. Nora's friend, Martina, had not been arrested, but her husband, who was now standing on the edge of a dusty-looking, uncurtained stage with a microphone in his hand, was the one who had made the initial welcoming speech in front of the house. Two of the Barnard students from my cell waved to me from across the room.

Nora and Martina lived on 119th Street in a building that was scheduled for demolition to make way for a new School of International Affairs. We exchanged phone numbers, and three days later in Nora's plant-filled kitchen, we decided to form a regular babysitting pool. Both women detested Columbia, whose role as the neighborhood's chief landlord they knew firsthand.

If Rick took away from his interview a reason to withdraw from our Columbia-saturated world, my new friends immersed me in it. The Community Action Committee was the tenant organization that had sponsored the 114th Street demonstration jointly with SDS. In the CAC office, a block below Harlem, I learned to type leaflets onto stencils and to run them off on the organization's ever-active mimeograph machine. Other mothers brought their children, so Kevin made friends as well. "I'm doing this because of you," I told Rick when he complained about my burgeoning social life. "*For* you, if you like. Isn't community activism what wives are supposed to do?"

At the end of June a letter for Rick arrived on Columbia College stationery. It apologized for being so long overdue and pleaded an extraordinary press of circumstances. "We regret to inform you," it went on, "that you have not been accepted for a preceptorship for the coming year. An exceptionally long list of highly qualified candidates has made the choice an unusually difficult one." The College Committee on Composition wished Rick the very best in his future teaching career, and that was that.

They're probably right was my first thought. Rick was too hard on himself to have much sympathy for those for whom learning was not easy. Perhaps Columbia College had fewer "slow learners" than other places but it would have some. How would they take to his beloved Wittgenstein, and would they really enjoy discussing the role of language in our apprehension of reality in a class about how to write a paper? When I first knew him, he read me his favorite passages from Wittgenstein's *Blue and Brown Notebooks,* and I was thrilled at being drawn into such an inaccessible corner of my lover's mind. But could he expect undergraduates to feel similarly honored? He had certainly not been patient when I hadn't immediately grasped his point.

Nevertheless, what I said was, "How dare they do such a thing to one of their star students?" I put my arm around Rick's waist, all too aware of how I might do in the same situation, and let my eyes take in the neat typing of the incriminating document.

"Apparently they don't share your high estimation of my abilities."

"Oh, this is absurd! It doesn't take a genius to teach freshman comp. What do they want from you anyway?" Seeing him attacked, I could be totally on his side. Hadn't I been learning, since that rainy Wednesday in April, how truly hateful Columbia was?

"Obviously I don't know what they want," he said, mustering a smile of appreciation. "But what am I going to do for next year?"

"Don't worry, we'll figure something out," I said. "You'll just do fabulously on your orals and show those idiots what a mistake they've made."

How Rick spent the next three months, I didn't ask, and he didn't tell. Perhaps he just went and sat in the park or stared into space in the library. Perhaps he went to the movies, though he'd never been much of a film enthusiast. At home he lay on the bed reading car magazines and science fiction, pleading that he didn't want to talk, that he needed an escape from all the pressure. We visited each of our families once, but being away from the city and from Columbia did not really break his mood. His food preferences narrowed to cereal, packaged fruit pies, and submarine sandwiches—the food of his college years. He was at his most confident when he played with Kevin, but as the exam drew near he did even that less and less.

When the October day we were both dreading finally arrived, Rick left early in the morning, his face nicked from shaving. Two hours later he came back and stood in the doorway between the hall and the living room, where I was sitting on the floor playing with Kevin. I got up and went toward him, but the expression on his face held me back. "How'd it go?" I almost whispered.

"I didn't go there," he said. "I called up the English department and said I wasn't coming."

"Did they say you could take it again later?"

"I'm not going to take it later." He punched each word into the space between us. "I've never been so miserable in my life as I've been these last six months. It's been absolute hell reading all this stuff and trying to figure out smart things to say about it. So I decided not to condemn myself to a lifetime of this kind of misery." He hung up his coat mechanically, lay back on the bed, and closed his eyes.

"But it's so easy for you to think of smart things to say," I moaned as Kevin climbed up beside his father.

"Maybe I think the whole business of 'smart things to say' is kind of nauseating," he said, giving Kevin a hug.

"What will you do if you don't try again?"

"I don't know. I'll lose the credits for my course work if I try to transfer to some other school and I'll lose my stipend if I drop out of here, so I said I would try again. But the truth is I hate graduate school. I've been doing it to please other people, but I'm torturing myself." I lay down beside him, angry at everyone who had made Rick hate himself and glad that Kevin was literally between us, hitting his father and me as I tickled him under the arms.

By this time I had a job as a grader for a class in the eighteenth-century novel taught by Professor Tayler's wife. I'd never read any eighteenth-century novels, so simply keeping up with the class was demanding. I looked after Nora's and Marina's children four hours a week, setting out Kevin's toys and Creative Playthings easel or taking the three of them to the park or the fountains on Low Plaza. For this I got eight hours of free time that I did not need to negotiate with Rick.

Danny's Liberation School class continued to meet weekly as a study group on Marx, and I went to it regularly. I also joined a class studying Franz Fanon, taught by two graduate students in history, one black, the other white, who had both been to Africa and were writing dissertations on colonialism. Raised on the coronation and the Queen's Christmas message, I was amazed by Fanon's view of the devastating psychological effects of colonial rule. I'd always liked the idea of being a British subject, and the new Canadian flag—a red maple leaf instead of the good old Union Jack—was not, in my opinion, an improvement.

Above all, I was conscious of needing to begin planning what to read for my own orals. By Christmas I had made a list of books to study and was moving toward the manic mode that consumed me as I battled my fear of doing what Rick had done. How had he gotten this disease of lethargy—and could it be contagious? I resurrected my bottle of speed, my old ally against this fear, but since methedrine was now much harder to get, I knew I would have to ration it carefully to make the pills last until the exam.

As my thesis advisor, Professor Tayler was the head of my committee. I know he had been impressed with Rick in our first-year classes, and because of this I suspected he felt as uncomfortable around me as I did around him. *I'm not going to fail you,* I wanted to say each time I saw him, but how could I be sure? It was hard to talk to anyone, though I did have one conversation with Meredith while Rick was out shopping with Kevin.

"He's probably better off doing something else," she said from the swing I now thought of as Simon's. "If you're going to survive in academia, you need to be tougher than Rick is. But you know, I remember what you said about him when you first met him. Do you?" I shook my head. "About how you admired him because he lived downtown and went off and ate lunch by himself."

"Yeah."

"Well, that's who you married," she said. "That guy."

Danny, too, was disturbed by what Rick now embodied: the possibility that immense intelligence did not guarantee success, even in the place that claimed to honor it most. But when Danny took his orals a month after Rick, he passed with distinction. Eight months later, jittery from the last of my speed, I passed mine with distinction too.

If the marriage ended on a particular day, it was when I decided to apply for the preceptor job for which Rick had been turned down. "Don't do it," said Martina, a faculty wife. But I did. When I was asked to come in for an interview, I didn't tell Rick. When the letter came offering me a job, I knew I had to ask him to move. I still believe that the confidence with which I described how I would use Orwell's "Politics and the English Language" as the starting point for a course on writing had come from marrying one of the program's smartest students. Or had I simply stolen my ideas from him? Perhaps confidence is the scarce resource that graduate study drains from its devotees, and a willingness to fake it is what you need to survive.

At any rate, Rick dug in his heels. "I have as much right to live with Kevin as you do," he insisted, and the fault line opened up right there. I didn't want my son growing up with his father's defeatist attitude. He didn't want his son growing up with a mother who didn't care about anyone but herself—my mother's curse "come round" to haunt me. This went on for a month: me, circling ads for apartments in the *Times* classifieds; Rick, throwing the ads away; and, Kevin, crying constantly.

Then one morning, out of the blue, Rick ripped the paper out of my hands, slapped me hard several times in front of Kevin, and then got himself, that very day, a one-bedroom apartment three blocks from where he had lived when I first met him. His new rooms had the same lack of light, the same almost nonexistent kitchen, the same exposed brick along one wall. Perhaps this move would be temporary, one more turn in a widening gyre. Perhaps a whole new relationship would emerge, beginning here.

We took Kevin with us while we painted and sanded and scraped windows that wouldn't move up and down—just as if this were a perfectly normal development in a marriage. I felt a burst of envy every time we got off the subway and walked east along Bleecker, *my* favorite street long before Rick had ever set foot on it. Wielding a roller and a hammer kept me from thinking about what I had done. Engaged in a common endeavor, we got along much better.

This camaraderie came to a climax on a warm, sunny Saturday afternoon. Rick and I went into our liquor store on Broadway, where I cashed a check. I had offered to cover the cost of half the paint and it was time to pay up. I wrote out a pale blue check with a design of clouds on it while the owner of the store, a rotund man in his fifties, observed an apparently happy couple caught in a pre-ATM-machine weekend financial crunch. As I handed Rick the check, he made a comment about the fluffy clouds. "They have a big selection of checks now," I said. "I suppose it's so you can express your personality."

"I've a better idea," said the owner. "They ought to make checks with your picture on them. That would solve your identification problem then and there. What d'ya think?"

"But suppose," said Rick, getting into the spirit, "you grew a beard, or shaved off the one you had? Then you'd be stuck with checks that didn't look like you anymore." I knew he was referring to the beard he had grown right after our wedding and to my pained response when he'd shaved it off when Kevin was born. "You just like a particular image of me," had been his complaint.

"Looks like an instance of *ars longa, vita breva*," I said brightly, to Rick as well as the store owner, referring to a phrase from Seneca, much quoted by the writers Rick and I had studied together in Professor Tayler's seminar. Art lasts longer than life. A handy phrase even now.

"*Vita brevis*," Rick said, accenting the final syllable. "*Brevis* is a third declension adjective, so the masculine and feminine forms are the same."

At that moment everything in me wanted to shout, "This is ridiculous! Let's go back and start all over. You can be the brilliant one and I'll be that girl you ate lunch with. The one who thought in interesting ways." But a force I only dimly understood was sending me in the opposite direction: some hope of being a different kind of heroine, to myself, and to other people. So I handed Rick the cash and he put it carefully into his billfold under a wallet-size picture of Kevin. "Okay," I said. "*Vita brevis* it is."

After Rick left it took a long time for me to feel the full impact of the change in my life, the loss of a sense of belonging to someone. For another two years I remained in the same world, in the same apartment, doing by myself the things I'd gotten used to doing by myself when Rick was still in my life, even if more and more in the background. It wasn't until I left New York with Kevin to take my job at Rutgers that *being alone* and *needing to do something about that* brought back the anxious person I was before I met him.

I wasn't literally alone, of course, as long as I lived with Kevin. But I knew I had abandoned his father, and I'd done so when he was wounded. For years, I believed it was I who'd been permanently damaged, and deservedly so. The only people I have ever heard speak about leaving a wounded buddy on the field in order to stay alive yourself are Vietnam vets, though perhaps if I asked my father, he could tell me similar stories. The analogy is not exact, of course, though I did begin to feel toward the end that if I stayed to take care of Rick I would lose my ability to keep myself alive. What does fit is the residue of sadness that never quite disappears.

14

Twenty years after the first student strike at Columbia in 1968 (a second strike was mounted two years later, as colleges all across the country protested Nixon's invasion of Cambodia), a xeroxed invitation that must have been sent to the names preserved on some ancient list arrived in my mailbox. "Bring friends," it said jubilantly. "Bring lovers, partners, kids." We would gather together, in the place where it all began, "for consideration and reconsideration, for reminiscence, for catching up with old friends, renewing alliances, carrying on old arguments, seeing where we were and where we are."

Hoping for some of that, I went by myself. In 1988, Kevin was in his last year at Stanford, but even if he'd been on the East Coast he would not have joined me. "Start the revolution without me, Mom" was a favorite expression of his. The sixties were now being simultaneously hyped and dismissed by the media and the view they put forward was also his: a time of overrated euphoria that had actually transformed very little. But "those of us who were part of the events of that year know that they had a significance which the media has missed," the invitation went on. We were going to take back our history from them.

The opening event at Teachers College was scheduled for a Friday evening in April, with a second panel the next day in Earl Hall, where an auditorium was surrounded by the offices of various religious denominations. I was actually part of the second panel, where people spoke of their lives in the interim. I'd been to the Soviet Union in 1987 and offered my year-old impression of that vast country just before it fell apart. To me it was still a source of possibility in the fading light of the Cold War, a place where bonds of comradeship could be forged in the face of repression, just as we had done during and after the strike.

After the panel on Saturday we partied in Earl Hall. "Brown Sugar," "I Heard It Through the Grapevine," and "You've Lost That Loving Feeling" brought back other parties, some of them at my apartment after Rick had moved out. "Gone . . . gone . . . gone" kept running through my head as I walked home. I saw people I hadn't seen in years and some, like Mark Rudd and Abbie Hoffman, who I'd never expected to see again. Walking down Broadway at midnight through a slight drizzle, implored for spare change by disheveled men and women on every block, I remembered the chant that captured the era whose passing we had gathered to mourn: THE STREETS BELONG TO THE PEOPLE!

The Friday event was supposed to start at seven. I think all of us chose outfits that night to emphasize our continuity with the past rather than distance from it. I wore a long, black skirt and a purple sweater I had knitted myself, the same one I had worn the night of my shooting eight years earlier. I never throw clothes away, and I could have worn a miniskirt or a pair of thirteen-button bellbottoms. But this was a reunion, after all, not a costume party.

By the time I got off the bus and made my way through the crowd outside the auditorium, the ground floor was filled with milling people I didn't recognize. Inside we were each handed a name tag and told we could put the name of the building we had occupied on it, along with our own names. The assumption that of course we had all been in a building annoyed me. It meant that we who could not give all of our time to the cause were still being set outside the "in crowd." Still, I printed my name and headed for the stairs to the balcony.

There I found a group of current Columbia students gathered around Seymour Melman, an activist during the strike and still a member of the political science faculty. Their reverential "Professor Melman" reminded me, as nothing else could have done, that a time warp was occurring around me. First names became the rule during the strike, a sign that hierarchy was history. Downstairs graying men and women faced toward us, scouting for arriving comrades. I picked out my friends Ruth and Mike, but they didn't see me, so I sat down and began envisioning a novel about *us* (that would of course be made into a movie) with this gathering as the opening scene. It was as if we'd fallen asleep for twenty years and had just woken up.

The invitation said we would first see the documentary film *Columbia Revolt*. Then the strike leaders were going to tell us "Why We Struck." But the ambivalence toward technology that had spooked sound systems past showed up again: the projector didn't work despite the urgency of stamping feet and shouts of "just like the old days!" I wanted the movie to start, to offer up a set of images where everyone would be connected to everyone else, a place that would take me in.

"Oh, shit," said the narrow-faced, bearded man seated on my right. He was probably feeling the same way I was, but on such grounds a conversation is hard to start. So for fifteen minutes the ceiling lights flicked on and off and the white screen glittered hopefully until finally Eric Foner, a striker then, a tenured member of Columbia's history department now, climbed up on stage, squinted into the light from the movie projector, and said, "I guess we'll have the panel first, so will the panelists please come forward."

Mark Rudd spoke first. He had recently come up from underground and, as he smiled out at his adoring audience, looked as though he had literally not seen light for a long time. He spoke about being a Jew at Columbia, a place where most people were "preppies," and about the Holocaust survivors in his family, people who had taught him that no crime is greater than carrying on "business as usual" when genocide is going on somewhere in the world. And he talked about two of his old friends: Ted Gold, killed by the bombs he had been making in a town house on West 11th Street, and Dave Gilbert, in jail for life for his part in a robbery that had left a Brinks guard dead. Mark felt responsible for what happened to them, he told us, and needed to get it all out.

The night was supposed to be a celebration but it felt like a memorial service. Eric kept interrupting with pleas to wind it up, and Mark's old

SDS buddies kept up a running response of friendly heckling—"just like the old days," as he observed from the stage. If it were up to me, I would have let him talk all night. It wasn't as if we were going to gather outside and march down Broadway together, with Mark in the lead, to take over a building. What was the rush that should keep him within a time limit?

The one woman on the panel was Nancy Biberman, whose Hollywood director-father had been a target of the House Un-American Activities Committee. She talked about being a Barnard "girl" in the years that gave rise to feminism. Next, Juan Gonzalez, then of the Young Lords, now of the *Daily News,* and Bill Sayles of the Student Afro-American Society reminded us that their communities had been the real leadership of the strike. The last speaker was a history grad student who'd climbed through an upper-story window in Fayerweather Hall rather than cross the picket line to take his orals. He pointed to Harlem a few blocks away—"the community," we had called it then, as if there could be only one. Had we been thinking of Harlem, he asked, a place that's almost as dangerous now as Saigon was back then, when we spoke about bringing the war back home?

It was a relief, after that, to turn to the movie, to slip back into the past, albeit through a very fragile print of *Columbia Revolt,* to listen to people gleefully identifying themselves and their friends on the screen. Then the lights came back on, and the people on either side of me began collecting their jean jackets and down windbreakers. I was about to put on my coat when my friend Ruth, her long hair now entirely gray, came up to the mike.

"I would like us to honor our dead the way they do in Nicaragua," she said. She waited for quiet. "Mark's already talked about Ted and Dave, but I want to tell you about Al Szymanski, my fellow grad student from sociology, who probably taught me more than any of the folks who were being paid to teach me and who took his own life a year ago."

"Presente!" came from those of us who had been to Nicaragua or who had been told about this way of honoring dead heroes. I'd heard it at an anti-apartheid rally at Rutgers when a black minister compared Reagan's treatment of his community to white rule in South Africa. At

the end of his speech, people in the crowd had called out the names of the "saints" who had been with us in our struggle—Nat Turner and Steve Biko, Bobby Kennedy and Martin Luther King—and we answered, "*Presente!*" till the assembly felt more like a prayer meeting than the "Ho! Ho! Ho Chi Minh!" style of demonstrating we'd done in the sixties.

Al Szymansky dead? He'd been one of the leader's in Danny's reading group and had taught me my first (and almost my only) lessons in Marxist theory, a subject none of us grad students in English knew much about before he came into our lives. His Polish working-class style of speaking and dressing set him apart in Columbia's Ivy atmosphere, even after the strike when wearing jeans and overalls to class became a political statement. Then someone got up and announced that more vets had died back here at home than in the jungles of Vietnam. Maybe all of us were survivors, at least those of us who weren't dead or "missing in action" by the age of forty.

When I got to the bottom of the stairs, I looked again for Ruth and Mike. Instead, I heard, over the eddying conversations around me, a voice that used to recite all four of T. S. Eliot's "Four Quartets" and Andrew Marvel's "To His Coy Mistress" with as much élan as he could rattling off the 1925 pitching lineup of the Brooklyn Dodgers. "Cathy Ellis! I'll be damned. What are you doing with yourself these days?"

"Danny Roth!" I turned to hug the man I had not seen since the dismantling of the reading group and who still knew me as Cathy, not Kate. Danny had been one of the few in our seminar whom Rick had judged to be "really smart." He was a good two inches shorter than me and still had the thick, plastic-rimmed glasses and pocked skin that called up the painful adolescence that brilliant people often live through. His red-and-black checked shirt looked soft and a little worn. Did I look as unchanged to him as he did to me?

"I'm teaching at Rutgers," I said. "What about you? Last I heard you were out in Cincinnati or someplace doing workplace organizing with—what was it called?—the Revolutionary Communist Party?"

"Good girl," he said. "It was Pittsburgh. I worked in a bunch of different steel mills calling myself a catalyst for the revolution, till things got so bad I couldn't get a job."

"Did you ever go back and finish your degree?"

"Nope. Never did."

"And now?"

"I'm on a year-to-year contract with the writing program at Essex County College. I've got an apartment in Jersey City, the new *in* place to live."

"I hear you got married." We moved away from the stairs so that other people could get by.

"Yep," he said, looking around. "Nadya's here someplace. We're not together anymore, but we have a couple of wonderful kids."

"Oh," I said, wondering if he was now unattached. "You know that Rick and I split up."

"Yeah. I don't know who told me. That was quite a while ago, though, wasn't it?"

"Yeah." I looked around and saw Abbie Hoffman talking to a group of black students. "Being back here with all these people makes it seem much closer."

"Some things have changed, but some things haven't," said Danny with a smile. "Are you still living in that great apartment?"

"No, I lost it when Rick and I went to court over custody of Kevin. But I still live in the neighborhood."

I didn't tell him that I'd just inherited some money from an aunt that, when added to the sum I'd won in my criminal negligence suit after the shooting, would give me enough to buy my apartment. For years I had been resisting this step, mainly because I did not want to return to the owner of the building the money my lawyer had extracted from him after four years of his stalling and trying to put the blame on me. We finally won $150,000, which was as much as I could expect to get, my lawyer said, given that I had recovered completely—but why should he have it?

Danny would be pleased to know that I had helped to organize the rent strike that had been going on when the shooting occurred, a strike that became evidence of the negligence I had alleged. The court case dragged on, and by the mid-eighties, prices for co-op apartments had skyrocketed. Had I bought sooner, I might have paid less than the sum I was about to lay out, but until my aunt's death I saw no reason to give up my status as a renter who could not be evicted, a thorn in the side of a man I still despise. Consorting with the class enemy, Danny would have called it. Would I still qualify as a comrade if I told him I was now about to do just that?

"That's too bad about your old place," he said now. "I have some happy memories connected with that living room."

"Anything specific?"

"The study group. Szymanski sitting on your wicker swing with your kid on his lap. Things like that."

"Well, the swing is in the new place."

"And the kid? I'm afraid I can't remember his name."

"Kevin."

"That's right. He must be practically grown up now. Is he college bound, as they say?"

"He's already there," I said, my spirits rising. "He's at Stanford."

"Well, isn't that something," said Danny, nodding his head in the wise, Talmudic fashion I remembered from our first graduate seminar. "Too bad he couldn't have come to this with you. I'd love to see him."

"It's not his kind of thing."

"A right-winger, huh?"

"No," I said sharply. "Kevin thinks we were marginal because we didn't understand the way things really worked. He's an international relations major."

"It's clear he's not going to make the same mistake," said Danny as we edged, with the rest of the crowd, toward the door. "Here's Nadya. Honey, I think I've spoken to you about Cathy." Nadya was Danny's height, with a plump face and a high forehead. She wore an engineer's cap fastened in the back under her long ponytail.

"Nice to meet you," I said. "Didn't I hear something about your being involved in a trial?"

"That's right," she said with obvious pride. "COINTELPRO. FBI surveillance at its best. The fuckers tried to stick us with several consecutive life sentences, but they were too damn incompetent to make 'em stick. So we won, and Danny and I split up three months later." She turned her pale, oval face toward him and smiled.

"That's my honey, tells it like it is." I wondered what had driven them apart. I'd worn striped overalls back then too. I'd even taught my composition sections at the College in them once or twice.

"It's funny," I said as we walked with the rest of the crowd down Broadway, wondering if I should suggest coffee. "For all the different things we did, we've ended up in similar places."

"Our paychecks are probably rather different." Danny's Brooklyn accent was completely free of the bitterness I might have expected. "But you've been doing it for a lot more years than I have. I had a rough day today or I'd take you both out for a drink. And Nadya has a sitter waiting at home."

"I know what that's all about," I said. I was walking between them, beginning to wish I could spend more time with her as well as him, when she spoke across me to her former husband. "Honey, is Cathy the person you told me about who got shot?"

"Oh, my God!" Danny exclaimed. "I completely put it out of my mind. Jesus, yes. I don't even remember who told me. I know they said you were okay, but shit, what was that all about?"

"A robbery," I said. "A bit more than that, actually."

"Where did they get you?" Nadya asked.

"In the lobby of my building."

"I mean, what part of you did they get?"

I ran my thumb along my scar, under my breast and shoulder blade.

"Whoa. Did they ever catch the guy who did it?"

"No. It's a long story. Once I was knocked out and on the operating table I couldn't remember their faces."

"Them, huh?" said Danny. Then hesitantly, "Black?"

"Yeah. Two young black kids."

"Well, girl, you're a survivor," said Danny, his arm around my shoulder. "But hell, this ain't the way we thought things were going to turn out, is it? Weren't you our liaison to the Black Panther office in Harlem?"

Just then the crowd behind us almost swept the three of us down the subway stairs. "That was me," I called out. "Look, my number's in the phone book. Give me a ring." Danny turned back toward me and shouted, "See ya," raising his right arm with a clenched fist. I raised my arm, too, and a cab swerved toward me. For a moment I thought of getting in. But *we* didn't ride in cabs in those days. Danny and Nadya probably still didn't. It looked as though they'd managed to hang on to something. Still, a shared sixties past had not been enough to keep their marriage together.

I continued down the familiar stretch of Broadway, my hands in my pockets, the fox collar of my dark green suede coat turned up. Halfway there, I passed the reclining statue of a Greek goddess that pays tribute to Ida Strau, a passenger on the *Titanic*, who refused a seat on a lifeboat to stay with her husband, Isador, the owner of Macy's. Serenely posed with her cheek against the back of her hand, she always reminds me of the grandmother I never met, who could have been on that boat but wasn't. Two blocks farther on was the Korean market where I might have gone for protection the night of the attack if had I realized what was happening.

When I reached the subway exit at 103rd Street, I was still thinking about Danny's question and wondering where the two young men were now. The chances of their even being alive eight years later were certainly not great. But unlike many people who ask about them, I knew that Danny did not believe in the efficacy of incarceration. His question was probably a way of getting at others that are harder to ask or answer. Had I recovered from my trauma? Did I blame all black people for it? If not, why not?

How would I know if I had recovered? Or, to put the question in a more familiar form, what *should* I be feeling? Over the years, I'd read several books on trauma and posttraumatic stress disorder, but my life in the eighties was not really marked by those symptoms. Politically, I was miserable, but so was everyone I knew. I'd tried various venues for connecting with a suitable man, and my failure there pressed down on my chest every morning when I woke up. But I'd never been afraid of going out after dark or of riding in the subway, and that didn't change. I couldn't summon much anger, nor was I deprived of sleep by uncontrollable flashbacks—although this felt like a failure as well, an indication of something missing.

In fact, the people toward whom I felt—and still feel—the greatest rage were my landlords, the ones who had fired our doormen in order to drive us renters out. I can't prove that the two boys were part of this drive, since their faces are still buried in my mind beyond recall, but back in the early eighties, avaricious landlords did hire thugs to terrorize tenants. My lawyer clipped newspaper articles describing fires in hallways, robberies at gunpoint, landlords who refused to repair boilers—a war on rental tenants far worse than anything we'd ever accused Columbia of doing. Even winning my lawsuit did not diminish my anger at them, and probably nothing will.

I also felt anger at my mother and father. For three years I carried on emotionally charged conversations with them in my head before I was able to ask them face to face about their speedy departure from the hospital. I was in Toronto, where the family that now included four grandchildren still gathered each year to open presents and eat the turkey, plum pudding with hard sauce, tangerines, mince pie, shortbread, and endless pots of tea that now welled up out of Ellen's kitchen every year. We all thought of Ellen as a saint for taking over Christmas in this way. It was a role she had always seemed destined to play.

I was probably wearing the slacks I had bought at Bonwit's with my credit slip. The spot on the pocketbook had never responded to leather cleaner, but my friend Florence, a fellow academic who was more courageous and less conflicted in stores than I was, took back the bag, claiming, I think, that the spot on its rim had always been there. Our friendship deepened over this transaction, and for years afterward I religiously packed the slacks I had acquired in the exchange whenever I went to Toronto.

It must have been in 1983, on the day after Christmas, that the confrontation with my parents occurred, because *Terms of Endearment* came out that year. I had gone alone to see it on Boxing Day, one of several major holidays that link Canada eternally to the British Empire. As I made my way back to the Park Plaza in Toronto, where my parents and

I always stayed over Christmas now that they lived in Ottawa all year round, I remember being unable to stop crying as I walked through the intricate underground mall whose stores were closed that day, by law, but whose well lit, sheltering corridors ran between the subway stops under Bloor Street that linked the theater and the hotel.

Watching the Debra Winger character (who would be dead by the end of the movie) take her three kids home to her mother when her marriage was in trouble—or listening to Shirley MacLaine screaming at the nurses, "My daughter's in pain! My daughter's in pain! Give her her shot, damn it!"—I got a sense of what a real bond between a daughter and her mother might be like. Her daughter's professor husband left her for another woman, but the mother never thought of that as failure.

I figured that my parents were having a drink or two before departing for a last round of Ellen's cooking, and I was right. "Come in," Daddy called out when I knocked on the door. "Can I get you anything?"

"No, thanks. I'd like to ask you a question, though."

"All right. Shoot." said Daddy.

"Are you wearing what you're going to wear to Ellen's tonight?" my mother wanted to know.

"Yes, I am. Do you remember coming down to the hospital when I got shot?"

"God, yes," said my father. "I think it was Kevin who called around two in the morning, and we couldn't get through to an airline till six. You can't imagine how it feels to wait like that after getting that kind of news."

I sat down on the neatly made bed. "So you came down the next day?"

"That's right. And we were darn lucky to get a flight that close to Christmas. I guess it's almost two years ago to the day, isn't it?"

"Yes, but what I want to know is why you left so soon."

"Your doctor told us to go home," my mother said. "He said there was nothing we could do for you, so there was really no reason for us to stay."

"And you left just like that?"

"Wouldn't you say he knew more about those sorts of things than two ordinary people like us?"

"Don't try and tell us we left because we don't love you," my father cut in, "because it's just not true." He was the one I'd always been closer to, the one who knew what it meant to risk everything and go after what you wanted, the one who'd left his own father's thriving business for political life, and who'd congratulated me when I got tenure at Rutgers a year before I was shot. He had left *his* beaten track, so he admired that tendency in me even though he couldn't quite put it together with my being a woman. He was the one who *did* things, once getting in the car in the middle of the night and driving to an all-night drugstore to get me some Coke syrup for a migraine.

In the cab ride to Ellen's, I saw that I would never get more than this from them. They'd had to leave the hospital because being there for others when the going got rough was not part of their training or their lives. They had not been there for each other, or even, one might say, for themselves. Escape had always been available and affordable, and they had never thought to do otherwise. Perhaps they saw withdrawal from the field of battle as the honorable thing to do, the brave posture of not displaying your feelings. Or perhaps it was simply the way they had been taught to be polite: doing as they'd been told.

So I might have told Danny that seeing Mummy and Daddy in this light—as people with limitations, produced and reinforced by the world they came from—was part of the recovery the shooting demanded. Maybe that doctor had been right. Or maybe he didn't know that "home" for my parents was not a brownstone on the Upper East Side but a four-story Tudor with signed photographs of the Queen and Prince Phillip in the foyer, and that going home meant crossing an international border.

But this new way of perceiving the world from which I had come was only a prelude to something even better, a train of events that began with the sound of a phone ringing into Florence's cluttered Park Slope apartment. She now taught at Medgar Evers, a part of the city university system. It had been ten years since her trip to Bonwit's with the bag and then my somewhat anticlimactic return with the credit slip to obtain the nice pair of slacks. "That was about one of my students," she said as she sat down in front of her half-eaten pasta and empty wine glass. "Apparently he was killed on the street right near the school."

As she went on telling about this young man, I was overtaken by an impulse that I was almost too embarrassed to voice. "Would it be okay," I finally said, "if I went to the funeral with you?"

"Why would you want to?"

I didn't know. It was one of those decisions one makes on the basis of input from sources unknown, the kind of directive that people sometimes describe as coming from a guardian angel or some such figure. In fairy tales someone chooses the leaden casket rather than the golden one, and the choice looks foolish but is, in fact, right. One wanders into a dark wood—*una selva oscura,* Dante calls it—and finds the light one is looking for. Florence was willing to give me the address of the funeral home only if I would adopt an appropriate disguise. "If anyone speaks to you," she finally said, "tell them you were one of his elementary school teachers. His name is Calvin Holmes."

I went to Calvin's funeral, and in the weeks following, I went to half a dozen others in the same place, the Woodward Funeral home in Bedford Stuyvesant. It wasn't easy to do this, but I was determined. I didn't want to go to just any funerals, only those of young men like the ones who had almost killed me. Once I knew the way to Woodward, the most difficult task was finding out which names from the list posted each day in the lobby of the low, stucco building were the right ones. The only way I could get this knowledge was to speak to the receptionist seated behind a wall of glass in front of a switchboard.

"Why do you want to know?" she asked. "What difference does it make to you how old they are?"

When I told her I was writing a book about funerals, she rolled her eyes. But as I continued to stand there, with no idea what I was going to say next, a very large woman came bursting into the lobby and let out a howl like I had never heard before. Two shorter women rushed up behind her, and the three of them stood pitched, like the famous statue of Laocoön and his sons, at the outermost edge of grief. After the funeral party had arranged themselves in limousines and cars, I asked the woman behind the glass whose funeral it was.

"A young woman," she said. "About twenty years old." Perhaps it was the thought of a mother grieving like that for her daughter, but I knew I was not going to leave without knowing the time of another service I could go to.

The exasperated receptionist finally summoned one of her bosses, a thin, soft-spoken African-American man named Michael Williams, who became my Virgil on this journey. "Let's go into my office," he offered when I gave him a brief version of my imaginary project. I also told him about my own shooting. This was not the first time I used the fact of being shot to open doors normally barred to me. *Something happened to me that isn't supposed to happen to people like me, only to people like you.*

The idea of someone writing about his place of work appealed to him, and he began calling me once a week for about two months to give me the lineup. The first time, I took the A train on my own. I was dressed in my most unobtrusive dark clothes—wary of being told, in looks if not in words, that I did not belong there. But my fellow mourners were preoccupied with their own grief, and by the time the service had gone on for ten minutes, I was sobbing along with everyone else. Of course my tears, like the tears we all shed for people we don't know, were not about him but about me. An elderly woman sitting next to me handed me a Kleenex. I had not come prepared.

When everyone got up to file past the casket, I followed this woman. I hadn't done this at Calvin's funeral. In fact, I had never seen an actual dead person up close. The round, soft face looked peaceful in death, but unformed. I thought of Jesse Jackson's words, "Be patient. The Lord's not finished with me yet." How could the Lord be finished with this teenager whose laughing picture beamed out from the front of the program I held in my hand?

He must have been a kid in trouble, and kids in trouble believe they can't go home, that nobody wants to hear what's really going on. I know about that. They do one thing and it leads to another, till they've got nowhere to turn and they're homeless for real. I know about that too. They rely on drugs to keep hopelessness from closing in on them. I also know about that. The kids who shot me started out as kids in trouble. I can't imagine what was in their heads when they turned and fired that shot, but there was something of me in their desperation.

I still have the announcements for each of the funerals I attended. The order of the service is inside, along with a short obituary. I once talked to Michael about the conventions that govern the phrasing of these obituaries. I was especially interested in the fact that, when there are children among "those he leaves to mourn," the obituary refers to the children's mother as "his fiancée." When several mothers of his children showed up, Michael told me, there could be a real fight at the funeral.

Part of Michael's job was to keep things like that from happening, and he was tremendously committed to that mission. He was also committed to our project, one that would end, we both knew, when my "research" was done. When we said good-bye he invited me to his church, a huge, redbrick building filled with vibrant voices, where he sang in the blue-robed choir. As the worshipers filed out after the service, Michael signaled me to wait, and he introduced me to his pastor and choir director. I told them I would come again, and I did. But back on the A train after the service, I knew that the journey that had begun at Calvin's funeral was now complete.

I felt connected, and still do, to the mothers of the young men who had been killed, but I was also *in* their shoes as the mother of a male child I could still lose at any moment. I must have been grieving, too, for the ones who came to the funerals of their friends and sat in the pews with me; for the medics who showed up with their stethoscopes and pressure suits; for the doctors who stayed on their feet for so many hours under the round, hot lights; and for the family I was born into, the one that never would have cried for me the way those families cried at the Woodward Funeral Home. It's a well of grief from which I can never be disconnected.

But lately I've been thinking that perhaps I cried not only as a mother but for a mother. I don't mean for her absence from my life. I mean I cried *for* her—let out the tears she'd never shed for her own mother, for the husband whose love affairs destroyed her world and her sense of safety in it, for her daughter lying in intensive care, perhaps even for the scared, defenseless self she buried again and again, the mother I never got to see.

I went back to Michael's church two or three times over the next six months. What drew me to it was precisely those parts of my Toronto self that had *seemed* so damaging to the dream I came to New York to realize. I'd been baptized and sent to two Anglican schools. I knew lots of hymns and Biblical passages. When I told Michael how much I liked the singing and preaching and the welcoming smiles but that it was a long trip out to Brooklyn on the Sunday morning subway, he suggested I check out churches closer to home. "You got Reverend Abernathy up there," he said. "Wyatt T. Walker too. Those are people who worked with Dr. King."

I'd heard of Reverend Abernathy's church, Abyssinian Baptist, and looked it up in the phone book. I like to cross boundaries, to go places that *people like me* are expected to avoid. Nevertheless when I put on a hat and walked along 138th Street the following Sunday, I was on the lookout for the annoyance I'd seen on the face of the receptionist the first time I went to Woodward. How dare I assume, that expression had told me, that I could go safely into anyone else's world? I'm not sure what I would have said had anyone asked me why I had come. But of course no one did.

Finding Wyatt T. Walker's church was more difficult, but I finally asked Felicia's secretary for help. "You want to come?" asked Marguerite. "That's where I used to go when I lived with my folks." She had to travel from Queens to meet me on 116th Street, but she was happy to do it. "We all went to Sunday school here," she said, meaning herself and her three brothers. It was easier going with a black friend, but I also wanted to be able to sit by myself in a row with wriggling children, hatted women fanning themselves, and a few men. So I went back.

In the middle of the service, people turned to their neighbors on either side to shake hands or give hugs and say, "Peace." I was a stranger and they took me in, but at first it was hard to reciprocate. Hand-shaking and smiling were what Daddy did when he wanted something in return: a vote on election day, for instance. His campaign literature featured pictures of him and his family leaving church on Christmas and Easter morning. When I came back home from Elmwood, after the disgrace that nobody talked about, I started going to the Quaker Meeting House near the university. Perhaps people at home thought it was an affectation, but I didn't care. When I lived at the Rehearsal Club, I sometimes went to St. Thomas's down the street, but shaking hands with the rector at the end of the service was as informal as things got there.

It was during one of Reverend Walker's services that I decided I wanted to reclaim the spiritual part of myself that I seemed to have lost, the person who knows psalms and hymns by heart and prays in moments of fear. I love the swaying choir at Canaan Baptist, their blue baptismal pool located where Episcopalians put their altar, the speakers mounted on the walls that blast the music right into you, the shouted responses, the drawn-out organ chords, the exhortations and assurances from the pulpit. Perhaps an African soul has selected my angular, Toronto-bred body this time around. But I needed a "church home" whose traditions were closer to mine. So I decided to go back to the one in my neighborhood with the beautiful Tiffany windows, and I kept going back.

Still, it's always when I've crossed a line that the blessings of my life have found me, and my welcome at that Baptist church reminds me of these blessings whenever I visit it, as I do from time to time. Making my way back out onto 116th Street after a service there, so different from the stately rituals that are part of my own history, I stand sometimes on the sidewalk for a moment and wonder why anyone would choose racism if they knew that this was available.

15

But did I really want, in Kevin's dismissive phrase, to "try again" after all these years? Foley and Rick were opposites in many ways. When I met Rick, I saw a brilliant mind whose sorrows I could dispel simply by becoming a part of his life. Depression would no longer sit on my chest because I could drive his away. And when it became clear that this magic of mine was not working, my powerlessness terrified me. I had dreams of failing my orals because I'd arrived in the wrong building or on the wrong day—and if I did fail them, I could become like the women with thinning hair and arms who shopped at my supermarket for small amounts of food each day.

Now everyone was calling me *iyawo* and again it seemed right to surrender. Yet my relationship with Foley escaped not only my mother's pattern for a relationship but even my own scenarios. I *was* more than a little tired of my culture's prescriptions for finding and keeping "the one," but Foley had grown up, not only beyond the reach of these, but indifferent—or so he insisted—to the measurements of masculine power that many wives and children provided in his culture. Whatever deficiencies he had, I sensed that he was not like my father, just as I'd sensed that about Rick. Perhaps he simply enjoyed the freedom of not having to check in with anyone that goes with being single. Well, I did too.

For women, the connection between being single and being unloved seems to be taken in at their mother's breast, or so it was with me. But like other feminists of my generation, I do not want to imitate my mother in allowing a man to control the way I spend my time. Clearly we'd have to make up our own rules, and keep making them up as we went along. Our plan was for Foley to spend six months in the States and for me to join him in Nigeria during the summer. That way, we could each pursue our goals while supporting one another and would spend some time on our own as well.

The closest we ever got to a "romance" conversation happened during the party in my apartment, shortly after Foley arrived in the Sates the first time, when Grace and her friends from Felicia's program passed a joint around my dining room table. Grace was helping Foley with the dishes after the spaghetti meal he had helped to cook, when she asked him how things were going between us two. He looked at her as if he didn't understand the question, so she said, in a tone of teenage exasperation, "I mean, Foley, do you love Kate?"

"Yes," he said, as if the answer to such a question was obvious. "I love her very well." Then he added, looking over at me, "and she loves me very well too." From that exchange I saw that for him love was a verb, not a noun; an activity, not an inner state; not something you felt so much as something you did. It wasn't "Some Enchanted Evening" for either of us, but I knew that something good lay in store for me if I let myself follow what seemed to be the line of least resistance.

The wedding ceremony in my New York apartment was the first of three (a final one for immigration purposes took place at City Hall in 1997) and, all in all, it remains my favorite. I did not initially plan to invite my sisters, but I'm glad now that I did. They, plus Liam, Kevin, Mitzi, several colleagues from Rutgers whom I labeled collectively "print culture," plus friends from the women's movement and the left made up the white contingent. Max and Felicia arrived late, annoying me with their eagerness to take credit for everything. "We introduced her to Nigeria," I heard them telling everyone they spoke to. But it was the half-dozen friends of Foley, dressed in embroidered satin, who turned the event I had planned into much more of a joining of cultures than I could ever have imagined.

This came about because the word *wedding* can have many meanings. Despite what I learned about colonialism from my class at the Liberation School during the strike, I can't help feeling grateful to the British for having brought the same language to Canada and Nigeria. Yet shared words don't always carry shared concepts. Foley comes from a world where ritual and ceremony are central, where family members can number in the hundreds, and where upcoming weddings are announced in the papers. In my world, no stranger would dream of showing up at your wedding. But if you invite fifty people to a wedding in Nigeria, you can expect five times that many to be there. Knowing the bride or groom is not a requirement for attendance. What counts (and is counted) is the number of cows killed and cases of beer consumed— and the more the better.

At the center of a Nigerian wedding, the bride and groom taste special foods that symbolize the elements of a good marriage. Like honey, which, when you are tired or upset, you have only to put on the tip of your finger and lick it to feel happy. Or salt, which banishes blandness. Or strong liquor, which releases you from your inhibitions, as must happen sometimes in a marriage. Or sweet palm wine that soothes, and pepper that's fire in your mouth. My favorite is the kola nut, which is bitter, they say, when you first bite into it but gets sweeter—even giving you a slight high, I'm told—the longer you chew on it.

Was there a lesson in this for me? My mother had told me in the Oak Room of the Plaza just before I got married the first time, how a bone is stronger after it's broken than it was before anything happened to it. If she had displayed increasing strength, it was expressed as an ability to endure in silence increasing levels of pain. But chewing on a kola nut is something you do *to* it, and by taking it in and chewing, you transform it into something sweet. This was an image of marriage that would make "trying again" worthwhile.

Since the New York event was for my friends and on my home territory, I assumed, without ever saying a word to Foley about it, that I would be planning it. So I recruited Marguerite to be my assistant, and we asked Calvin, a fellow volunteer in Felicia's organization, to be our master of ceremonies. As Marguerite and I focused on chairs, candles, flowers, food, and CDs, I threw my anxiety into the slipstream of her enthusiasm. I was grateful for her mood, too, remembering my exchange with Jean at the Lagos airport and our promise of a future conversation about black women's views of white women with black men, a talk that had not, in fact, taken place.

Marguerite and I joined forces to make the three-layer cake: separating thirty-two eggs, mixing the yolks and stiffly beaten whites with ground hazelnuts and melted chocolate, and icing these layers with the whitest possible cream-cheese frosting to contrast with the dark chocolate inside. We ordered food from a Caribbean restaurant up the street and planned to end the ceremony with everyone clapping and singing "Rock-a My Soul in the Bosom of Abraham," the finale of Alvin Ailey's superb dance piece *Revelations,* done to a series of spirituals beginning with "I've Been 'Buked and I've Been Scorned." But most of all, I wanted my guests to talk, to say something about their history with one or the other of us. I wanted a highly verbal, participatory ceremony.

Foley did tell me that he had invited his friend Jagun to "do something" with kola nuts, but I guess I was far too enveloped in my own vision of a community joining together across lines of race, age, occupation, and culture to take in his news. Only my sisters had been at my Western "traditional" wedding (when I married Kevin's father) with its striped awning and four-piece band, its caterers and bouquet-throwing, and I certainly didn't want the focus of this, my second wedding, to be on my *finally getting another husband.* Most of all, I didn't want to crow, in front of my single women friends, about my departure from their ranks.

So the event that I had in mind was to be primarily symbolic, a gesture toward multicultural harmony that might someday exist in the world. Almost all the guests had arrived, and I was sending someone out to get plastic glasses, which I'd forgotten to buy, when Calvin, who had studied to be a preacher and who I thought was in charge, came up to me looking grave. I knew that the male Nigerians had gathered in my bedroom, but Calvin, a black American, had slipped in among them. "I think they have a rather different agenda from ours, Kate," he said. "And I recommend we just let them run with it."

Then Foley came up and told me I should come back to the bedroom with him. I was by then wearing a four-piece *asoke* outfit, a shiny blue and white, hand-woven fabric made into a wrapper, top, head tie, and sash. These had been given to me by Tall Foley and his Nigerian girl-friend, Lara, whose triumph over the wiles of Zoe reassured me that even men raised under a patriarchal regime like Nigeria's are not auto-matically "impossible." Everyone in the bedroom was in *asoke* also, an assembly of brilliant colors and embroidery even more spectacular than mine.

"She needs to cover her head," Jagun announced, so Foley draped one of my own scarves over my head tie, covering my face. Well, okay. When I'd walked up the aisle on my father's arm to the strains of Purcell's lovely "Trumpet Voluntary," my face was covered by a much more transparent veil until the minister announced, "The groom may now kiss the bride." This time two of Foley's friends started beating their talking drums as he arranged us into a procession, with the two of us more or less in the middle. Then we all walked slowly, surrounded by drums and chanting, from one end of the long apartment to the other.

When we got to the living room, Calvin and Marguerite were sitting on either side of the two high director's chairs that were waiting for us, on loan from Felicia. As soon as we were settled, Jagun began to speak. "The extended family is at the heart of Nigerian culture," I heard him say. "So for us marriage is a truly sacred institution."

For *us* but not for whom? In this gathering of mainly Americans, could he be holding up Nigerian marriages as superior to American ones? "We don't need divorce courts," he went on. "We settle everything within the family." I wished at that moment that I could have seen through my scarf and caught the eye of any of my women friends in the room. *Right*, our eyes would be saying. *At the expense of how many women's silence?*

Then Jagun began to talk about fertility. "May these two be blessed with many children. A thousand children." Well, okay, an exaggeration—though it is also true that in many African cultures, the people you help and nurture or who are "junior" to you in any way call themselves your children and call you their mother: *iya*. So Foley's friends often refer to me as "our mother in New York: *Iya Katie*."

To some extent I resent this, partly because it implies that I will do things for my "children," but mostly because it makes a point of the fact that I am older than most of them.

Nigerian culture is highly deferential. The younger kneel to greet the older, run their errands, do their laundry, and sweep their floors. Mine is a highly antideferential culture that holds up youth for all to imitate; the amount of money this idolatry has extracted from my bank account over the years is information I can't reveal because, quite honestly, I've blocked it from my mind. So I bridle in silence when a young Nigerian woman takes from my hands a package I've been carrying. But sometimes I can hardly keep from yelling, "Leave me alone, for God's sake! I'm not feeble!"—or even sometimes, "Damn it, I'm not *that* much older than you!"

While my thoughts were taking me away from the friends gathered around me, Jagun rambled on about what a wonderful life Foley and I and our many children would have. By the time forty-five minutes of his oratory had elapsed, I could almost feel steam rising from under my scarf. Everyone in the room surely knew that I could not have more babies, so enough about fertility and all the lucky people (younger than me, of course) to whom I was, or would become, a mother!

"Foley," I said firmly, "tell this guy to shut up."

"Don't worry, he is almost finished."

"I want him to be finished now."

"Kate, calm down," said Calvin. "Let us handle things."

"Well, do it, then."

After five more minutes, Calvin interposed, and "my" part of the ceremony began. Taking turns, my friends spoke about their past history with me, their joy in meeting Foley, their wishes for our future together. Foley's friends spoke again too; Nigerian's love to make speeches! "Rock-a My Soul" didn't have quite the polish it does when the Ailey company dances to it but it led into the high point of the evening, a moment not part of anyone's plans.

We had gathered in the dining room to cut the cake, and my son announced that he wanted to speak. Kevin looks like an ad from the *Times* men's fashion section: drop-dead casual WASP. I once gave him a button that said: PEOPLE WHO THINK THEY KNOW EVERYTHING REALLY ANNOY THOSE OF US WHO DO. He cleared his throat and began.

"Most families have a pattern in which the parents are out ahead—setting an example and all that—and the children follow along behind. Well, in this family it's been pretty much the other way around. For instance, my mom used to be way, way out on the left, with—uh—some of you here, you know, never let a week go by without a demonstration. But now we're both supporting Bill Clinton, and that's because she's moved in my direction, not the other way around."

He paused while people laughed. Then he gave some more examples: he'd spent his junior year abroad in Leningrad, and lo and behold, the following year I decided to see the Soviet Union for myself. Perhaps he stretched the point a bit, but then came the punch line: "Two years ago I got married." I laughed happily along with everyone else, but his words sent me a blessing no one else heard: I could have my husband without losing my son.

Our Nigerian ceremony the following August was much longer and of course much less tightly choreographed. Jean was there with her video camera, and as each part of the day unfolded, I judged it by how my friends back in the States would view the video version. Of course they would hate the sight of a dog being killed, but they would love the spectacular dancers who had come to perform at the Osun festival and stayed on for our wedding the next day. They'd surely be repelled by the custom of "dashing" the bride and groom so publicly, plastering *naira* on our foreheads. Yet having been pressured, as Americans in Nigeria always are, to spend more than I'd brought, I was glad to have the several thousand *naira* we took in.

Still, none of these public displays entirely dispelled my fear that a conspiracy was going on somewhere beyond my range of vision. Rather, by drawing so many people into the picture, they raised the specter of an ever more devastating humiliation. In my head I still struggle to explain to my son, to my women friends, to my colleagues at Rutgers, why I want in my life this man who has never read a book and who, according to his passport, is twenty-two years younger than I am. "God brought us together," Foley likes to say, and with this one-time Catholic altar boy who now goes sometimes to night vigils, who prays under his breath in Yoruba while I sit for twenty minutes in front of a lighted candle, I can only agree.

In the middle of the following summer, a year after the wedding ceremony, Foley told me he had been invited to Zimbabwe to do some carving. He promised, as always, to come back to Nigeria soon, but the weeks went by and that did not happen. Several times I got a message that he had called the school when I wasn't there, but none of the arrangements I tried to make worked out and we did not speak again until I was back in the States two months later. I was feeling utterly forsaken well before that, but since no one else seemed to notice that a serious breach had occurred, I revealed my feelings only to my computer. How like my mother, I said to it, waiting grimly and in silence for the other shoe to drop.

While I stayed on in Nigeria without Foley, putting up a brave front that nobody seemed to notice, an unexpected ally appeared in the form of Nike's now official *oko,* the police commissioner who'd made a wonderful speech at our Nigerian wedding as the stand-in for my father. I was sitting with the two of them at Nike's now familiar dinner table, the place where my relationship with Foley had first been spoken into existence. "We feel concern for you," he said, "with Foley running off the way he does. He doesn't seem to want to be responsible for being married, and we want to help you if we can."

Tears welled up as I looked from one to the other of them, the commissioner in rose-colored satin, Nike in a burgundy silk *boubou* with a large off-center design she had put there herself. While she was younger than me and the commissioner was about my age, they were my parents in Africa, at whose table I could eat with my hands and say what I pleased.

"How can you help?"

"I don't know if we can," said the commissioner gravely. "This way of doing things and not telling your wife is the Nigerian way. When Nike was married to Twins, he never told her what he was doing or where he was going."

"That's true," said Nike, a piece of chicken in her left hand, the one Nigerians eat with. "But you know, I never told him where I was going either." She smiled at her *oko* at the head of the table.

"But now we tell each other everything," he said, "and I now think it's the best way."

"I wish you would tell Foley that."

"We will," said Nike. "We will speak to him in his own language. But you need to speak to him too."

"You should ask to see his passport," the commissioner added, a self-satisfied smile on his face. "He says he's in Zimbabwe. So just say to him, 'My dear, let me see your passport.'"

I was a little shocked that he would recommend such a course. But he also assured me that he had his spies and would use them to check Foley out. "You can't ask people from the school," he said. "They all cover for one another."

When I finally spoke to Foley on the phone from the States, he was very contrite and promised to come to me as soon as I sent him an invitation. "Why don't you stay there and work," I said. "I've always wanted to spend Christmas in Nigeria." Explaining his absence to my American friends had been difficult, but I didn't want to send Foley another invitation till we'd had this out, and though my thinking seems strange to me now, I decided I wanted this to happen on his home territory. In the meantime, I could concentrate on my work, and Nike and the commissioner could talk to him. If he didn't have a good explanation for why he'd been out of touch for so long, I could leave him there, and that would be it.

At Christmastime, Foley met me at the airport and took me to a house he had rented in Osogbo with Emmanuel and two of their younger siblings—his extended family encompassed brothers older than me and younger than Kevin. The small living room was filled with an over-stuffed couch, two matching maroon chairs, and a TV set with a VCR, standard items in Nigerian homes that belong to everyone but the very poor. And as always happens in Foley's presence, the person who is con-vinced that she has been abandoned and who still lives in the center of her mother's worst nightmare disappeared as completely as the mi-graine headaches that occasionally incapacitate me, and left me as elated, as unable to imagine my former pain as I would feel after a day of cold washcloths and throwing up.

To what could I attribute my sudden serenity? And what in Foley's upbringing, so different from mine, produced happiness not just on special occasions when someone or something had *made* him happy, but as a ground of being? Not all Nigerians are this way, but being around Foley never failed to give me what in my pot-smoking days I called a "contact high." At the same time, I couldn't help but notice how natural it was for me to feel unhappy—unwanted, disappointed, hope-less of any future I could not spell out. Had he been sent to be my teacher? Could I actually learn to let go of the need to know and control? For Foley, happiness is a habit, and habits are not always transferable.

We spent Christmas day and evening in Nike's house, and every-thing was so jolly I concluded that the commissioner, Felicia's husband, had subjected Foley to his own brand of lie detector test, and that he had passed it. The commissioner was a Nigerian man par excellence and one who wore a police uniform to boot. I decided, at any rate, to believe what Foley had told me. This removed a barrier between us and he felt it. "I think you like me now," he said as we got into bed that night.

"What do you mean by that?"

"You're not asking me if I like you." This was an odd way of putting it, but it was extraordinarily astute. I had stopped, at least at that mo-ment, checking for signs of conspiracy. We had a wonderful three weeks together.

Back in New York, the walls of mistrust went up and came down again, crumbling a bit faster each time, a bit less sturdy each time they were rebuilt. Through a Nigerian friend living here, Foley got a job restoring a church in Philadelphia during the week. Emmanuel joined him there, and it was understood, at least by me, that they would spend weekends in New York. But I couldn't count on that, and when I did, I sometimes found myself disappointed—and furious. I didn't want to live by myself again but I could do it. If this was his idea of marriage, he could take it and shove it. These were the words I'd always wished my mother had said, and I rehearsed them, to myself, with vehemence.

I thought about what I would tell people, but I knew they'd understand. I'd remind myself that there were no watches or phones where Foley grew up. The distance between our two cultures was simply too great. Then he would appear, uncomprehending when he found out that he'd had the power to upset me, since I clearly did not have that power over him. Trying to pin him down to being at a particular place at a particular time was futile, no matter where he was. He'd invariably turn out to have lost track of the time and I invariably found myself unable to hold on to my anger in his presence. To be angry, one must hang on to the past, and the past is no match for Foley.

Tossed back and forth like this by an energy I could not control, I forgot all about the commissioner's suggestion that I check out Foley's passport. Instead, getting a green card for him became our next project, and I had to explain to a skeptical lawyer, seated behind an immense desk covered with photographs of a young-looking wife and two teenagers, that Foley hadn't married me in order to obtain this precious piece of plastic. If anything, it was a sign of his heightened commitment to me that he was willing to stay in the States for the one to two years the process now required. With him in Philadelphia during the week, I was enjoying solitude as a defined, but temporary, state and looked forward to the weekends.

One day when he was away, I was looking through my top drawer and came across his passport, left in my safekeeping. The commissioner's words came back into my mind as I held the all-revealing document, and though I had until that moment put behind me any thought that Foley had lied about his activities the previous summer, I opened it. There was his made-up birth date, testament to the lack of records in Osi. There were stamps for his various trips to the States and one to Kenya. There was a photograph on every page of a face I recognized, but barely. But no stamps from Zimbabwe.

My first impulse was to call Philadelphia. Yet even as I flipped through these strange, watermarked pages, I knew that the bond between us was not about to be shattered by anything on them. It might grow denser, like the net of lights that had held me up in intensive care at St. Luke's. Or, it might even break at some point, but it was my marriage now, not my mother's. The announcement that she had spent most of her married life anticipating, the lightning flash that could at any moment reveal its entire landscape to be made out of cardboard, was not going to knock me to the ground. I had friends—and not just one—who weren't bound by the rules that had kept Alice Grayson silent. I had my teaching. And like Alice—though perhaps my definition would not be the same as hers—I had God.

It is enough, I decided, as my mother must have done when my father, after six months of silence, told her he was not going to leave after all. She'd had a big wedding, too, and a three-month honeymoon in Europe. An enormous home and three maids to take care of it; a man her friends must have seen as a real catch; beautiful clothes and parties to which to wear them; a house in the country with a swimming pool and room for a dozen guests—what more did she want? My grandmother had probably told her what she had told me: not to come running home to mother. That night in the Oak Room, she was only passing on to me a piece of her history.

The silver band on the fourth finger of my left hand—and I admit I don't leave home without it—is a reminder that I no longer inhabit a place where, I suspect, my mother thought I would always live: the country of the unloved. It's a place that exists only in the mind, and others besides Foley have helped me to pitch my tent outside it. Still, I feel lucky to be connected to someone whose voice, even over the phone, has the power to bring me back from there. I like it, too, that we each have lives that are not the other's. Perhaps I couldn't handle being with someone to whom I could really talk about all the areas of my life— things and events whose existence Foley knows nothing about—the contents of this book that he'll probably never read. I come from a long line of nontalkers, after all, and perhaps I will always, in some way, be theirs.

"I went to Zimbabwe," Foley said the following Friday night, seated on our bed, the light from my bedside lamp behind him. "They gave me a paper with a stamp on it. I have it somewhere."

There was no anger or hesitation anywhere in his face or in his body. *I don't want to kill myself,* he had said in the car. *What's for me is for you,* he'd said in my kitchen. Of course. Lying to me, he would damage himself, and I know, as clearly as I can know anything, that Foley would never intentionally do that. I would simply have to choose, and trusting him seemed to offer more possibility for good than not trusting him. They don't stamp *my* passport, after all, when I cross the border into Canada. Perhaps there was a paper somewhere, and perhaps he still had it. Perhaps this was the truth that Africa had finally brought home to me: that only intuition will get me to the place I want to be. For how clear it was that what I could know for a fact would never be what I needed.

Kate Ellis teaches women's studies, creative writing, and eighteenth-century literature at Rutgers University in New Brunswick, New Jersey. She is the author of *The Contested Castle: Gothic Novels and the Subversion of Domestic Ideology*. Her fiction and poetry have appeared in *The Village Voice* and *Ms.* magazine. She lives in New York City and Osogbo, Nigeria, and is currently working on a collection of essays that further explore several of the themes touched on in this memoir.